Communications
in Computer and Information Science　468

T0214197

Pavel Klinov   Dmitry Mouromtsev (Eds.)

Knowledge Engineering and the Semantic Web

5th International Conference, KESW 2014
Kazan, Russia, September 29 – October 1, 2014
Proceedings

 Springer

Volume Editors

Pavel Klinov
University of Ulm
Institute of Artificial Intelligence
89069 Ulm, Germany
E-mail: pavel.klinov@uni-ulm.de

Dmitry Mouromtsev
Saint Petersburg National Research University
of Information Technologies, Mechanics and Optics
Saint Petersburg, Russia
E-mail: muromtsev@mail.ifmo.ru

ISSN 1865-0929   e-ISSN 1865-0937
ISBN 978-3-319-11715-7   e-ISBN 978-3-319-11716-4
DOI 10.1007/978-3-319-11716-4
Springer Cham Heidelberg New York Dordrecht London

Library of Congress Control Number: 2014948937

Typesetting: Camera-ready by author, data conversion by Scientific Publishing Services, Chennai, India

Printed on acid-free paper

Springer is part of Springer Science+Business Media (www.springer.com)

Preface

These proceedings contain the papers accepted to oral presentation at the 5th Conference on Knowledge Engineering and Semantic Web (KESW 2014). The conference was held in Kazan, Russia, during September 29 – October 1, 2014.

The principal mission of the KESW conference series is to provide a discussion forum for the community of researchers currently under-represented at the major International Semantic Web Conference (ISWC) and Extended Semantic Web Conference (ESWC). This mostly includes researchers from Eastern and Northern Europe, Russia and the former Soviet republics, as well as the Middle East. Another important part of the mission is to help this community get used to the common international standards for academic conferences in order to increase chances of publication at other top events. To this end KESW 2014, as its last year's predecessor, featured a rigorous reviewing process in which every paper was reviewed by at least three members of the Program Committee. The PC was truly international representing a range of EU countries, USA, and Russia.

The strict reviewing policy resulted in only 18 (41%) full size research and industry papers being accepted for publication in the proceedings. Additionally we accepted 4 shorter system description papers which discuss practical issues of using and implementing semantic technologies. The authors represent the EU, various Russian regions, and even such distant countries as Ecuador, Oman, or New Zealand.

Besides the paper presentations, the KESW program featured invited talks by established researchers: Julia Taylor (Purdue University, USA), Stefan Dietze (L3S Research Center, Germany), and Vladimir Gorodetski (SPIIRAN, Russia). It also included posters and position paper presentations to help attendees, especially younger researchers, discuss immature ideas and possible PhD topics.

KESW 2014 could not have taken place without the hard work of a large group of people, especially the local organizers from the Kazan Federal University: Ayrat Khasyanov, Vladimir Ivanov, Alik Kirillovich, and Darya Galeyeva. We are also extremely grateful to our sponsors whose support cannot be overestimated: the Russian Foundation for Basic Research, the St. Petersburg State University of Information Technologies, Mechanics and Optics, and STI International. Special thanks are extended to our Web designer Maxim Kolchin for his energy and willingness to help and Easychair for helping with preparation of this volume.

July 2014

Pavel Klinov
Dmitry Mouromtsev

Organizing Committee

General Chair

Dmitry Mouromtsev   St. Petersburg National Research University of
Information Technologies, Mechanics and
Optics, Russia

Program Chair

Pavel Klinov   University of Ulm, Germany

Local Organizers

Ayrat Khasyanov   Kazan Federal University, Russia
Vladimir Ivanov   Kazan Federal University, Russia
Alik Kirillovich   Kazan Federal University, Russia
Darya Galeyeva   Kazan Federal University, Russia

Program Committee

Alessandro Adamou   ISTC-CNR, Italy
Sören Auer   University of Bonn, Germany
Samantha Bail   The University of Manchester, UK
Sergey Balandin   Finnish-Russian University Cooperation in
Telecommunications, Finland + Russia
Mathieu D'Aquin   The Open University, UK
Chiara Del Vescovo   The University of Manchester, UK
Ivan Ermilov   University of Leipzig, Germany
Timofey Ermilov   University of Leipzig, Germany
Tatiana Gavrilova   St. Petersburg State University, Russia
Rafael S. Gonçalves   The University of Manchester, UK
Vladimir Gorovoy   St. Petersburg State University, Russia
Daniel Hladky   Ontos AG, Switzerland
Martin Homola   Comenius University, Slovakia
Matthew Horridge   Stanford University, USA
Konrad Höffner   University of Leipzig, Germany
Dmitry Ignatov   Higher School of Economics, Russia
Natalya Keberle   Zaporizhzhya National University, Ukraine
Ali Khalili   University of Leipzig, Germany
Evgeny Kharlamov   Oxford University, UK

Jakub Klimek	Charles University, Czech Republic
Boris Konev	The University of Liverpool, UK
Roman Kontchakov	Birkbeck College, UK
Dmitry Kudryavtsev	St. Petersburg State Polytechnical University, Russia
Jose Emilio Labra Gayo	Universidad de Oviedo, Spain
Yue Ma	Technical University of Dresden, Germany
Nicolas Matentzoglu	The University of Manchester, UK
Elena Mozzherina	St. Petersburg State University, Russia
Andriy Nikolov	fluid Operations AG, Germany
Bijan Parsia	The University of Manchester, UK
Rafael Peñaloza	Technical University of Dresden, Germany
Denis Ponomaryov	University of Ulm, Germany
Svetlana Popova	St. Petersburg State University, Russia
Mariano Rodriguez-Muro	IBM T.J. Watson Research Center, USA
Valery Rubashkin	St. Petersburg State University, Russia
Marvin Schiller	University of Ulm, Germany
Daria Stepanova	Technical University of Vienna, Austria
Anna Szkudlarek	Grenoble Ecole de Management, France
Darya Tarasowa	University of Bonn, Germany
Julia Taylor	Purdue University, US
Ioan Toma	STI Innsbruck, Austria
Trung-Kien Tran	University of Ulm, Germany
Dmitry Tsarkov	The University of Manchester, UK
Joerg Unbehauen	University of Leipzig, Germany
Serge Yablonsky	St. Petersburg State University, Russia
Amrapali Zaveri	University of Lepzig, Germany
Dmitriy Zheleznyakov	University of Oxford, UK
Nikita Zhiltsov	Kazan Federal University, Russia

Additional Reviewers

Martin Brümmer	Fan Chaosheng
Ruslan Fayzrakhmanov	Mofeed Hassan
Ernesto Jimenez-Ruiz	Liubov Kovriguina
Edgard Marx	Muhammad Saleem

Sponsors

Platinum Sponsors

Russian Foundation for
Basic Research

NRU ITMO

Gold Sponsors

STI Innsbruck

Table of Contents

Research and Industry Track Papers

Text Categorization for Generation of a Historical Shipbuilding
Ontology 1
    Galina Artemova, Kirill Boyarsky, Dmitri Gouzévitch,
    Natalia Gusarova, Natalia Dobrenko, Eugeny Kanevsky, and
    Daria Petrova

Domain Categorization of Open Educational Resources Based on
Linked Data.. 15
    Janneth Chicaiza, Nelson Piedra, Jorge Lopez-Vargas, and
    Edmundo Tovar-Caro

Cloud Sensor Ontology and Linked Data to Support Autonomicity in
Cloud Application Platforms 29
    Rustem Dautov, Iraklis Paraskakis, and Mike Stannett

Construction of Personalized Information Services for Researchers 44
    Viktoria Foteyeva and Michail Panteleyev

Towards Building Wordnet for the Tatar Language: A Semantic Model
of the Verb System 57
    Alfiya M. Galieva, Olga A. Nevzorova, and Ayrat R. Gatiatullin

Access Control, Triggers and Versioning over SPARQL Endpoint 67
    Sergey Gorshkov

Return on Investment in Linking Content to CRM by Applying the
Linked Data Stack 76
    Daniel Hladky, Svetlana Maltseva, Dmitriy Ogorodniychuk,
    Grigory Drobyazko, Martin Voigt, and Jon Jay Le Grange

Creating Cognitive Frames Based on Ontology Design Patterns for
Ontology Visualization 90
    Pavel Lomov and Maxim Shishaev

$OntoMath^{PRO}$ Ontology: A Linked Data Hub for Mathematics 105
    Olga A. Nevzorova, Nikita Zhiltsov, Alexander Kirillovich, and
    Evgeny Lipachev

Semantic Analysis and Prediction of Various Risks of Diabetic
Patients 120
    Sherimon P.C., Vinu P.V., Reshmy Krishnan, and Youssef Takroni

Interaction History Based Answer Formulation for Question
Answering 128
    Rivindu Perera and Parma Nand

Automatic Term Extraction for Sentiment Classification of Dynamically
Updated Text Collections into Three Classes 140
    Yuliya Rubtsova

Distributed Knowledge Acquisition Control with Use of the Intelligent
Program Environment of the AT-TECHNOLOGY Workbench 150
    Galina V. Rybina and Yury M. Blokhin

A Feature Selection Approach for Anchor Evaluation in Ontology
Mapping 160
    Frederik C. Schadd and Nico Roos

Linked-Data Integration for Workflow-Based Computational
Experiments... 175
    Pavel A. Smirnov and Sergey V. Kovalchuk

Ontology for Resource Self-organisation in Cyber-Physical-Social
Systems 184
    Nikolay Teslya, Alexander Smirnov, Tatiana Levashova, and
    Nikolay Shilov

Words Worth Attention: Predicting Words of the Week on the Russian
Wiktionary.. 196
    Dmitry Ustalov

Deriving of Thematic Facts from Unstructured Texts and Background
Knowledge 208
    Nataliya Yelagina and Michail Panteleyev

System Description Papers

A Collaborative Development of Ontology-Based Knowledge Bases 219
    Oleg Dyachenko and Yury Zagorulko

A Tool to Convert Linked Data of E-Learning System to the SCORM
Standard 229
    Fedor Kozlov

OntoFast: Construct Ontology Rapidly 237
    Abdul-Mateen Rajput, Marzio Pennisi, Santo Motta, and
    Francesco Pappalardo

Mathematical Content Semantic Markup Methods and Open Scientific
E-Journals Management Systems 242
   Alexander Elizarov, Evgeny Lipachev, and Denis Zuev

Author Index 253

Text Categorization for Generation of a Historical Shipbuilding Ontology

Galina Artemova[1], Kirill Boyarsky[1], Dmitri Gouzévitch[2], Natalia Gusarova[1], Natalia Dobrenko[1], Eugeny Kanevsky[3], and Daria Petrova[1]

[1] Saint Petersburg National Research University of Information Technologies, Mechanics and Optics (ITMO University), Saint Petersburg, Russia
[2] Centre d'Etudes du Monde russe, caucasienne centre-européen, École des hautes études en sciences sociales, Paris, France
[3] Saint Petersburg Institute for Economics and Mathematics, Russian Academy of Sciences, Saint Petersburg, Russia

Abstract. This paper deals with the task of developing a text corpus for the automatic generation of a historical shipbuilding domain ontology. Standard methods of analysis produce unsatisfactory results due to the limited nomenclature of available texts and lexical evolution of language. In this work, a parser developed by authors is used for lemmatization and word-sense disambiguation. The parser is based on an external classifier and provides the unambiguous relationship between each lexeme and class. The documents are represented as vectors in the topic space. The experiments show that the proposed method of categorization produces results very close to the expert opinion and at the same time is sufficiently resistant to the historical dynamics of the vocabulary.

Keywords: Text categorization, historical shipbuilding domain, ontology, parsing, space of topics.

1 Introduction

Intensive introduction of ontologies in education and production is connected with automation of their construction that found reflection in definition: "Ontology Learning (also named ontology generation or ontology extraction) is a knowledge acquisition activity that relies on (semi-) automatic methods to transform unstructured (e.g. corpora), semi-structured (e.g. folksonomies, html pages, etc.) and structured data sources (e.g. data bases) into conceptual structures (e.g. T-Box)".[1]

The given definitions, in essence, predetermine the statement of problems of creating the ontologies as one of the variants of natural texts processing (NLP) in a class of methods of mathematical statistics and machine learning. The various approaches of machine training used at the solution of NLP tasks have an extensive bibliography. Text categorization (classification) [18,7,10,12,19,28],

---

[1] http://semanticweb.org/wiki/Category:Topic_ontology_learning

P. Klinov and D. Mouromtsev (Eds.): KESW 2014, CCIS 468, pp. 1–14, 2014.

text clustering [7,13,16], thematic modeling [3,14,26,11], and also various combined options [10,12,23] are among these approaches. Specifics of use of the text corpora as the solution of NLP tasks are considered in [2,29].

Key moments defining efficiency of procedures of machine learning are the choice and formation of feature space. That is why before using machine learning algorithms text preprocessing is needed, such as text marking, normalization and commenting. However the other important factor of machine learning efficiency is the formation of training and control sets which are responsible for training accuracy. Training and control in problems of NLP are carried out on specially created text collections (text corpora). Such collections have to contain the sufficient volume of the linguistic data supplied with expert interpretation, which meets the requirements of a statistical representativeness [22].

Analysis carried out by the authors has shown that in the majority of the published research the representativeness is interpreted as uniform distribution of controlled linguistic units (words, word usage, lexemes) within all training corpus. At the same time for concrete domains this interpretation can be insufficient, and sometimes even incorrect. In works [6,21] the problems arising at a stage of text preprocessing of concrete domains are formulated as follows:

– Categorizations of units in formal ontology languages and in a natural language are, as a rule, semantically various.
– In complex domains each step of classification can take in consideration some new classification features and make them actual.
– Formal interpretation can't be identified with encyclopedic definitions of terms; that is why the use of the domains dictionaries for ontology formation becomes complicated.
– In domains with complex structure there can be sections which are described in different, but similar systems of concepts.
– Specifics of structure of a field of knowledge of the expert in concrete domain (and, respectively, his view of domains ontology) depend on its experience and specific features and amplify with growth of qualification of the expert.

The listed problems are especially characteristic for poorly formalized, butt and high-dynamic domains which, as a rule, are objects of the greatest scientific, economic and social interest. The historical shipbuilding (HS) which is the object of this research, can be referred to such domains. HS is the construction of models-copies of historical vessels of different eras. Today in Russia, as well as around the world, the priority is given to the best quality models, characterized by the maximum historical reliability.

A number of the ontologies connected with a perspective of shipbuilding is so far developed (see for example [27]), however they are focused on modern vessels and, respectively, are based on modern sources of information. At the same time the development of design and technological documentation for the construction of model-copies is carried out on the basis of the historical reconstruction which are carried out on remained archival materials, pictures and documents of the corresponding eras. It adds specifics of HS to the above listed problems:

- considerable historical dynamics of terminology;
- quite small nomenclature of texts available to analysis, a great difference of their lengths and heterogeneity.
- small frequency of occurrence of special terms (up to 12 in the single text);
- it is difficult for the expert to join basic Russian-speaking terminology with a big flow of newly entering foreign-language terms.
- all above mentioned significantly complicates text categorization for building of HS ontology.

Thus, there is a task – text corpus formation (texts clustering) for the automated building of HS ontology: besides traditional statement, there is the additional subtask – selection and structuring of an initial collection of documents in order to form the processed text corpus from them.

In order to solve the problem of text categorization under consideration we suggest to pass from the creation of model of the text "by words" to the model "on topics" – that is to the integrated blocks of words with similar semantics. We use semantic classes based on V. A. Tuzov qualifier [24] as such topics.

The rest of this paper is organized as follows. In Section 2 the short review of approaches to a problem of text categorization is provided and possibilities of their application to our objective are estimated. In Section 3 texts which can be used for creation of ontology of HS are characterized. In Section 4 the results of pilot research of their statistical properties are given. In Section 5 the approach proposed in our work is reasoned, and experimental estimates of quality of text categorization are given. In the conclusion the received results are summarized and the directions of further researches are outlined.

2 Related Work

2.1 Construction of Text Corpuses for Machine Learning Purposes

In the majority of research on NLP the probabilistic model of generation of the document [26] prevails as shows the analysis. Let W – a set of words w (dictionary); D – set (corpus, collection) of text documents d; T – a set of topics t, which can be compared to the document, and each word w in the document d is connected with some (probably, not one) topics t. The probabilistic model of generation of the document is defined as

$$p(w|d) = \sum_{t \in T} p(w|d,t)p(t|d) = \sum_{t \in T} p(w|t)p(t|d),$$

and works within standard hypotheses:

- order of words in the document and order of documents in a collection are not important (a hypothesis of conditional independence) $p(w|d,t) = p(w|t)$;
- all the words in different forms are considered as the same word (that means that at a preprocessing stage text lemmatization, i.e. reduction to a form of lemmas has been carried out);

– the words met in the majority of texts as well as too rare words are not important (that means that at the preprocessing stage stop words and too rare words have been removed).

According to these hypotheses in practical research the frequency estimates of conditional probabilities are used:

$$\hat{p}(w|d) = \frac{n_{dw}}{n_d}; \qquad \hat{p}(w|t) = \frac{n_{wt}}{n_t}; \qquad \hat{p}(t|d) = \frac{n_{dt}}{n_d}$$

where n_{dw} – number of occurrences of the term in the document; n_{wt} – number of the terms defining a topic; n_{dt} – number of the topics compared to the document; n_d – document length; n_t – "the topic length"; n – collection length. Such model received the name of "bag of words". It corresponds to the training set formed on the basis of common lexicon corpora in which various periods, genres, styles, authors, etc. are represented in proportion. This means that these words are distributed evenly within all the collection according to the frequency of their occurrence in real language. As a rule, it is various national or specialized research corpora.

Limitation of "bag of words" model is overcome in much research by its parametrization [9], [12]. However, despite obvious complication of processing procedures, overall performance of the qualifier remained rather low and significantly depended on style features of the processed text.

One more direction of enrichment of the NLP models is their binding to external qualifiers (ontologies). In works [16], [17] text linkage with external bases of knowledge like Wikipedia, Google, Tipster corpus is used for their categorization. All in all the idea of external parametrization for NLP models adaptation should be considered very perspective, but its practical application for specialized domains is limited. The developed and multilevel ontology of domain is necessary for this purpose which we, actually, plan to construct.

2.2   Accounting for Historical Development of Domain Lexicon

Approaches applied here can be divided into two groups: using meta-information about the text and allocation of characteristic structural units directly in the text. As an example of the first approach we can take the work [15] in which changes in a marking of New York Times articles corpus during 1987–2007 are considered.

In work [25] the problem of creation of historical ontologies is considered in order to simplify researchers access to historical documents and artifacts. For this purpose each document is supplied with the most detailed meta-information, which registers in the Attempto Controlled English language and can be automatically processed with the first order logic. The same approach is realized in the ontologic standard of historical heritage of CIDOC CRM [1]. However this approach is focused mainly on preservation and search of information on artifacts of culture and historical heritage and does not assume automation of their substantial structuring that represents the main interest in our work.

Within the second approach it is possible to allocate work [12] in which the episode concept is used. Dynamics of development of episodes is traced that allows to reveal and include not taxonomical relations in domain ontology.

3   Statistical Properties of the Texts

Considering available sources it is advisable to build HS ontology as domain ontology, but with possibility of expansion to ontology of tasks. [5] and [20]] were used as the main text sources.

The book [5] of 544 pages is considered to be the encyclopedia of modern ship modeling around the world. The book is available in public libraries.

The book [20] is one of the earliest printing editions about shipbuilding technology in Russia. The book consists of two parts of 542 and 355 pages respectively. The book belongs to rare editions.

For research of statistical properties of the selected texts thematically relative fragments were allocated from both books. During the selection it was revealed that thematical estimates of separate structural components of books made by experts not always coincide with books headings; in these cases the preference was given to expert estimates of proximity. The fragments chosen for research are presented in Table 1.

Table 1. Analyzed fragments of texts

Fragment designation	Source	Chapter	Volume of a fragment (word usage)
[F1]	[43]	Hull Construction	5400
[F2]	[43]	Hull Construction of Shipmodel	8700
[F3]	[43]	Sails	2400
[F4]	[51]	About Ship Plans	4100
[F5]	[51]	About Sails and Ropes	5800

Available texts in domain have small volume and are narrow in thematic, that is why their statistical characteristics are far from normal, and any assumptions of "accident" words emergence in the text are obviously unfair. For example, in [F1] the word "vessel" (in all word forms) takes the fourth place on occurrence frequency, conceding to only syntactic words "and", "on", "in" and advancing all words of the general lexicon. Its frequency is about 103000 ipm (instances per million words) that is 14 times higher than in the National Russian Corpus and the frequency of the word "frame" is 224 times higher.

Besides, these frequencies sharply change from chapter to chapter. The relation of frequencies of the word "vessel" determined by [F1] and [F2], is equal 1.5, and the words "frame" – 0.015. It predetermines the specifics of lexical and statistical processing of the specified texts.

For lemmatization and disambiguation the SemSin parser developed by the authors [8] is used in work. The parser is constructed within the concept of dependency parsing and implements the lexicalized model of the sentence analysis. The expanded and modified V. A. Tuzov dictionary [24] is used as a base, containing about 190000 lexemes broken into 1600 semantic classes. Operation of the parser is based on application of a set of production rules [4], the parser makes the full syntax and semantic analysis for each sentence and builds a tree of dependences.

Firstly, such text analysis allowed to solve the problem of a homonymy and, secondly, to exclude from consideration not only the stop word, but also to sharply narrow a circle of possible candidates for the terms of the domain already at a preliminary stage. At the first stage of work as those only the nouns were considered, however used technology allows changing structure of terms easily, including groups of the words standing separately in text.

In further analysis for each analyzed fragment the list (frequency word book) of nouns entering it ordered on frequency was received.

The analysis of the selected fragments was carried out. The frequency structure of three fragments for which the experts determined the general thematic as "the hulls of the ships and their models" is given in Table 2. In the table it is designated: a1 – number of words with relative number of occurrences more than 0.005; a2 – number of words with relative number of occurrences from 0.001 to 0.005; a3 – number of words with relative number of occurrences less than 0.001.

Table 2. Frequency structure of nouns of fragments of group "cases of the ships and their models"

Fragment	a1	a2	a3
[F1]	31 (6.6%)	204 (43.4%)	235 (50.0%)
[F2]	11 (2.3%)	142 (29.1%)	335 (68.6%)
[F4]	39 (17.0%)	81 (35.4%)	109 (47.6%)

Despite the fact that only nouns are used in the analysis, statistical characteristics of the text do not change significantly. So, the Zipf's law (the return proportionality of frequency and quantity of the lexemes entering the text with this frequency) is carried out.

Table 3 characterizes total sample of 10 most frequent words from each fragment: frequencies of their occurrence are specified as a percentage; the normalized vectors are constructed which components of d_i were determined by a formula

$$d_i = \frac{p(w_i)}{\sqrt{\sum_i p(w_i)^2}}$$

where p_i is the frequency of emergence of i-th word in this fragment.

Table 3. Statistics of the most frequency words of fragments of "the hulls of the ships and their models" group"

	lexeme	[F1] frequency	[F1] vector	[F2] frequency	[F2] vector	[F4] frequency	[F4] vector
1	vessel	0.063	0.685	0	0	0	0
2	hull	0.024	0.254	0.072	0.686	0	0
3	frame	0.025	0.277	0.043	0.406	0.037	0.319
4	planking	0.030	0.328	0.022	0.213	0	0
5	model	0	0	0.034	0.324	0	0
6	deck	0.024	0.260	0.021	0.201	0	0
7	plank	0.019	0.204	0.024	0.228	0	0
8	part	0.023	0.249	0	0	0	0
9	keel	0.018	0.198	0.015	0.146	0	0
10	sickness	0	0	0.021	0.198	0	0
11	lap	0	0	0.019	0.181	0	0
12	beam	0.017	0.181	0	0	0	0
13	stern	0.013	0.141	0	0	0	0
14	cut section	0	0	0.018	0.169	0	0
15	plane	0	0	0	0	0.047	0.412
16	ribband	0	0	0.017	0.160	0.046	0.397
17	wood	0	0	0.015	0.149	0.039	0.341
18	point	0	0	0	0	0.037	0.326
19	lines	0	0	0.015	0.143	0.033	0.284
20	figure	0	0	0.013	0.128	0.033	0.284
21	line	0	0	0.012	0.114	0.032	0.277
22	mould	0	0	0.011	0.108	0.028	0.241
23	projection	0	0	0.011	0.108	0.026	0.227

The hypothesis that the frequency structure of the dictionary defines a measure of thematic proximity of texts is checked. As an integrated assessment of texts similarity cosine measure is taken:

$$sim(d_i, d_j) = cos(\angle(d_i, d_j)) = \frac{\sum_k d_{ik} d_{jk}}{\sqrt{\sum_k d_{ik}^2}\sqrt{\sum_k d_{jk}^2}}$$

On the basis of tab. 3 data we received for fragments [F1] and [F2] $cos\varphi = 0.48$, and for fragments [F1] and [F4] of $cos\varphi = 0.09$, i.e. the thematic similarity of fragments practically is absent that, certainly, is not true.

The same analysis is made for fragments [F3] and [F5] for which the experts determined "sails" thematic. The most frequency lexemes covering 45% of all word usage are selected. For [F3] these are 26 lexemes with rate 7 and above,

Table 4. Statistics of the most frequency words of fragments of parusa ("sails") group

[F3]				[F5]			
lexeme	number of entrances	frequency	vector	lexeme	number of entrances	frequency	vector
sail	116	0.284	0.872	sail	111	0.144	0.585
vessel	27	0.066	0.203	block	70	0.091	0.369
yard	24	0.059	0.180	fig.	50	0.065	0.263
jib	22	0.054	0.165	rope	48	0.062	0.253
bolt rope	20	0.049	0.150	angle	48	0.062	0.253
angle	17	0.042	0.128	end	46	0.060	0.242
canvas	15	0.037	0.113	leech rope	41	0.053	0.216
mizen	14	0.034	0.105	eyelet hole	37	0.048	0.195
side	12	0.029	0.090	leech	36	0.046	0.119
mast	11	0.027	0.083	length	24	0.031	0.126
sails	10	0.024	0.075	bolt rope	23	0.030	0.121
stay sail	10	0.024	0.075	main sail	20	0.026	0.105
edge	9	0.022	0.068	part	20	0.026	0.105
form	9	0.022	0.068	bolt	19	0.024	0.100
bowline	8	0.020	0.060	cloth	19	0.024	0.100
detail	8	0.020	0.060	cordage	19	0.024	0.100
end	8	0.020	0.060	sheet	19	0.024	0.100
man rope	8	0.020	0.060	ship	17	0.022	0.090
leech rope	8	0.020	0.060	image	16	0.021	0.084
topsail	8	0.020	0.060	lap	16	0.021	0.084
reef	8	0.020	0.060	hight	15	0.019	0.079
reef hole	8	0.020	0.060	tack	15	0.019	0.079
main sail	7	0.017	0.052	strand	15	0.019	0.079
eyelet hole	7	0.017	0.052	nock	14	0.018	0.074
reef becket	7	0.017	0.052	middle	14	0.018	0.074
bridle	7	0.017	0.052				

for [F5] – 25 lexemes with rate 14 and higher (see Table 4). It appears that from the selected lexemes only 7 are met in both selections.

On the selected lexemes (tab. 4) vectors (3) are constructed and the thematic proximity (4) fragments of [F3], [F5] is calculated. The value of $cos\varphi = 0.63$ is received and, excluding "sail" lemma, $cos\varphi = 0.25$. In other words, the calculation shows some similarity between the chosen fragments, but actually it is based only on one word. Similarity calculated using other lexicon is very low.

On the example of a fragment [F5] the frequency of occurrence of special terms (names of sails) within analyzed texts is estimated (see Table 5). It is visible that in a fragment [F5] among 15 names of sails only 1 (main sail) gets to the selection described above and only 4 have rate higher than three (tab. 4). Many special terms have small frequency (to 1–2 on a fragment).

Table 5. Names of sails and their rate in the text

name of sail	rate	name of sail	rate
main sail	17	main under studding sail	2
studding sail	10	stay sail	2
main top sail	9	mizen	1
top sail	6	main royal sail	1
topgalant sail	3	topgalant studding sail	1
main top studding sail	3	main sail	1
topgalant sail	2	studding boom	1

4   The Text Clustering Approach

The results presented in the Section 4 allow to formulate the problems arising at the text categorization of considered domain:

- Even among lexemes with a big weight there are those which hardly can become terms (water, foot, crossing).
- Some special terms have small frequency (to 1–2 on a fragment). At the same time among low-frequency lexemes there are as obvious candidates in terms of subject domain (fore mast, the boat cutter, sail vessel), and casual words (barbarian, time). That complicates selection even more. As a result the candidates in terms remain imperceptible among lexical noise.
- The condition of uniform distribution of lexemes on the text isn't satisfied.

For overcoming of these problems it is offered to turn from vector representation of documents in space of words into vector representation in space of topics, having reduced thereby dimension of vectors. But then there is a new problem – how to correlate the word and a topic. To solve this problem in completely automatic mode semantic classes of the V.A. Tuzov qualifier are used. In this case together with sentence analysis and creation of a tree of dependences correlation of each lexeme with any class is made.

In order to check the efficiency of the offered thematic allocation of lexemes we used the same groups of text fragments, as in Section 4: [F1], [F2] and [F4] – thematic "the hulls of the ships and their models", [F3] and [F5] – "sail" thematic.

The results of thematic group of lexemes in texts of the first group and the corresponding vectors calculated from the formula (3), are given in Table 6.

Table 6. Results of thematic group of lexemes in group texts "the hulls of the ships and their models"

classes	[F1]		[F2]		[F3]	
	words	vector	words	vector	words	vector
Floating boats (vessel, corvette)	140	0.261	42	0.079	26	0.134
Parts_of_vessels (bowsprit, keel, stern)	498	0.929	402	0.755	102	0.525
Rooms (cabins, powder-room)	73	0.136	4	0.007	1	0.005
Part_of_room (planking, bulkhead)	44	0.082	26	0.049	12	0.062
Details (rivet, strut)	53	0.099	188	0.353	4	0.020
Hatch (hatch, hole)	45	0.084	51	0.096	0	0
Building materials (rail-post, whetstone)	84	0.156	162	0.304	69	0.355
Drawing tools (pencil, curve)	4	0.007	16	0.030	46	0.237
Borders (edge, leech)	12	0.022	17	0.032	50	0.257
Figures (plane, half ring)	17	0.032	138	0.259	118	0.608
Contour (contour)	1	0.002	11	0.020	40	0.206
Wood (wood, oak)	13	0.024	16	0.030	39	0.201
Hull (hull, base)	16	0.030	150	0.282	2	0.010
Model (model)	0	00	111	0.208	2	0.010

Table 7 shows the estimation of similarity between the fragments in the group. In both cases we calculated the cosine measure of the similarity (4), however compared vectors of di were received in the first case by frequency allocation of lexemes (Table 3), and in the second case – by thematic allocation of lexemes (Table 5).

Table 7 shows that the measure of similarity is significantly higher while using thematic allocation of lexemes, than using frequency allocation. This means that the thematic allocation of lexemes closer corresponds to expert opinion, than frequency allocation.

Similar check was performed on a group of text fragments with "sail" thematic. The results of the thematic allocation of lexemes in texts of "sail" group and the vectors constructed by the formula (3), are shown in table 8.

Table 7. Similarity estimates between fragments in-group

By topics By Words	[F1]	[F2]	[F4]
[F1]	—	0.57	0.87
[F2]	0.48	—	0.76
[F4]	0.10	0.40	—

Table 8. Results of thematic allocation of lexemes in texts of "sail" group

classes	[F3] words	[F3] vector	[F5] words	[F5] vector
Sails	262	0.837	175	0.441
Parts of vessels	161	0.514	322	0.812
Position	0	0	48	0.121
Floating boats	38	0.121	0	0
Cordage	28	0.089	104	0.262
Figures	26	0.083	68	0.171
Side	0	0	47	0.118
Blocks	0	0	54	0.136
Fabrick	20	0.064	0	0

The thematic proximity (4) of fragments [F3] and [F5] was calculated using the results of tab. 8. The value $cos\varphi = 0.83$ is received and excluding a lemma "sail", $cos\varphi = 0.81$. Comparing these values to the similar data obtained above on the basis of tab. 4, it is possible to see that the use of thematic allocation of lexemes significantly increases the stability of results and characterizes the cumulative semantic similarity of texts and not only their coincidence by one word.

5   Conclusion

The problem of construction of text corpus (text categorization) for the creation of domain ontology of historical shipbuilding was solved in this work.

As shown in the work, the texts on scope of historical shipbuilding are difficult objects for processing by methods of computational linguistics and machine learning. They greatly vary in length (from 1–2 phrases to 1600 pages of the full-scale book text), and also in frequency of occurrence of special lexicon.

As it was experimentally shown in this work, traditional methods of texts categorization, based on the ranging of lexemes on the frequency of occurrence and the comparison of the corresponding vectors, provide unsatisfactory results for the domain "Historical Shipbuilding". These failures can be understood. Over the decades separating the dates of creation the texts on identical topics, the authors lexicon has changed dramatically. Besides, due to the domain specifics the total volume available for the analysis of texts is limited, and it does not allow to apply the traditional methods of regularization for machine learning that give excellent results on large text corpora.

Thus, it is necessary to have a formal method of texts categorization on statistically uniform areas. To do this it is suggested in this work to turn from vector representation of the documents in space of lexemes into vector representation in space of topics (thus significantly reducing vectors dimension).

Results of using of the SemSin parser on texts of historical shipbuilding domain were quite satisfactory. Thus, the accuracy of definition of lemmas was not worse than 97% even on historical texts. The accuracy of identification of nouns, which first of all are considered as candidates in terms, was approximately the same order.

The efficiency of the offered method of a clustering of texts was checked experimentally. For this purpose based on an expert opinion (substantially) the groups of texts forming the general category were allocated, and categorization quality was compared in each of groups using two methods – traditional (frequency allocation of lexemes) and offered (thematic allocation of lexemes). As experiments showed, in all cases the offered method yielded the results that were much closer to expert opinion, than the traditional method.

Thus, the application of the method of texts categorization offered by the authors for creation of domain ontology provides a number of advantages:

– the texts (be detected)come to light characterized by cumulative semantic similarity, instead of simple coincidence on separate, though very frequency, terms;
– the stability of categorization significantly increases; it allows adding easily new text fragments to already created categories, expanding this way the base for ontology creation;
– the processed fragments contain not only almost all candidates for terms, but also very small amount of noise in the form of foreign words;
– there aren't basic difficulties in order to extent the list of terms to two- and three-word combinations received from a tree of dependences. It significantly facilitates a problem of further creation of ontology;
– for more exact allocation of the fragments belonging to one category, on long texts it is possible to use "a sliding window" that is the direction of further researches of authors.

References

1. The CIDOC conceptual reference model (CRM), www.cidoc-crm.org/
2. Bekkerman, R., El-Yaniv, R., Tishby, N., Winter, Y.: Distributional word clusters vs. words for text categorization. Journal of Machine Learning Research 3, 1183–1208 (2003)
3. Blei, D., Lafferty, J.: Topic models. Text Mining: Classification, Clustering, and Applications, 71–94 (2009)
4. Boyarsky, K.K., Kanevsky, E.A.: Rules language for creation of a syntactic tree. In: Internet and Modern Society: XIV All-Russian Joint Conference, pp. 233–237. Multi Project System Service Publishing, Sankt-Petersburg (2011)
5. Curti, O.: Modelli Navali. Encyclopedia del Modellismo Navale. Sudostrojenie Publishing (1977)
6. Gavrilova, T.A., Horoshevsky, V.F.: Knowledge bases of intellectual systems. Piter Publishing, Sankt-Petersburg (2000)
7. Isa, D., Kallimani, V.P., Lee, L.H.: Using the self organizing map for clustering of text documents. Expert Systems with Applications 36, 9584–9591 (2009)

8. Kanevsky, E.A., Boyarsky, K.K.: Semantic-syntactical analyzer semsin. In: International Conference on Computational Linguistics Dialog 2012, Bekasovo, May 30-June 3 (2012), http://www.dialog-21.ru/digest/2012/?type=doc

9. Karlgren, J., Cutting, D.: Recognizing text genres with simple metrics using discriminant analysis. In: Proc. 15th Int. Conf. on Computational Linguistics (COLING), Kyoto, vol. 2, pp. 1071–1075 (1994)

10. de Knijff, J., Frasincar, F., Hogenboom, F.: Domain taxonomy learning from text: The subsumption method versus hierarchical clustering. Data & Knowledge Engineering 83, 54–69 (2013)

11. Korshunov, A., Gomzin, A.: Topic modeling in natural language texts. In: Works of Institute of System Design of the Russian Academy of Sciences (2012)

12. Lee, C.S., Kao, Y.F., Kuo, Y.H., Wang, M.H.: Automated ontology construction for unstructured text documents. Data & Knowledge Engineering 60, 547–566 (2007)

13. Luo, C., Li, Y., Chung, S.M.: Text document clustering based on neighbors. Data & Knowledge Engineering 68, 1271–1288 (2009)

14. Mashechkin, I.V., Petrovsky, M.I., Tsarov, D.: Methods of calculation of relevance of text fragments using topic models in a problem of automatic annotation. Computing Methods and Programming 14, 91–102 (2013)

15. Mozzherina, E.: Approach to improving the classification of the new york times annotated corpus. In: Klinov, P., Mouromtsev, D. (eds.) KESW 2013. CCIS, vol. 394, pp. 83–91. Springer, Heidelberg (2013)

16. Nasir, J.A., Varlamis, I., Karim, A., Tsatsaronis, G.: Semantic smoothing for text clustering. Knowledge-Based Systems 54, 216–229 (2013)

17. Newman, D., Lau, J.H., Grieser, K., Baldwin, T.: Automatic evaluation of topic coherence. In: Human Language Technologies: The 2010 Annual Conference of the North American Chapter of the ACL, Los Angeles, California, pp. 100–108 (June 2010)

18. Nouman, A., JingTao, Y.: Comparison of term frequency and document frequency based feature selection metrics in text categorization. Expert Systems with Applications 39, 4760–4768 (2012)

19. Pinheiro, R., Cavalcanti, G., Correa, R., Ren, T.I.: A global-ranking local feature selection method for text categorization. Expert Systems with Applications 39, 12851–12857 (2012)

20. Romme, C.: L'Art de la marine, ou principes et prceptes gnraux de l'art de construire et d'armer les vaisseaux. Sea military school Publishing (1793, 1795)

21. Rubashkin, V.S.: Ontologic semantics. Knowledge. Ontologies. Ontologically focused methods of the information analysis of the text. Fizmatlit Publishing (2013)

22. Rykov, V.V.: Text corpus as realization of an object-oriented paradigm. In: Workshop Dialog 2002. Nauka Publishing (2002)

23. Song, W., Li, C.H., Park, S.C.: Genetic algorithm for text clustering using ontology and evaluating the validity of various semantic similarity measures. Expert Systems with Applications 36, 9095–9104 (2009)

24. Tuzov, V.A.: Computer semantics of Russian. Sankt-Petersburg State University (2004)

25. Varfolomeyev, A., Ivanovs, A.: Representation of historical sources on the semantic web by means of attempto controlled english. In: Klinov, P., Mouromtsev, D. (eds.) KESW 2013. CCIS, vol. 394, pp. 177–190. Springer, Heidelberg (2013)

26. Vorontsov, K.B.: Probabilistic topic models of text documents collections, http://www.machinelearning.ru/wiki/images/7/7e/Voron-ML-TopicModels-slides.pdf

27. de Vries, G., Malaisé, V., van Someren, M., Adriaans, P., Chreiber, G.: Semi-automatic ontology extension in the maritime domain. In: Proceedings of the Twentieth Belgian-Dutch Conference on Artificial Intelligence, University of Twente, Faculty of Electrical Engineering, Mathematics and Computer Science, pp. 265–272 (2008), http://dare.uva.nl/en/record/315959

28. Yang, J., Liu, Y., Zhu, X., Liu, Z., Zhang, X.: A new feature selection based on comprehensive measurement both in inter-category and intra-category for text categorization. Information Processing and Management 48, 741–754 (2012)

29. Zagidulin, I.: Methods and means of an automatic text categorization (2008), http://www.cv.imm.uran.ru/uploads/f1/s/0/299/basic/7/858/Metodyi_i_sredstva_TK.pdf

Domain Categorization of Open Educational Resources Based on Linked Data

Janneth Chicaiza[1], Nelson Piedra[1], Jorge Lopez-Vargas[1], and Edmundo Tovar-Caro[2]

[1] Departamento de Ciencias de la Computación
Universidad Técnica Particular de Loja
1101608 San Cayetano Alto S/N (Loja-Ecuador)
{jachicaiza,nopiedra,jalopez2}@utpl.edu.ec
[2] Dpto. Lenguajes y Sistemas Informáticos e Ingeniería
Universidad Politécnica de Madrid
edmundo.tovar@upm.es

Abstract. One of the main objectives of open knowledge, and specifically of Open Educational Resource movement, is to allow people to access the resources they need for learning. The first step to that a learner starts this process is to find information and resources according to his/her needs. One of the reasons why OERs could stay hidden and therefore to be underutilized is that each institution and producer of this kind of resources, labels them using tags or informal and heterogeneous knowledge schemes. This issue was identified in the Open Education Consortium (until recently called OpenCourseWare Consortium) study, where respondents noted that one way to improve the courses is to make a "major better categorization of courses according to subject areas". In previous works, the authors present the Linked OpenCourseWare Data project, which published metadata of courses coming from different open educational datasets. So far there are over 7000 indexed courses associated to 626 topic names or knowledge fields, however, appear different names meaning similar areas or they are written in different languages and also correspond to different detail level. The semantic lack in the relations between areas and subjects make it difficult to find associations between topics and to list recommendations about resources for learners. In this work, authors present a process to support semi-automatic classification of Open Educational Resources, taking advantage from linked data available in the Web through systems made by people who can converge to a formal knowledge organization system.

Keywords: OCW, linked data, classification, knowledge area, discovery of resources, web of data, thesaurus, DBPedia.

1   Introduction

In the last years, the amount of Open Educational Resources (OER) on the Web has increased dramatically, especially thanks to initiatives like OpenCourseWare (OCW) and Massive Online Open Course (MOOC).

In e-leaning there are a huge amount of educational resources to be used; however, in most cases it is very difficult and cumbersome for users (teachers, students and

P. Klinov and D. Mouromtsev (Eds.): KESW 2014, CCIS 468, pp. 15–28, 2014.

self-learners) find or explore these resources, among other reasons due to the diversity of data and repositories, and partly by the reduced use of agreed metadata schemas and knowledge organization systems.

In [1, 4], the problem of the access to OER repositories is analysed. In 2013, by scrappy techniques we extracted the metadata of the available resources in OCW sites. From the review of the extracted data, it was possible to check that each institution and producer of this kind of resources labels them using tags or informal and heterogeneous knowledge schemes or academic subjects.

In that case, there are over 7000 indexed courses associated to 626 unique category names or knowledge fields, many names correspond to similar areas written in different ways or different languages and also correspond to different detail level. The semantic lack in the relations between areas and subjects make it difficult to find associations between topics and to list recommendations about courses for self-learners. This issue was identified in the Open Education Consortium (until recently called OpenCourseWare Consortium) study [2], where respondents noted that one way to improve the OCW is to make a "major better categorization of courses according to subject areas".

With the aim of improve the OERs localization, the use of thesauri and semantic models provide a controlled source of terms or concepts, it is an essential precondition to guarantee quality in document indexing and retrieval [3]. In this work, the authors propose to categorize OERs according to the organization capacity of the formal classification systems, and the data enrichment capacity that could be provided by open vocabularies and repositories created socially.

Continuing with the paper, in section 2 appears: the systems of knowledge organization, as controlled or formal ones as open and social ones, and the current approaches for the classification of resources. Later, in the section 3 describes our proposal based on Linked Data to characterize Open Educational Resources. A proof of concept, it is explained in the section 4. Finally, in the section 5 the conclusions and future works appear.

2   Theoretical Background

Tasks associated with Information Retrieval (IR) are experimenting with processes that integrate linked data available in the Web and that are codified by means of semantic technologies. This is the main approach used in this work.

Semantic Web technologies and Linked Data are changing the way information is stored, described and exploited. The term "Linked Data" refers to a set of best practices for publishing and connecting structured data on the Web [5]. In summary, the Linked Data Design Issues, outlined by Tim Berners-Lee back in 2006, provide guidelines on how to use standardized Web technologies to set data-level links between data from different sources [6].

In Web Semantic, the resources are described according to a metadata schema called vocabulary or ontology. Each resource and property are identified by a unique resource identifier (URI) with a dereferencing option. Resources descriptions and relations are encoded in RDF language (Resource Description Framework) and are stored in a repository. Finally, a query language is used to retrieve data. Thus, through the life cycle of Linked Data can be enrich, disambiguate, connect and retrieve data from heterogeneous domains, repositories or systems.

Then, we describe the potential use of knowledge organizational systems and linked data in order to classify the Web resources according to a domain.

2.1   Knowledge Organization Systems

2.1.1 Traditional Systems
Knowledge Organization Systems, such as thesauri, have traditionally been used to improve the organization and retrieval of documents. In the academic field, there are some thesauri to classify knowledge, which listed in Table 1.

Table 1. Thesauri

System name	Language	Last year of update	Context of use
Dewey Decimal Classification (DDC)	Over 35	2011	Libraries
Universal Decimal Classification (UDC)	Over 40	In English, 2005	Libraries, bibliographic, documentation and information services
UNESCO Nomenclature	English, Spanish, French and Russian	2008	Retrieval of documents and publications in several fields
Joint Academic Coding System (JACS)	English	2012-2013	Higher Education in United Kingdom
European Training Thesaurus (EuroVoc)	Over 22		European legislation and other legal texts

The DDC decimal system and UDC are of the most widely used in libraries; however, they are proprietary schemas. JACS is one of the most complete thesaurus and updated, though it is available only in English and its adoption has been restricted to the United Kingdom. Finally, EuroVoc and UNESCO thesauri are multilingual and multidisciplinary systems, however, the first one covers the activities of the European Parliament and the second one is more popular.

It is not an aim of this work analyses which of the knowledge organization systems is the best, since the decision will depend on the context and of the criteria of selection that are considered; nevertheless, as it will explain here in after, nomenclature UNESCO has been considered as case of implementation.

2.1.2 Semantic Approach for Knowledge Organisation
In Semantic Web, SKOS (Simple Knowledge Organization System) is used for representing mapping relationships among systems [15]. It provides a standard way to

represent knowledge organisation systems using RDF to describe concept schemes
such as thesauri, classification schemes, subject heading lists, taxonomies and other
types of controlled vocabulary, thus guaranteeing interoperability among applications.

In 2009, SKOS reached Recommendation status at W3C. It is a popular ontology
to organize knowledge; in the Datahub site[1], 149 datasets was found for "format-
skos"[2]. Practically all the thesauri named in the Table 1, are mapping to SKOS.

In SKOS, the elements of a thesaurus are represented by means of concepts among
which there are established hierarchic relations. In figure 1, appears the representation
of the 12 field (Mathematics) of UNESCO nomenclature and the two following levels
of disciplines that it covers. The properties skos:broader and skos:narrower are
used to assert a direct hierarchical link between two SKOS concepts.

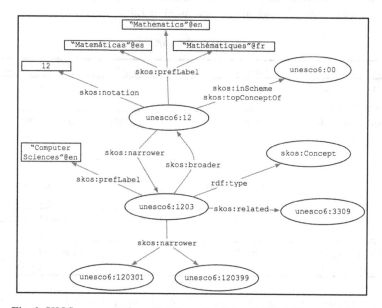

Fig. 1. SKOS representation of Mathematics field of UNESCO nomenclature

2.1.3 Sources of Social Knowledge

In the Web, the lack of update and maintenance could limit the use of a traditional
thesaurus. Therefore a formal classification system can be enriched with categories
that people spontaneously shared on social sources. Wikipedia, the encyclopedia created by the people, is the main case of success of this approach.

Therefore, sources of social knowledge specified in SKOS are being used for the
data enrichment of Web entities as people, organizations, products and knowledge
categories.

---

[1] Datahub is a data management platform from the Open Knowledge Foundation. In the site, there is the
possibility of getting a wide rage of information available in more than 9 thousand datasets.

[2] http://datahub.io/dataset?q=format-skos

In [7] are described some of the features of social data sources when organizing knowledge: i) they are the largest repositories built in a collaborative way, ii) provide an up-to-date channel of information and knowledge on a large number of topics. Thus, one should expect a high coverage of subjects that are emergent [8].

If in the Social Web, the Wikipedia is one of the major cases of success; in the Semantic Web, DBPedia is the most popular structured Web data sources.

The DBPedia ontology enables a broad coverage of entities in the world, and allows entities to bear multiple overlapping types; it includes RDF data derived from Wikipedia; each resource is harvested from a Wikipedia article (which content is maintained by thousands of editors and it broad and multilingual) [7]. In addition DBPedia resources are linked to other data sources and ontologies such as Geonames, YAGO, OpenCyc, and WordNet, providing more semantic information in the form of relations such as typeOf and sameAs. [9]

In some works the use of DBPedia is addressed to annotate, to enrich and to classify content; in the following point, some approaches are outlined in this area.

2.2   Current Techniques to Categorization in Subject Areas

Identifying the main topics and concepts associated with a document is a task common to many applications including classification, retrieval and recommendation. [10]

One of the basic approaches that can be applied to classification of an information objects into domains is to identify and to group the entities that are mentioned in his content. That is to say, this activity implies the use of i) methods for the processing text, ii) lexical data sources or mechanisms for identification of entities in the text, and iii) techniques for grouping the entities found. The text pre-processing is not covered in this paper. Next, proposals to address the points ii) and iii) are highlighted.

To perform the entity recognition, traditionally have been used approaches based on Natural Language Processing, lexical databases such as WordNet, and domain ontologies. In an open platform as the Web, the effectiveness of these methods can be reduced and the complexity can increase because there may be high topical diversity and irregular and ill-formed words [7]. In conclusion, this task is time consuming and error prone. [8]

With respect to techniques used for grouping entities, the most popular ones are based-on: i) learning machine: Bayesian Network and Semantic Vector Model (SVM) to classify or k-means to clustering and ii) probabilistic: Latent Dirichlet Analysis (LDA), Latent Semantic Analysis (LSA) and Latent Semantic Indexing (LSI). We can also quote the Hierarchical Relational Models, which are based on text analysis in order to identify topics from the words of a document [16]. In [8] and [9] some of these approaches are analysed.

Thanks to the growth of the open linked data, new methods based on this paradigm are emerging; then, some works are outlined.

In [7], the structured knowledge of DBPedia and Freebase are used for the contextual enrichment of a Tweet's entities by providing information that can help to disambiguate the role of a given entity in a particular context. This enrichment is based on a developed technique for deriving semantic meta-graphs from different sources.

To identifying the topics in posts published in social media [9] presents a method that combines NLP (natural language processing), tag-based and semantic-based techniques, and unsupervised method, which learns from Wikipedia corpus avoiding the need of training data that is difficult to gather in environments such as the social web where the vocabulary is in constant change.

A proposal with a similar objective to the previous one is presented in [8]. It classifies blog posts by topics with supervised learning machine techniques (distance supervision and Network Bayesians). To obtain training data for the classifier, this work uses Wikipedia articles labelled with Freebase domains.

However, if a supervised approach is adopted, a considerable training effort can be required. To avoid this problem, in [11] a method to categorize blogs using a domain dictionary is proposed, it there is not used the machine learning. Authors of [11] find their classification method to be up to 99% accurate.

Finally, [10] uses Wikipedia articles and categories, and article link graphs to predict concepts common to a set of documents. In this work, uses spreading activation technique to predict a very generalized category.

In summary, all the mentioned works are based on a social data source as the Wikipedia or on sources structured as DBPedia or Freebase. Nevertheless, these works, except [10], do not take advantage of the hierarchic relations between categories of concepts and resources.

Unlike the traditional methods of classification, in this work we propose the use of an algorithm to exploitation of graph structures and semantic relations between entities. The experimentation result of [10], which uses this approach, supports our method.

Probably the method that is proposes in [10] is similar the method that we propose in this paper, though they differs in the intention and [10] does not include a phase of enrichment of a thesaurus based on a source of social knowledge.

2.3   Use of Spreading Activation to Traverse a Graph

Spreading activation method is a class of iterative algorithms for relevancy propagation, local search, relationship/association search, and computing of dynamic local ranking. [12]

The main idea of spreading activation is that it is possible to retrieve relevant resources if they are associated with other resources by means of some type of connection [10]. For this reason, it is one of the approaches used for recommendation in graph-based systems.

The spreading activation algorithm is based on the breadth first expansion from seed nodes in the graph data structure. It employs iterative steps where activation is propagated between neighbour nodes. [12]

In Figure 2, there appear two forms of spread of the algorithm: i) from a seed node crosses the graph to activate other nodes and to find related entities, and ii) from several seed nodes, the nodes that are directly related are activated until come together in one or more top level nodes.

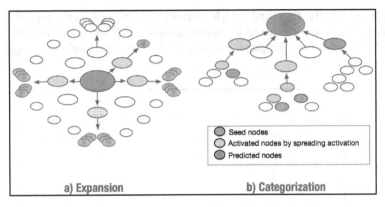

Fig. 2. Graph propagation by spreading activation algorithm

a. Expansion of graph: This task can be performed for finding related entities to a given resource, i.e. the semantic relations graph helps by predicting more specific concepts [10]. In information retrieval, this approach can be used to expand a user's query, to annotate semantically a resource or to recommend related entities.

b. Categorization of concepts: According to [10] the Wikipedia (or DBPedia) category graph can be used to predict generalized concepts. To achieve this aim, the key factor is the navigation by the path defined by the hierarchic relations that SKOS proposes.

In the following section, we explain the framework proposed to classify OERs that takes advantage of data, relations and structure of directed graph of social knowledge sources.

3   Process for Domain Categorization of OER

To initiate a learning process, OERs must be described, classified and characterized so that those could be suggested to the learners. This work is part of a major initiative that aims to improve access and use of open educational resources, by self-learners, through different discovery services.

In figure 3, appears the general process to be implemented to categorize OERs and further provide the resources that need a self-learner.

In [1] we proposed a framework based on Linked Data to describe and interoperate data from distributed and heterogeneous OCW-repositories. The result of this work was the repository of linked data, LOCWD (Linked OCW Data). From this source of OCW metadata and OERs was implemented a platform to discover and visualize open educational resources, named Serendipity[3] [4]. However, when users search OER

---

[3]   Serendipity, the search engine is available in: http://serendipity.utpl.edu.ec. Serendipity, the service for visualization is available in: http://serendipity.utpl.edu.ec/map.

through Serendipity, they find a high diversity of data, especially, topical. For this reason, in this paper, we extend the previous work and propose a method for categorizing OERs exploiting the graph structure of the Data Web and knowledge created collaboratively.

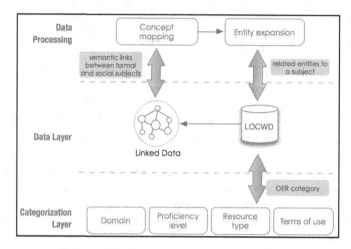

Fig. 3. General Framework for categorize OERs

3.1   Data Processing

At this stage as seen in Figure 4, two tasks are performed in an offline way: i) mapping between formal classification system (controlled) and social organization system (open), and ii) expansion of main concepts of formal thesaurus through categories existing in social data sources.

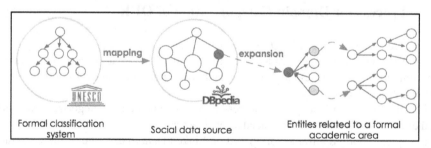

Fig. 4. Tasks of Data Processing: mapping and expansion

3.1.1 Concept or Topical Mapping
To achieve the semantic interoperability among different collections or schemes [3, 13] propose to create links between equivalents objects.

During the creation of links between entities it must face key challenges as: name variation, entity ambiguity or absence of data [14]. For the first case, a previous task of pre-processing text is needed; to solve ambiguity issues, it will be necessary to obtain or to provide additional information. As for the third aspect, it can happen due to the fact that some sub-disciplines of the chosen thesaurus it has lost force, therefore, it does not produce major impact, if it is not possible to find the equivalent resource.

Considering this problematic, the main objective there is not automate this activity, rather, a semi-automatic system could support to expert who realize this work.

As mentioned earlier, in this work it has been chosen the system of 6-digit of the nomenclature UNESCO. Since 2013, there is an implementation of this thesaurus according to SKOS, which groups the different categories of the nomenclature in a only scheme of concepts (skos:ConceptScheme). On the other hand, the selected target scheme is DBPedia; an approach of multiple sources to enrich, disambiguate and get better results can be adopted. [7]

From the found associations, semantic relations must be created and stored in a semantic repository. In the future these equivalences will be used to categorize resources.

SKOS defines certain properties in order to define mappings between SKOS concepts from different concept schemes, where the links are inherent in the meaning of the linked concepts. In an academic environment, we propose to use the skos:exactMatch transitive property to link two concepts (formal-to-open), it indicates a high degree of confidence that the concepts can be used interchangeably across a wide range of information retrieval applications [15].

3.1.2 Entity Expansion

In order to find entities related to each of the sub-disciplines of the formal system, the spreading activation method is applied. Of recursive form, the graph of the social and structured repository is traversing; with each iteration, the nodes related to the active node are visited. In this point, relevant relations that link the nodes should be chosen.

Also for purposes of categorization, we propose to associate a weight to each semantic relationship so that the nodes can be sorted. To finish this task, descriptive attributes of every entity (as label, abstract and comment in several languages) could be recover them. All this information is stored in the knowledge repository.

Moreover, data obtained in this stage have been used to annotate and connect digital resources that will be offered for the learning of self-learners. The recognized entities on the text of the educational resource are stored in the knowledge repository for a later query on the part of the services oriented to final user.

3.2   Categorization Layer

At this point, the goal is organize the OERs according to at least 4 categories: i) knowledge area according to a formal classification system, ii) proficiency level that allow achieve, iii) type of resource, and iv) rights for use and reuse. In Table 2, it can be seen a set of possible values that can take each of these categories.

Table 2.   Categories for OER organization

Category	Range of possible values
Knowledge area	Each field of the chosen thesaurus
Proficiency level	Introductory
	Intermediate
	Advanced
OER type	Activity
	Coursework
	Lecture Note
	Syllabus
	Learning Guide
	...
Rights for use and reuse	According to the specification of Creative Commons Licenses[4]:
	Share: copy and redistribute the material in any medium or format.
	Adapt: remix, transform, and build upon the material.
	For any purpose, even commercially.

As it explains in the following section, OERs' categorization of agreement to areas of knowledge is possible using linked data. As shown in the following rule, from the subjects related to an entity recognized in the OER content, it is possible to converge to more general concepts, such as the disciplines or fields of a knowledge organisation system.

```
forall(?R)
[rdfs:Resource(?r) AND skos:Concept(?c1) AND
skos:Concept(?c2)
AND dcterms:subject(?r, ?c1) AND skos:broader(?c1, ?c2)
]->
  [dcterms:subject(?r, ?c1)]
```

As for the categories: license, type of resource and proficiency level, the range of values is more limited, therefore, an approach based on technologies of natural processing and supervised learning can be cash. In the LOCWD repository, we analyze the value space of each metadata and identify patterns to create groups as indicated in Table 1. Next, a subset of the possible values for the category "Activity" of the metadata OER type is indicated.

```
domain(Activity) = {"Assignment"@en | "Ejercicio"@es |
"Exam"@en | "Exercise"@en | "Práctica"@es | "Prueba"@es |
"Project"@en | "Assignment"@en | "Examen"@es | ...}
```

---

[4] http://creativecommons.org/licenses/by/4.0/

After to this stage, some services that allow locating relevant educational resources can be implemented. Currently, we are building applications, orientated for the final users, based on services Web that maximizes the reutilization of components and sharing of data.

4   Proof of Concept

A proof of concept of the proposed method is presented below. The test scenario includes: i) type of categorization: according to a UNESCO nomenclature, specifically, the Computer Science field, ii) DBPedia as open repository and iii) corpus of OERs: a subset of resources collected on LOCWD project.

4.1   Data Processing

4.1.1 Data Collection

The nomenclature UNESCO in SKOS format is accessible in http://skos.um.es/ sparql/. A script implemented in Python has allowed recovering information of every subject. The following query was executed to retrieve data from external dataset. `<%s>` represents each of the properties of a SKOS concept.

```
PREFIX u: <http://www.w3.org/2004/02/skos/core#>
SELECT DISTINCT ?concept ?label
WHERE {
GRAPH <http://skos.um.es/unesco6>
{ ?concept a u:Concept.
  ?concept <%s> ?label
}
}
```

On the basis of the following query we have recovered: 17480 units of RDF information (tripletes), 5 SKOS properties for every concept (`prefLabel`, i.e, prefered name of each area in three different languages, `narrower` that links a discipline to a top field, `broader` inverse relation of narrower and the properties `notation`, `inSchema`), and 2504 UNESCO categories.

From the categories' titles, the service Sem4tags[5] was used to choose the DBPedia semantic entity that better defines each concept. Applying this method of the 27 sub-disciplines of the Computer Science field, 16 were found based on similarity of titles between the two sources, 10 were mapped manually using Wikipedia and Google to find the best candidates, in one case no equivalent category was found in DBPedia (Sensors systems design), finally, the general category "Other (specify)" was not considered.

---

[5] http://grafias.dia.fi.upm.es/Sem4Tags/

4.1.2 Entity Expansion

Then, to find entities (topics, tags, people) related to each of the sub-disciplines of Computer Science, the scripting language Gremlin[6] was used to traverse DBPedia according to spreading activation method.

Applying this method, the categories with more related resources were: Artificial Intelligence (1215), Data Banks (1416) and Hybrid Computing (4205). By contrast, the categories for which fewer resources were found are: Accounting (20), Automated manufacturing systems (36), and Computer and software (39).

For the "Programming language" category, 437 entities were found belonging to different types of resources. Table 3 enlists the entities that reached the top ten.

Table 3. Top ten entities recommended for the "Programming Language" sub-discipline

DBPedia URI	Position
http://dbpedia.org/resource/Category:Programming_language_topics	1
http://dbpedia.org/resource/Category:Procedural_programming_languages	2
http://dbpedia.org/resource/Category:Computer_programming	3
http://dbpedia.org/resource/Category:Computer_languages	4
http://dbpedia.org/resource/Category:Academic_programming_languages	5
http://dbpedia.org/resource/Category:Multi-paradigm_programming_languages	6
http://dbpedia.org/resource/Category:Programming_language_theory	7
http://dbpedia.org/resource/Category:Data-structured_programming_languages	8
http://dbpedia.org/resource/Category:Object-based_programming_languages	9
http://dbpedia.org/resource/Category:Dependently_typed_languages	10

4.2   Categorization According a Sub-discipline

A set of OERs indexed by search engine Serendipity was annotated through KIM platform, which was customized to recognize the DBPedia entities extracted in the previous step.

To illustrate the principle of categorization using the spreading activation algorithm, we expose a case of a resource entitled " Connecting Java and Matlab". Through the process of annotation, were found as main entities: Java [http://dbpedia.org/resource/Java_(programming_language)] and MatLab [http://dbpedia.org/resource/MATLAB]. From these two resources recognized in the content of the resource starts the traversing through the hierarchical relationships that link resources. The iterative process should end when it is found a DBPedia category equivalent to a UNESCO sub-discipline. Fig. 5 shows the path between annotated entities and the goal category "Programming Language".

After the preliminary results obtained, we continue by testing and improving the defined activities. Later, authors hope to share with the community the implemented code.

---

[6] https://github.com/tinkerpop/gremlin/wiki

5   Conclusion

For an Open Educational Resource (OER) to be used as learning strategy into a formal or informal learning process must have specific characteristics and pedagogical information, in order to supply their discovery of searching tools and their use for people. In this work, four forms are proposed to organize OERs; concretely, we have proposed a method to categorize resources in a specific domain.

Through a concrete case, we tried to demonstrate that is possible to find semantic relationships between a formal knowledge organisation system and a social knowledge source. Creating links between these two systems is done with the aim of expanding the network of concepts of a formal and static system, by means of the spontaneous categories and dynamic that occurs in social systems like Wikipedia and DBPedia.

Moreover, this work demonstrate that it is possible to support semi-automatic classification of OCW courses, taking advantage from linked data available in the Web through systems made by people who can converge to a formal knowledge fields classification system. The representation of areas or subjects and their relationships through semantic technologies, will help the discovery of such kind of resources for students and self-learners at worldwide.

Different systems or applications could make inference on subject demanded by a learner and could display recommendations to get more relevant resources to support learning. In order to deliver more relevant results to the learners, we are currently designing a recommendation service that will use the categories defined for a resource and the top-concepts encountered during the expansion phase.

Acknowledgment. The work has been partially funded by scholarship provided by the "Secretaría Nacional de Educación Superior, Ciencia y Tecnología e Innovación" of Ecuador (SENESCYT).

References

1. Piedra, N., Tovar, E., Colomo-Palacios, R., López, J., Chicaiza, J.: Consuming and producing linked open data: The case of Opencourseware. Program: Electronic Library and Information Systems 48, 16–40 (2014)
2. OpenCourseWare Consortium: OCWC User Feedback Survey Results » Announcements (2013), http://www.openedconsortium.org/news/2013/06/ocwc-user-feedback-survey-results/
3. Francesconi, E., Faro, S., Marinai, E., Perugi, G.: A Methodological Framework for Thesaurus Semantic Interoperability. In: Proceeding of the Fifth European Semantic Web Conference, pp. 76–87 (2008)
4. Tovar, E., Piedra, N., López, J., Chicaiza, J., Martínez, O.: Linked OpenCourseWare Data: a demonstration of the potential use of OCW Universia linked Data. OpenCourse Ware Consortium Global Meetings, Cambridge, U.K (2012)
5. Bizer, C., Heath, T., Berners-Lee, T.: Linked Data - The Story So Far. International Journal on Semantic Web and Information Systems 5(3), 1–22 (2009)

6. Bizer, C.: The Emerging Web of Linked Data. IEEE Intelligent Systems 24(5), 87–92 (2009)
7. Cano, A.E., Varga, A., Rowe, M., Ciravegna, F., He, Y.: Harnessing Linked Knowledge Sources for Topic Classification in Social Media. In: Proceedings of the 24th ACM Conference on Hypertext and Social Media, pp. 41–50 (2013)
8. Husby, S.D., Barbosa, D.: Topic Classification of Blog Posts Using Distant Supervision. In: Proceedings of the 13th Conference of the European Chapter of the Association for Computational Linguistics, pp. 28–36 (2012)
9. Muñoz-García, O., García-Silva, A., Corcho, O., de la Higuera, M., Navarro, C.: Identifying Topics in Social Media Posts using DBpedia. In: Proceedings of the Networked and Electronic Media Summit (NEM summit 2011), Torino, Italia (2011)
10. Syed, Z., Finin, T., Joshi, A.: Wikipedia as an ontology for describing documents. In: Proc. of the Second Int. Conference on Weblogs and Social Media. AAAI Press (2008)
11. Hashimoto, C., Kurohashi, S.: Blog Categorization Exploiting Domain Dictionary and Dynamically Estimated Domains of Unknown Words. In: Proceedings of ACL 2008: HLT, pp. 69–72 (2009)
12. Troussov, A., Parra, D., Brusilovsky, P.: Spreading Activation Approach to Tag-aware Recommenders: Modeling Similarity on Multidimensional Networks. In: Proceedings of Workshop on Recommender Systems and the Social Web at the 2009 ACM Conference on Recommender Systems, RecSys 2009, New York, NY, October 25 (2009)
13. van Gendt, M., Isaac, A., van der Meij, L., Schlobach, S.: Semantic Web Techniques for Multiple Views on Heterogeneous Collections: A Case Study. In: Gonzalo, J., Thanos, C., Verdejo, M.F., Carrasco, R.C. (eds.) ECDL 2006. LNCS, vol. 4172, pp. 426–437. Springer, Heidelberg (2006)
14. Olieman, A.M.: Mastery Profiling through Entity Linking, to Support Project Team Formation in Higher Education. Graduate Thesis - University of Amsterdam - Information Studies (2013)
15. W3C: SKOS Simple Knowledge Organization System Reference (2009), http://www.w3.org/TR/skos-reference/
16. Chang, J., Blei, D.: Hierarchical Relational Models for Document Networks. The Annals of Applied Statistics 4(1), 124–150 (2010)

Cloud Sensor Ontology and Linked Data to Support Autonomicity in Cloud Application Platforms

Rustem Dautov[1], Iraklis Paraskakis[1], and Mike Stannett[2]

[1] South-East European Research Centre (SEERC),
CITY College — International Faculty of the University of Sheffield,
Thessaloniki, Greece
{rdautov,iparaskakis}@seerc.org
[2] Department of Computer Science, University of Sheffield, UK
m.stannett@sheffield.ac.uk

Abstract. Cloud application platforms with their numerous deployed applications, platform and third-party services are becoming increasingly complex, dynamic and data-intensive, and require novel intelligent approaches to be applied in order to maintain them at an operational level. By treating cloud application platforms as distributed networks of software sensors and utilising techniques from the Semantic Sensor Web area, we have developed a monitoring framework which allows us to detect, diagnose and react to emerging critical situations in complex environments of cloud application platforms in a dynamic manner. In this paper, we focus on our use of a Sensor Cloud Ontology to: (i) represent cloud-based logical software sensors; (ii) homogenise monitored sensor data in the form of RDF streams; and (iii) apply stream and static reasoning to these monitored values in order to detect critical situations. We also explain how utilisation of Linked Data principles can help achieve a more flexible and extensible architecture to define diagnosis and adaptation policies. We discuss benefits associated with our approach, as well as potential shortcomings and challenges.

Keywords: Cloud Computing, Autonomic Computing, Semantic Sensor Web, SSN Ontology, Linked Sensor Data.

1 Introduction and Motivation

Since its emergence nearly 15 years ago [3,4], the Semantic Web stack has developed into a wide range of solutions and technologies whose purpose is no longer limited to providing computer-readable meaning to the Web, but now encompasses a range of problem domains, not necessarily related to the Semantic Web, where existing challenges dictate a need for novel intelligent approaches.

One such area is the domain of Cloud Application Platforms (CAPs). These are a group of Platform-as-a-Service (PaaS) cloud offerings, characterised by

P. Klinov and D. Mouromtsev (Eds.): KESW 2014, CCIS 468, pp. 29–43, 2014.

extensive customer support for developing, testing, deploying and maintaining software. CAPs not only provision their customers with an operating system and run-time execution environment, but additionally offer a range of generic, reliable, composable and reusable services, following the principles of Service-Oriented Computing (SOC) [22,27]. For example, Google App Engine[1] currently offers 41 services (or "features"), Microsoft Windows Azure[2] provides 17 built-in services and 46 add-ons (i.e., third-party services registered with the platform), and Heroku[3] offers over 100 add-on services.

However, such a flexible model for application development, in which complex application systems are assembled from existing components, has its pitfalls. Cloud platform providers increasingly find themselves in a situation where the ever-growing complexity of resulting environments poses new challenges as to how large volumes of actively streaming, heterogeneous and uncertain data should be dynamically analysed to support situation assessment and run-time adaptations. Accordingly, our research focuses on how Semantic Web technologies (specifically, OWL ontologies, SWRL rules, RDF streams and continuous SPARQL query languages) can be utilised to define semantic streams of monitored data which will then be queried and reasoned over in order to perform situation assessment and suggest further adaptation strategies. Using these technologies has allowed us to develop a small-scale prototype self-adaptation framework which enables dynamic monitoring and intelligent analysis of flowing data within CAPs to support run-time adaptations.

The rest of the paper is organised as follows. Section 2 is dedicated to background information, outlining both the context of the research presented in this paper, and some of our earlier findings. It briefs the reader on: (a) our approach to treating CAPs as distributed networks of software sensors; and (b) the self-adaptation framework for CAPs. In Section 3 we study existing ontologies for modelling cloud environments and sensor-enabled domains, and position our work at the intersection of these two domains. Section 4 describes the Cloud Sensor Ontology which lies at the core of our self-adaptation framework, and illustrates its role in the definition of RDF streams, C-SPARQL queries and SWRL rules using an example based on Heroku add-on services. In Section 5 we elaborate on the presented semantic approach and explain how it can be further extended utilising Linked Data principles. Section 6 concludes the paper.

2   Background

2.1   Cloud Application Platforms as Sensor Networks

A fundamental underpinning of our approach is our interpretation of CAPs as distributed networks of "software sensors" – that is, services, deployed applications, platform components, etc., which constantly emit raw heterogeneous data

---

[1] https://cloud.google.com/products/app-engine/
[2] http://azure.microsoft.com/
[3] https://heroku.com

which has to be monitored and analysed to support run-time situation assessment.[4] This enables us to apply existing solutions developed by the Semantic Sensor Web (SSW) community, which address the requirements of Sensor Web Enablement [8] by combining ideas from two research areas, the Semantic Web and the Sensor Web; this combination enables situation awareness by providing enhanced meaning for sensor observations [28]. In particular, we were inspired by the Semantic Sensor Networks (SSN) approach to express heterogeneous sensor values in terms of RDF triples using a common ontological vocabulary, and have created our own Cloud Sensor Ontology (CSO) to act as the core element of a self-adaptation framework for CAPs.

2.2 Self-adaptation Framework for CAPs

Fig. 1 demonstrates a high-level architecture of the self-adaptation framework, taking the established MAPE-K model [21] as an underlying model for self-adaptation. In order to support both self-awareness and context-awareness of the managed elements (i.e., software sensors within CAPs), we needed to develop certain modeling techniques to define the adaptation-relevant knowledge of the cloud environment (e.g., platform components, available resources, connections between them, entry-points for monitoring and execution, adaptation and diagnosis policies, etc.). In particular, we wanted to ensure:

- separation of concerns;
- the ability to make flexible modifications through declarative definitions;
- enhanced reuse capabilities, automation and reliability (as opposed to traditional hard-coded approaches).

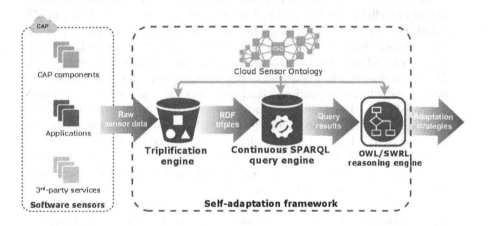

Fig. 1. High-level architecture of the self-adaptation framework

Our solution was to develop a Cloud Sensor Ontology, which also serves as a common vocabulary of terms, shared across the whole managed system, and

---

[4] For a more detailed overview of our approach we refer interested readers to [12].

corresponds to the Knowledge component of the MAPE-K model. Accordingly, our ontological classes and properties serve as "building blocks" for creating RDF streams, C-SPARQL [2] queries and SWRL rules. By annotating monitored values with semantic descriptions, we enabled the framework to combine observation streams with static ontological knowledge and perform run-time formal reasoning. This work in turn opened promising opportunities for performing run-time analysis, problem diagnosis, and suggesting further adaptation actions [14]. In this paper we focus on the Semantic Web aspects of our approach.

3   Related Work

There has been a considerable amount of research efforts in the direction of conceptually modelling cloud environments with ontologies and thus benefit from declarative definitions, human-readability, built-in reasoning capabilities, standardised languages, interoperability, easy accessibility, etc. [35]. In [1] Androcec et al. provide a holistic view on the existing works and presents a systematic review of 24 cloud ontologies. According to this review, the whole body of work can be classified into four main categories:

- *Cloud resources and services description* – studies in this category describe cloud delivery models (i.e., IaaS, PaaS, SaaS), resources and services, pricing models, etc. Examples of ontologies belonging to this category include [7,15,24,33,37]. However, broadly speaking, all cloud ontologies can be classified under this categor et al.y, since they all describe cloud resources to certain extend.
- *Cloud security* – this category of ontologies looks at clouds from a perspective of modelling security- and privacy-related aspects. For example, in [32] Takahashi et al. devised an ontology based on cyber-security operational information of cloud systems, and developed the Countermeasure Knowledge Base – a set of assessment rules with scoring methodologies and check-lists.
- *Cloud interoperability* – studies in this category use ontologies to achieve interoperability among various cloud providers, their services and APIs (often based on existing standards and proposals for software interoperability), and thus minimise the so-called "lock-in" effect. A notable example in this category is the cloud ontology, which was derived in the frame of the mO-SAIC project [25] and aims at providing a transparent and simple access to heterogeneous cloud resources and avoid locked-in proprietary solutions. Other examples also include [5] and [18].
- *Cloud services discovery and selection* – this category consists of ontologies which facilitate the process of discovery and selection of best cloud services. Typically, an ontology serves as a unified common benchmark against which the comparison of various heterogeneous services is performed. Examples of such ontologies include [11,17,19,20,31,38].

Another cluster of related research efforts comprises studies which utilise ontologies to formally describe sensor-enabled domains, collectively referred to as

Semantic Sensor Web (SSW) [28]. Compton et al. [9] provide a survey of 12 SSW ontologies, which provide vocabularies of concepts, relationships between those concepts and built-in reasoning techniques to facilitate semantic interoperability, and compare these ontologies with respect to such criteria as main purpose of use, expressive power, underlying technology, etc.

In this light, a particularly notable and representative example of an ontology used to model sensor networks of any complexity via a common and standardised vocabulary is the Semantic Sensor Network (SSN) ontology, developed by the SSW community. It is a product of careful analysis and comparison of existing sensor ontologies by a group of established researchers and experts in the field [36]. The SSN ontology comprises ten modules, and includes 41 concepts and 39 object properties, which describe sensors, the accuracy and capabilities of such sensors, observations and methods used for sensing, as well as other related concepts [10]. Despite this coverage, the ontology remains domain-independent, as it does not describe domain concepts – these are intended to be defined separately, and included from other linked resources. Such domain independence allows for potential applications of the ontology to a wide range of sensor-enabled domains (for example, the emerging area Internet of Things [29]), and is exploited in the work described in this paper.

Nevertheless, none of the existing cloud ontologies features the sensor-related dimension, and none of the existing sensor ontologies captures the "logical" sensors of CAPS (albeit they offer ways of extending them with relevant concepts). Given this situation, we have developed our own Cloud Sensor Ontology[5] (CSO), which combines the two aforementioned domains, and in the next section we explain how it can be used to express software sensors within CAPs.

4   Cloud Sensor Ontology (CSO)

The principles underpinning the development of the CSO reflected existing insights, best practices, and recommendations as to how sensor-enabled domains should be modeled using ontologies (apart from the SSN ontology, which was the main point of reference in our work, other important influences were OntoSensor [16] and Ontonym [34]). Moreover, when developing the CSO, we tried to follow established ontology engineering principles [26,30], such as clarity, coherence, consistency, extensibility and adoption of naming conventions.

Having outlined some of the key structures defined within CSO, we demonstrate by example how the resulting ontology can be used to define RDF streams, C-SPARQL queries and SWRL rules, thereby helping to detect excessive numbers of client connections to Heroku's Postgres database add-on service.

4.1   Structure of the CSO

When shifting focus from the conventional physical sensor devices of the Sensor Web domain to the "logical software sensors" of CAPs, many of the concepts

---

[5] Available at http://seerc.org/ikm/docs/cso.owl.

defined in existing sensor ontologies become irrelevant and may be omitted. Mainly, these are the concepts related to the physical placement and environment of sensor devices. Additionally, since existing ontologies primarily target sensor observations, they do not include concepts related to situation assessment and adaptations, and this was another challenge for us when developing the CSO.

Logically, CSO can be divided into an upper (i.e., platform-independent) and a lower (i.e., platform-specific) level. The former contains high-level concepts which are potentially reusable across multiple CAPs, whereas the latter contains domain-specific knowledge, such as actual cloud service names and their properties. Accordingly, as far as the principle of *ontology completeness* is concerned, our work on these levels is still ongoing: we are investigating various case studies (one of which will be demonstrated below) with a view to extending and optimising both the upper and the lower parts of the ontology, e.g., to capture concepts relevant to a specific CAP and its services.

The upper ontology includes 5 modules:

- Sensor (Fig. 2) – this is the main class used to describe sensors within CAPs, and includes such subclasses as Service, PlatformComponent, Application, User, etc.
- Property (Fig. 3) – this class describes various qualities of software sensors to be observed, such as Size (further sub-classed into DatabaseSize, QueueSize, etc.); Time (further sub-classed into ExecutionTime, QueuingTime, StartingTime, FinishTime, etc.); and NumberOfConnections. The Property class is related to Sensor through the hasProperty object property, which is further sub-classed into hasTime, hasSize, hasNumberOfConnections, etc. In adopting this structure we have followed the *Sensor-Observes-Property* pattern adopted by the SSN, OntoSensor and Ontonym ontologies. This pattern facilitates conciseness and

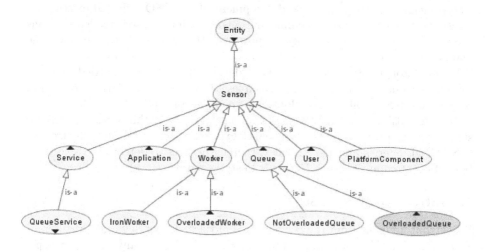

Fig. 2. Upper ontology: the Sensor module

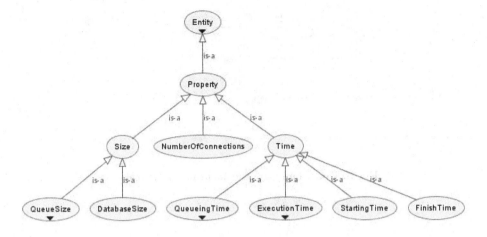

Fig. 3. Upper ontology: the `Property` module

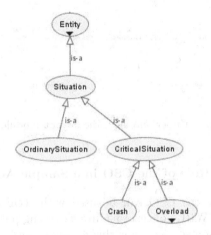

Fig. 4. Upper ontology: the `Situation` module

enables defining the upper concepts (i.e., `Sensor`, `hasProperty`, `Property`) first, and then extending them with required subclasses and sub-properties, thus avoiding redundancy and repetitions.

- `Situation` (Fig. 4) – this class contains the subclasses `CriticalSituation` and `OrdinarySituation`, which are used to classify observations as either requiring or not requiring adaptation actions. `CriticalSituation` includes such subclasses as `Crash`, `Overload`, and `ClientConnectionViolation`.
- `Adaptation` (Fig. 5) – this class defines possible adaptation actions in response to detected critical situations, and includes such subclasses as `ResourceProvisioning`, `ResourceDeprovisioning`, and `Substitution`.
- `Object` (Fig. 6) – this is an auxiliary class to model all other entities within CAPs which should not necessarily be modeled as `Sensors`.

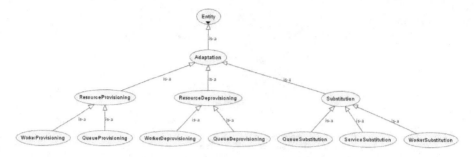

Fig. 5. Upper ontology: the `Adaptation` module

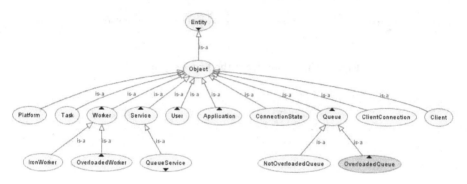

Fig. 6. Upper ontology: the `Object` module

4.2 Example: The Role of the CSO in a Sample Adaptation Loop

We now illustrate how the CSO can be used with RDF sensor streams, C-SPARQL queries and SWRL policies to address existing potential shortcomings of Heroku and its add-on services. For this example, we focus on the Postgres database service[6], one of several data storage services offered by Heroku.

Heroku's pricing model offers customers a range of subscription plans, each offering a different level of service. In particular, a typical metric relating to data storage services is the *number of simultaneous client connections*. However, customers are not currently notified in advance when the number of active connections is reaching 'danger levels', and this can result in further connection requests being unexpectedly rejected. Accordingly, our goal in this case study was to equip data storage services with sensing capabilities, so that application providers can be notified in advance whenever a threshold is approaching, allowing them to take appropriate preemptive actions – for example, by closing down low-priority connections or by automatically upgrading their subscription plan.

Using our framework we manually annotated sensor data (in this case, the current pool of client connections and the current state of the database backup

---

[6] https://www.heroku.com/postgres

process) with semantic descriptions defined in the CSO to generate a homogeneous data representation, and then streamed these RDF values to the C-SPARQL querying engine.[7] The following RDF stream captures the situation when the number of client connections increased from 15 to 18 (the connection limit is 20 for the initial subscription plan), and no backup process is running – this is important because the backup process establishes two client connections to the database, but typically lasts for less than a minute, and therefore should not be considered as a threat.

```
cso:postgres-service-10 rdf:type cso:StorageService
cso:postgres-service-10 cso:hasNumberOfConnections
     cso:number-of-connections-122
cso:number-of-connections-122 rdf:type cso:NumberOfConnections
cso:number-of-connections-122 cso:hasValue "15"^^xsd:int

cso:postgres-service-10 rdf:type cso:StorageService
cso:postgres-service-10 cso:hasNumberOfConnections
     cso:number-of-connections-122
cso:number-of-connections-122 rdf:type cso:NumberOfConnections
cso:number-of-connections-122 cso:hasValue "16"^^xsd:int

cso:backup-service-8 rdf:type cso:BackupService
cso:backup-service-8 cso:accesses cso:postgres-service-10
cso:backup-service-8 rdf:isActive "false"^^xsd:boolean

cso:postgres-service-10 rdf:type cso:StorageService
cso:postgres-service-10 cso:hasNumberOfConnections
     cso:number-of-connections-122
cso:number-of-connections-122 rdf:type cso:NumberOfConnections
cso:number-of-connections-122 cso:hasValue "18"^^xsd:int
```

In order to assess current situation and detect violations we registered a standing C-SPARQL query, which is evaluated every second and triggered whenever the number of client connections during the previous minute reaches the threshold of 18, provided there is no backup process running – that is, there are indeed 18 client connections, and there is a potential threat to the application stability.

```
REGISTER QUERY PostgresClientConnectionViolation
AS PREFIX cso:<http://seerc.org/ontology.owl#>
SELECT ?service1, ?noc
FROM STREAM <http://seerc.org/stream> [RANGE 1m STEP 1s]
WHERE { ?service1 rdf:type cso:HerokuPostgresService .
     ?service1 cso:hasNumberOfConnections ?noc .
     ?noc cso:hasValue ?v . FILTER (?v >= 18) .
```

---

[7] To extract these metrics from the Postgres service we relied on standard mechanisms offered by this database. See [13].

```
?service2 rdf:type cso:PGBackupService .
?service2 cso:accesses ?service1.
?service2 cso:isActive "false"^^xsd:boolean }
```

Once the C-SPARQL query is triggered, the corresponding critical values are instantiated in the CSO as instances of HerokuPostgresService and CriticalNumberOfConnections, and reasoning over SWRL rules is applied. The following two rules define that: (a) a situation when a Postgres service has a critical number of client connections should be classified as critical under the ClientConnectionViolation class; and (b) such a critical situation requires an adaptation – in this case a subscription plan upgrade.

```
HerokuPostgresService(?ser), CriticalNumberOfConnections(?noc),
    hasNumberOfConnections(?ser, ?noc), Situation(?sit)
            -> ClientConnectionViolation(?sit)


HerokuPostgresService(?ser), ClientConnectionViolation(?sit),
    isInSituation(?ser, ?sit)
            -> needsSubscriptionPlanUpgrade(?ser, true)
```

5   Next Steps: Linked Data

Our original motivation to employ the Semantic Web technology stack was to move away from rigid, hard-coded approaches and introduce a flexible, easily maintainable, and platform-independent way of expressing diagnosis and adaptation policies for the domain of CAPs. Our self-adaptation framework offers CAP providers an opportunity to define policies in a declarative and human-readable manner by using the underlying Cloud Sensor Ontology as a common vocabulary of terms.

However, as illustrated in the Postgres example above, this approach implies that cloud providers are responsible for maintaining adaptation-related knowledge which concerns not only the internal platform components, but also third-party services, which are registered with the given CAP. In reality, however, this is not necessarily the case. Typically, third-party service providers, having deployed their software on a cloud and exposing the API to the users, take on the responsibility to maintain the software and associated resources, and provide customers with required support. This means that CAP providers treat third-party services as black boxes and need not be aware of their internal architecture and organisation. Accordingly, this may result in situations where adaptation policies are incomplete, imprecise, or even invalid, which in turn may lead to incorrect adaptations, non-optimised resource consumption, and even system failures.

As a potential solution to this problem we are currently investigating how *Linked Data* principles can be utilised in this context. The primary goal of Linked Data is to enable discovery and sharing of semantically-enriched data over the Web using standardised technologies, such as URIs and RDF [6]. In other words, Linked Data implies the ubiquitous re-use of existing distributed data, which is exactly what we need in order to separate various pieces of adaptation policies between CAP owners and third-party service providers.

Accordingly, we believe that using Linked Data principles will enable us to create a distributed two-level ontological framework, which would consist of:

- *Platform Adaptation Ontology*: a core OWL ontology containing all the necessary concepts, relations and default SWRL rules needed to define the default adaptation-related behaviours of platform components and services.
- *Extension Adaptation Ontologies*: a set of linked OWL ontologies and SWRL rules developed by third-party service providers and deployed on the Web, which specify diagnosis and adaptation policies for respective services registered with a CAP. These ontologies may either extend or overwrite the default behaviour specified in the core Platform Adaptation Ontology.[8]

The main benefits of Linked (Open) Data are that it is *sharable, extensible,* and easily *re-usable*. In the context of a distributed ontological framework for adaptation policies, we also postulate the following additional benefits:

- Linked extensions are distributed and easily accessible over the Web by means of URIs and/or SPARQL endpoints. In this sense, software services become "self-contained" as they inform the autonomic manager about their diagnosis/adaptation policies by providing a link to the corresponding policies. The autonomic management system need not know about them in advance, but can access them at run-time using Linked Data principles.
- Linked extensions are easily modifiable. Since third-party service providers have full control over their segment of policies, they can seamlessly change them so as to reflect ongoing changes.
- Linked extensions are potentially re-usable across multiple CAPs. Indeed, it is quite common for third-party service providers to offer their services on several CAPs. For example, CloudAMQP[9] – a messaging queue service – is offered on 10 different CAPs (including Amazon Web Services[10], Heroku, Google Cloud Platform[11], etc.). Accordingly, under certain assumptions one and the same policy definition can be re-used across all of those CAPs.

Moreover, there is no need to restrict oneself to exposing as Linked Data only the schemas. In the future we may consider publishing historical CAP sensor observations (as homogenised RDF triples) in public repositories. Indeed, we already record these datasets for the purposes of post-mortem analysis, in

---

[8] It should be perhaps noted that typically the term "Linked Data" refers to published RDF datasets (or "instance data"), rather than to OWL, RDFS and SWRL vocabularies. Nevertheless, there is ongoing research aimed specifically at linking, sharing and re-using the underlying schemas, not just the datasets themselves. See, for example, Linked Open Vocabularies - LOV (`http://lov.okfn.org/dataset/lov/`) for a representative example of this research initiative.

[9] `http://www.cloudamqp.com/`

[10] `https://aws.amazon.com/`

[11] `https://cloud.google.com/`

order to identify critical failures or suboptimal behaviours. We are also planning to apply machine learning techniques so as to detect underlying trends and patterns, which will hopefully lead to more precise and accurate diagnosis, and more efficient adaptation policies. Exposing this information as Linked Data will, we believe, provide access to real-world performance measurements, and will have the potential to facilitate comparison between different CAPs.

6   Summary and Conclusions

In this paper we have presented our Cloud Sensor Ontology (CSO), and illustrated how it lies at the core of our semantic self-adaptation framework for cloud application platforms. Having Despite thoroughly studied studying related ontologies in the domains of SSW and cloud computing, we were unable to find one, which would satisfy our the requirements of sensor-enabled cloud application platforms "out of the box", and therefore opted to define our own. Taking the established SSN ontology as a reference, we developed this ontology by treating CAPs as networks of distributed "logical" software sensors. We employed the CSO as an underlying semantic architecture model of cloud environments as well as a shared vocabulary of terms for defining RDF sensor streams, C-SPARQL continuous queries for performing situation assessment, and SWRL rules for the final diagnosing and adaptation planning. We have argued that this approach allows us to benefit from an extensible architecture to introduce new software services, flexible and declarative declaration of adaptation policies, and powerful reasoning capabilities to analyse critical situations and suggest possible adaptation strategies. Accordingly, we believe that the CSO might be of interest to academic or industrial researchers willing to ontologically model complex software environments as networks of distributed logical sensors.

On the other hand, we can also identify potential shortcomings of the approach. These include the general scalability issue of formal reasoning, which in presence of large amounts of monitored data within CAPs needs to be properly addressed [23]. We are planning to perform a more formal evaluation of the CSO with respect to its scalability and "queriability" – that is, how the shape of the ontology affects the performance, and whether potential downgrades can be tolerated in favour of increased analytical and reasoning capabilities of the described approach.

We are also planning to experiment with another CAP to prove flexibility and agility of our approach. In these circumstances, another issue to be considered is the proprietary software standards, which may restrict us from inserting probes into applications to extract monitoring data.

To address the potential shortcoming associated with CAP providers being not necessarily in a position to define policies concerning a particular third-party service registered with the given CAP, we also proposed utilising Linked Data principles so as to decouple semantic knowledge concerning the CAP per se from knowledge concerning external services. This approach has the potential to create an open extensible architecture where a cloud sensor network consists of independent self-contained sensors (i.e., platform components and services), described by a two-tier distributed set of interacting ontologies.

References

1. Androcec, D., Vrcek, N., Seva, J.: Cloud Computing Ontologies: A Systematic Review. In: MOPAS 2012, The Third International Conference on Models and Ontology-based Design of Protocols, Architectures and Services, pp. 9–14 (2012)
2. Barbieri, D.F., Braga, D., Ceri, S., Della Valle, E., Grossniklaus, M.: C-SPARQL: SPARQL for continuous querying. In: Quemada, J., León, G., Maarek, Y.S., Nejdl, W. (eds.) Proceedings of the 18th International Conference on World Wide Web, WWW 2009, Madrid, Spain, April 20-24, pp. 1061–1062. ACM, New York (2009)
3. Berners-Lee, T.: Semantic Web on XML (2000),
   `http://www.w3.org/2000/Talks/1206-xml2k-tbl`
4. Berners-Lee, T., Hendler, J., Lassila, O.: The Semantic Web. Scientific American 284(5), 34–43 (2001)
5. Bernstein, D., Vij, D.: Intercloud Directory and Exchange Protocol Detail Using XMPP and RDF. In: 2010 6th World Congress on Services (SERVICES-1), pp. 431–438 (July 2010)
6. Bizer, C., Heath, T., Berners-Lee, T.: Linked Data – The Story So Far. International Journal on Semantic Web and Information Systems (IJSWIS) 5(3), 1–22 (2009)
7. Böhm, M., Leimeister, S., Riedl, C., Krcmar, H.: Cloud computing – outsourcing 2.0 or a new business model for it provisioning? In: Keuper, F., Oecking, C., Degenhardt, A. (eds.) Application Management, pp. 31–56. Gabler (2011)
8. Botts, M., Percivall, G., Reed, C., Davidson, J.: OGC® Sensor Web Enablement: Overview and High Level Architecture. In: Nittel, S., Labrinidis, A., Stefanidis, A. (eds.) GSN 2006. LNCS, vol. 4540, pp. 175–190. Springer, Heidelberg (2008)
9. Compton, M., Henson, C.A., Neuhaus, H., Lefort, L., Sheth, A.P.: A Survey of the Semantic Specification of Sensors. In: Proc. Semantic Sensor Networks 2009, pp. 17–32 (2009)
10. Compton, M., Barnaghi, P., Bermudez, L., Garcia-Castro, R., Corcho, O., Cox, S., Graybeal, J., Hauswirth, M., Henson, C., Herzog, A., Huang, V., Janowicz, K., Kelsey, W.D., Phuoc, D.L., Lefort, L., Leggieri, M., Neuhaus, H., Nikolov, A., Page, K., Passant, A., Sheth, A., Taylor, K.: The SSN Ontology of the W3C Semantic Sensor Network Incubator Group. Web Semantics: Science, Services and Agents on the World Wide Web 17 (2012),
    `http://www.websemanticsjournal.org/index.php/ps/article/view/312`
11. Dastjerdi, A.V., Tabatabaei, S.G.H., Buyya, R.: An Effective Architecture for Automated Appliance Management System Applying Ontology-Based Cloud Discovery. In: 10th IEEE/ACM International Conference on Cluster, Cloud and Grid Computing (CCGrid 2010), pp. 104–112 (May 2010)
12. Dautov, R., Paraskakis, I.: A vision for monitoring cloud application platforms as sensor networks. In: Proceedings of the 2013 ACM Cloud and Autonomic Computing Conference, pp. 25:1—25:8. ACM, Miami (2013)
13. Dautov, R., Paraskakis, I., Stannett, M.: Towards a Framework for Monitoring Cloud Application Platforms as Sensor Networks. Cluster Computing Journal (in press, 2014)

14. Dautov, R., Kourtesis, D., Paraskakis, I., Stannett, M.: Addressing Self-management in Cloud Platforms: A Semantic Sensor Web Approach. In: Proceedings of the 2013 International Workshop on Hot Topics in Cloud Services, HotTopiCS 2013, pp. 11–18. ACM, New York (2013)

15. Fortis, T.F., Munteanu, V.I., Negru, V.: Towards an ontology for cloud services. In: 2012 Sixth International Conference on Complex, Intelligent and Software Intensive Systems (CISIS), pp. 787–792 (July 2012)

16. Gruber, T.R.: Toward Principles for the Design of Ontologies Used for Knowledge Sharing. Int. J. Hum.-Comput. Stud. 43(5-6), 907–928 (1995)

17. Han, T., Sim, K.M.: An ontology-enhanced cloud service discovery system. In: Ao, S.I., Castillo, O., Douglas, C., Feng, D.D., Lee, J.A. (eds.) Proceedings of the International MultiConference of Engineers and Computer Scientists 2010, IMECS, Hong Kong, March 17-19, vol. I, pp. 644–649. Newswood Limited/International Association of Engineers (2010)

18. He, K.Q., Wang, J., Liang, P.: Semantic Interoperability Aggregation in Service Requirements Refinement. Journal of Computer Science and Technology 25(6), 1103–1117 (2010)

19. Kang, J., Sim, K.M.: Towards Agents and Ontology for Cloud Service Discovery. In: 2011 International Conference on Cyber-Enabled Distributed Computing and Knowledge Discovery (CyberC), pp. 483–490 (October 2011)

20. Kang, J., Sim, K.M.: Cloudle: An Ontology-Enhanced Cloud Service Search Engine. In: Chiu, D.K.W., Bellatreche, L., Sasaki, H., Leung, H.-F., Cheung, S.-C., Hu, H., Shao, J. (eds.) WISE Workshops 2010. LNCS, vol. 6724, pp. 416–427. Springer, Heidelberg (2011)

21. Kephart, J.O., Chess, D.M.: The vision of autonomic computing. Computer 36(1), 41–50 (2003)

22. Kourtesis, D., Bratanis, K., Bibikas, D., Paraskakis, I.: Software Co-development in the Era of Cloud Application Platforms and Ecosystems: The Case of CAST. In: Camarinha-Matos, L.M., Xu, L., Afsarmanesh, H. (eds.) Collaborative Networks in the Internet of Services. IFIP AICT, vol. 380, pp. 196–204. Springer, Heidelberg (2012)

23. Le-Phuoc, D., Dao-Tran, M., Xavier Parreira, J., Hauswirth, M.: A native and adaptive approach for unified processing of linked streams and linked data. In: Aroyo, L., Welty, C., Alani, H., Taylor, J., Bernstein, A., Kagal, L., Noy, N., Blomqvist, E. (eds.) ISWC 2011, Part I. LNCS, vol. 7031, pp. 370–388. Springer, Heidelberg (2011)

24. Ma, Y.B., Jang, S.H., Lee, J.S.: Ontology-based resource management for cloud computing. In: Nguyen, N.T., Kim, C.-G., Janiak, A. (eds.) ACIIDS 2011, Part II. LNCS, vol. 6592, pp. 343–352. Springer, Heidelberg (2011)

25. Moscato, F., Aversa, R., Di Martino, B., Fortis, T., Munteanu, V.: An analysis of mOSAIC ontology for Cloud resources annotation. In: 2011 Federated Conference on Computer Science and Information Systems (FedCSIS), pp. 973–980 (September 2011)

26. Russomanno, D.J., Kothari, C.R., Thomas, O.A.: Building a Sensor Ontology: A Practical Approach Leveraging ISO and OGC Models. In: The 2005 International Conference on Artificial Intelligence, Las Vegas, NV, USA, pp. 637–643 (2005)

27. Rymer, J.R., Ried, S., Matzke, P., Magarie, A., Anderson, A., Lisserman, M.: The Forrester Wave™: Platform-As-A-Service For Vendor Strategy Professionals, Q2 2011 – A BT Futures Report: Identifying The Best Partner Choices For ISVs And Service Providers. Business report, Forrester Research (May 19, 2011)

28. Sheth, A., Henson, C., Sahoo, S.S.: Semantic Sensor Web. IEEE Internet Computing 12(4), 78–83 (2008)
29. Soldatos, J., Serrano, M., Hauswirth, M.: Convergence of Utility Computing with the Internet-of-Things. In: Sixth International Conference on Innovative Mobile and Internet Services in Ubiquitous Computing (IMIS 2012), pp. 874–879 (2012)
30. Stevenson, G., Knox, S., Dobson, S., Nixon, P.: Ontonym: A Collection of Upper Ontologies for Developing Pervasive Systems. In: Proceedings of the 1st Workshop on Context, Information and Ontologies, CIAO 2009, pp. 9:1–9:8. ACM, New York (2009)
31. Tahamtan, A., Beheshti, S., Anjomshoaa, A., Tjoa, A.: A Cloud Repository and Discovery Framework Based on a Unified Business and Cloud Service Ontology. In: IEEE Eighth World Congress on Services (SERVICES 2012), pp. 203–210 (2012)
32. Takahashi, T., Kadobayashi, Y., Fujiwara, H.: Ontological approach toward cybersecurity in cloud computing. In: Proceedings of the 3rd International Conference on Security of Information and Networks, SIN 2010, pp. 100–109. ACM, New York (2010)
33. Tsai, W.T., Sun, X., Balasooriya, J.: Service-Oriented Cloud Computing Architecture. In: Proceedings of the 2010 Seventh International Conference on Information Technology: New Generations, ITNG 2010, pp. 684–689. IEEE Computer Society, Washington, DC (2010)
34. Uschold, M., Gruninger, M.: Ontologies: Principles, methods and applications. Knowl. Eng. Rev. 11, 93–136 (1996)
35. Uschold, M., Gruninger, M.: Ontologies and semantics for seamless connectivity. SIGMOD Rec. 33(4), 58–64 (2004)
36. W3C Semantic Sensor Network Incubator Group: Review of sensor and observations ontologies (June 17, 2011)
37. Youseff, L., Butrico, M., Da Silva, D.: Toward a Unified Ontology of Cloud Computing. In: Grid Computing Environments Workshop, GCE 2008, pp. 1–10 (November 2008)
38. Zhang, M., Ranjan, R., Nepal, S., Menzel, M., Haller, A.: A Declarative Recommender System for Cloud Infrastructure Services Selection. In: Vanmechelen, K., Altmann, J., Rana, O.F. (eds.) GECON 2012. LNCS, vol. 7714, pp. 102–113. Springer, Heidelberg (2012)

Construction of Personalized Information Services for Researchers

Viktoria Foteyeva and Michail Panteleyev

St. Petersburg Electrotechnical University "LETI", Russia
{vnfoteyeva,mpanteleyev}@gmail.com

Abstract. As the amount of information available on the Internet is growing very rapidly (including Linked Data, in particular Linked Open Data), creation of customized tools for knowledge management is becoming increasingly important. The paper proposes an approach to construction of personalized information services that can be customized to the needs of different users. The approach is based on two models: model of user's information needs and information environment model (types of data sources). An implementation of the approach is considered on the example of system which is intended for concrete category of users: researchers in the area of the Semantic Web. Three basic types of users queries have been identified: news, general and analytical. Designing the personalized service is considered from the standpoint of the main stages of the queries lifecycle: its construction and execution. Two types of ontologies are used for initial query constructing: basic ontology of research activity and the domain ontology. Query execution algorithms include obtaining data from different types of sources (HTML, HTML+RDFa, RSS, SPARQL endpoints) and its processing depending on the features of the query. In addition the design pattern for effective building of queries management module is proposed. In conclusion future directions of prototype improvement are discussed.

Keywords: Personalized information services, queries to semantic data sources, information services for researchers.

1 Introduction

Currently the volumes of information available on the Internet and a variety of data representation formats preserve the tendency to rise. In this environment effective knowledge management is possible by means of personalization of information services. To do this, services should take into account individual user requests and be able to handle different types of sources, including semantic ones. It is especially important for researchers, who spend lots of time searching and processing information to stay up to date in their area of interest.

In [1] the following definition of personalized information service is given: "A personalized information service is a service towards a customer comprising (a) filtering of information out of former gathered and qualified information regarding users textual interest (b) presentation of this information using a user defined time schedule and media appropriate with recent user environment".

P. Klinov and D. Mouromtsev (Eds.): KESW 2014, CCIS 468, pp. 44–56, 2014.
© Springer International Publishing Switzerland 2014

2   Related Work

To help researchers to follow the news in their area (new publications, dissertations, upcoming conferences,etc.) social networks for researchers are designed, such as Academia.edu [2], Researchgate [3], Mendeley [4] etc. Since the main function is communication and search of researchers with similar interests, such systems have limited options for customizing news notifications and support a small number of predefined formats (text formats, no support for semantic sources). Search is focused on internal databases (also available in a fixed number of external ones), new sources for updates tracking cannot be added.

At present a number of approaches to semantic data aggregation are proposed. In particular, "Sigma" system [5] provides an automatic search for sources (pages with embedded RDF, RDFa, Microdata and Microformats), an integration of data from different types of sources, removing repeated data, ranking results and presenting them to user who may refine the results by adding or removing sources. ECSSE (Entity Centric Semantic Search Engine) [6] provides mashups from sources that contain structured data using large scale Semantic web indexing, logic reasoning, data aggregation heuristics and other methods. In [7,8] an aggregators of public professional events are described. The first one utilizes microblogs (e.g. Twitter) as data sources. The second one collects and integrates data in XML and utilizes RDF data model as a repository.

Some aspects of the research and development of a prototype of personalized service for researchers (including review of existing systems, the general architecture, agent-based approach to service construction) have been described in previous papers of authors [9,10,11]. Compared with other systems, the main purpose of the construction of described prototype is personalization for a particular user, the ability to extend the functionality and customization for the required information environment. This paper discusses aspects of queries preparation (on the example of news and general queries) and data collection from different types of sources, including semantic ones.

3   User Information Needs

The first step towards building a personalized service which would help to improve the efficiency of searching and processing information is to find out the information needs of users. Since different categories of users have different needs let us consider researchers as an example.

There are several human-centered models of information seeking [12], including anomalous states of knowledge model [13] in which the information needed to solve a problem are not clearly understood by a seeker. In this paper we focus on professional events to help researchers stay relevant in their area of research and plan their activities (e.g., upcoming conferences, new publications, projects, etc.), for this reason searching for answers in some specific domain is omitted. In that case users realize their information needs which in context of our prototype may be represented as a set of information queries:

$$IN = \{IQ_j\}, \tag{1}$$

where IN - information needs and IQ_j - j-th information query.

3.1 Basic Model of User Information Needs

The second step is to identify possible categories of queries and its features. The initial motivation of our project was to improve the efficiency of scientific research and educational process at the Department of Computer Engineering of SPbETU "LETI" within masters' program "Distributed Intelligent Systems". Therefore, the basic set of information needs were identified and structured based on a survey of graduate and postgraduate students and professors of the department, working in the field of Semantic web and multi-agent systems. Based on the analysis of the survey three basic categories of information queries were identified:

1. News - report about new events significant for a user. For example, an announcement of a new conference, new publication, etc;
2. General - find the set of entities with specified properties. For example, "Researchers in the field of descriptive logic", "Projects related to the Semantic Web technologies over the last 3 years", "Conferences on Artificial Intelligence in 2013";
3. Analytical - related to statistical parameters measurement ("Distribution, i.e. number of researchers, interested in the Semantic Web in the EU countries") or the dynamics ("Increase in the number of publications about the LOD for the last 5 years").

Considering selected categories user's information needs may be presented as:

$$IN = IQi = \{NQ_j\} \cup \{GQ_k\} \cup \{AQ_l\} \tag{2}$$

where NQ - news query, GQ - general query and AQ - analytical query.

News and general queries are similar, they only differ in a set of contained entities, in a set of properties (the determining factor in this case is a date) and a method of determining if the requested data is new for the user. Analytical queries do not directly contain the required data but it can be obtained by executing special operations.

3.2 Query Life Cycle

The life cycle (LC) of a user query, in general case, includes three phases:

1. query preparation (construction);
2. query execution (processing);
3. query results presentation to a user.

The life cycle phases are important for refinement of requirements to software and on the design phase.

On the query preparation phase, a user constructs a query in accordance with the selected category and sets modes of its processing. In details the preparation of a query includes:

- selection of query category;
- construction of the query;
- choosing and setting a set of external sources of data;
- setting the query processing modes (frequency and method of activation, methods of extraction / processing of required data, etc.);
- specifying form of results presentation to a user.

When constructing the query a user should specify its attributes. A news query may be generally characterized by two main attributes:

- type of a new event for user (such as the announcement of a conference, a competition, publication of a monograph, etc).
- subject (theme, topic) of event (e.g., the Semantic web, multi-agent systems).

Thus, a news query can be presented as:

$$NQ_j =< ET_j, ES_j >, \tag{3}$$

where ET_j - event type and ESj - event subject.

When preparing the general query, the user must specify the basic entity of the query (e.g. person, project, publication etc.), the topic (descriptive logic, linked data etc.), and perhaps some additional constraints (time, location, etc.). Thus, a general query can be formally presented as:

$$GQ_j =< BE_j, QT_j, AC_j >, \tag{4}$$

where BE_j - basic entity of general query, QT_j - query topic and AC_j - additional constraints.

Furthermore, on the step of query construction user forms a list of sources to be processed at each cycle of query implementation.

On the query execution step it is processed in accordance with the specified execution mode. Query processing generally includes:

- collection of information from sources;
- selection of required facts from sources;
- further processing according to the query type.

On the last step the query result is presented to a user.

3.3 Model of the Information Environment for the Personalized Service

To provide flexible customization of the service to the dynamically updated global information environment it is necessary to determine the model of the environment.

This model should describe the properties of the environment, such as types of sources, protocols to access them, formats of queried data, etc. The Internet contains a huge number of distributed heterogeneous sources and the way they may be collected depends on their type. In our project the following types of sources are selected for consideration:

1. News RSS feeds.
2. SPARQL-endpoints.
3. Pure HTML web pages (without microformats, microdata or RDFa).
4. HTML + RDFa (or with microformats or microdata).

Thus, basic data for general or news query are:

- a query;
- a list of external sources.

A number of popular sources of scientific information, in particular [14,15,16], provide the opportunity to proactively inform users in accordance with specified requirements. In our project we are planning in particular provide a single interface to configure them.

4   Architecture of the Personalized Service and the Used Ontologies

As shown on Fig. 1 the main modules of the prototype are the web application, the client and service agents and a knowledge base (containing three types of ontologies).The prototype that is developing as a Java web application is at an early stage. Ontologies are stored in PostgreSQL database. To deal with ontologies Jena framework [17] is used. Agents are built with the help of Jade framework [18].

Since the service prototype for researchers aims to help them in their everyday work, types of ontologies were selected based on the analysis of their activities.

Ontology of informational environment (IE). Describes the information environment in which the service works: data sources, document formats and access protocols to them (based on the model of information environment). Due to ontology of informational environment and the service architecture user have the ability to choose and add new types of sources.

Basic ontology of research activities (BRA). Contains information about interesting to user events and describes infrastructure of scientific and educational activities (based on the categories of information queries for this group of users). This ontology allows users to customize the types of followed up events and related data (e.g., for the event "publication of a new paper" data about authors are related).

Domain ontology (DO). Describes the structure of a particular domain and provides a flexible configuration of the service. Due to the domain ontology, service is not tied to a particular domain and may be customized to the user

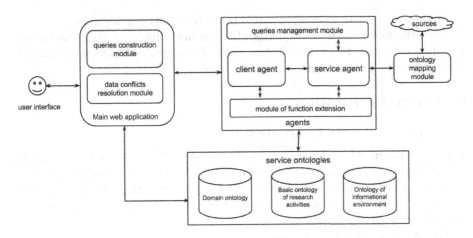

Fig. 1. General architecture of the prototype

interests. To do this during the setup phase of the service ontology mapping is required that is quite a tedious task, but it may be partially automated.

For each user customized versions of ontologies of three types are created (user ontologies). Query is constructed using described ontologies: types of events are selected from the BRA, query themes from the DO, data sources from the IE. Service agent is an important module of the prototype which is used to construct queries and collect data from different types of sources.

5   Query Management Module

For efficient processing of user queries a module should be constructed which main objectives would be:

- to make the process of getting query result transparent for service agent regardless of data source type;
- to provide an ability to add new types of sources without changing the architecture of the service.

This module (called "Query Management Module") is used in several ways:

1. On a query processing step. The input of the module is a query q of appropriate type (in the prototype - SPARQL or a string query) and a type of source or a particular source s (if specified). As a result, the module returns triples T containing the result data. The module defines the access method to the source of a particular type: it sends a query to the appropriate source, receives the response and brings it to a format suitable for storage in the user ontologies (triples). The module has two work modes: user queries processing in real time and scheduled data updates collecting (e.g., once a day).
2. On a query construction step to the source of a specified type - for configuration and the query's initial data retrieve.

At the architecture level this module is located in the service agent.

Next, the first two steps of queries life cycle are considered: its construction and data collection from the selected types of sources, and implementation of these steps using the queries management module.

6 Query Preparation

6.1 SPARQL Query Preparation

For scientific and educational purposes it is proposed to select a list of typical SPARQL queries with the possibility of user configuration for a specific endpoint. Typical queries are constructed in terms of the service ontologies. By configuration we mean the imposition of restrictions on selected by user properties available in a specific endpoint.

The algorithm of query preparation:

1. User selects a typical SPARQL query and an endpoint. Ontologies used in the endpoint and the service ontologies should be previously mapped. In this case it is possible to select an entity class with meaning similar to the ones described in a typical query using such properties as sameAs, skos:closeMatch and skos:exactMatch for a particular endpoint. For this task ontology mapping module is used.
2. Queries management module selects all the properties for the requested entity class from the selected endpoint. For each query a binding to a basic entity is stored (BE for general query or ET for news query, see 3.2).
3. User selects the properties on which he would like to put restrictions.
4. Types of selected by user properties (e.g., string, date) are defined.
5. User is asked to input values of selected properties as restrictions for the query.
6. Ready to run query is stored in the knowledge base of the service.

Let us notice that ontology mapping is going to be done in semi-automatic way by the user since nowadays the process cannot be fully automated. Currently COMA 3.0 [19] is used for mapping in the prototype. Various algorithms may be used for this purpose and every year Ontology Alignment Evaluation Initiative presents comparison results of the best ones (e.g., results of 2013 year [20]).

6.2 News Feeds (RSS)

To get updates from the RSS-sources RSS-aggregators are commonly used. Data collection from this type of source has little scientific interest, but as the format is very common its support is added to the service prototype. So far RSS has two most popular versions: 1.0 is based on XML standards and RDF, and the 2.0 has a simpler syntax and is not an RDF-format. Version 2.0 may be converted to the RDF using XSLT.

To provide the ability to process SPARQL queries for this type of sources an initial extraction of the RSS-feed should be performed on the step of adding the source to the service for:

– mapping between dictionaries (RSS modules) and services ontologies;
– storing data about feed content in the service (used classes and properties).

The initial extraction is performed by the queries management module. After that the algorithm of a query creation to the news feeds is similar to the one described in Section 6.1.

6.3 HTML+RDFa

In order to process SPARQL queries to HTML+RDFa documents an initial extraction of the RDF-triples from the document should be performed. To do this various libraries for RDFa extraction may be used in the query management module (in the prototype Semargl [21] was used). After triples extraction the information about ontologies used for defining the RDFa will be saved. Next task is to build a SPARQL query. To do this it is necessary to map the entities of the typical query and the entities used in RDFa. The algorithm is similar to one described in Section 6.1.

6.4 HTML Documents

For this source type there are two basic approaches:

– processing using a structure of a particular site, i.e. the specific predefined HTML markup of the site.
– general processing without considering the peculiarities of a particular site. In this case the text queries are applicable. Selection of news facts may be performed using text mining.

In this paper only the first case is considered. In our opinion the optimal way would be to offer users to add their own markup to pages (e.g., RDFa or microformats). For convenience, an interface to help a user add a markup to elements of HTML pages containing specific information (such as conference title, start date, etc.) is required. This approach brings HTML processing to HTML+RDFa case. The most well-known tool that works in a similar way is Structured Data Markup Helper [22] from Google (supports schema.org, partially JSON-LD and microformats).

In the service prototype the following steps should be completed for querying HTML-pages using the proposed method:

1. At the step of adding HTML page user marks it by adding RDFa properties using the service interface.
2. Markup for this page is stored in the service.
3. After that user creates queries the same way as he does it for HTML+RDFa.

7 Data Collection Using the Query Management Module

Data collection from sources of different types has its own features considered below.

7.1 Data Collection from SPARQL Endpoints

The module of queries management in order to work with sources of this type should provide execution of SPARQL queries based on ETj and ESj, taking into account the features of the specific endpoint. Processing algorithm of this type of source is the following:

1. execute the query for a given SPARQL-endpoint;
2. get the triple from the SPARQL-endpoint;
3. save results to user ontologies.

To save the triples to the user ontologies a particular query pattern should be used which universally chooses a subject, object, predicate and a text label if available. The pattern of the general SPARQL-query for data collection is the following:

```
SELECT ?subj ?prop ?obj ?label
WHERE {
   ?subj a prefix:OntologyClass.  #event type
   #get property to filter value
[  ?subj prefix:OntologyProperty ?property. ]
   ?subj ?prop ?obj.
[  OPTIONAL  { ?objrdfs:label ?label.}
   #filter property value
   FILTER regex(?property, "propertyValue", "i")   ]
}
LIMIT N
```

Optional parts of the query are in square brackets. Values filtering is held in different ways depending on the type of values in the query (in the example by string value).

7.2 Data Collection from RSS Feeds, HTML+RDFa Documents and HTML

Since for a particular RSS-feed and a HTML+RDFa document SPARQL queries were constructed during the setup step, data collection from these types of sources is described in 7.1.

In the service prototype the following steps should be performed for the collection of data from HTML documents:

1. the queries management module downloads a page and adds the saved RDFa markup (see 6.4);
2. the queries management module collects data from HTML+RDFa (with the help of external libraries integrated into the prototype) using a predefined user queries.

8   Design Patterns for Data Collection

To be effective the implementation of the queries management module should provide (see Section 4):

- abilities for adding a new type of data source without changing existing classes in the module;
- separation of service agent class from the specific implementation of source classes: service agent should receive and forward a query but should not have the information about how to get data from the source of a particular type.

Analysis of software design patterns showed that it is advisable to adapt the pattern Command [23] for data collection in real time (Fig. 2). For each operation (e.g., retrieve data from a source by a query execution, get all properties of an entity class) of a particular source type (SPARQL endpoint, RSS, HTML+RDFa, HTML, search engine and semantic search engine) classes are created (e.g., the class for retrieving data from a SPARQL endpoint is "GetFromEndpointCommand"). They contain instances of the corresponding source class (let us call it a "controller" of the source, Fig. 2 shows "SPARQLController" as an example). The "SPARQLController" class contains all the methods for retrieving data from a specific source type (a SPARQL-endpoint). A "RequestDistributor" class is responsible for the distribution of user requests to appropriate controllers.

For scheduled data collection it is important to set a sequence of queries for update collection and maintain high performance. The command pattern can be used to handle a situation where there are a number of jobs (commands) to be executed but only limited resources available to do the computations [23]. In this case objects that implement the ommand interface are queued and program threads sequentially extract commands and call their execute() method, and after that go back for the next command object.

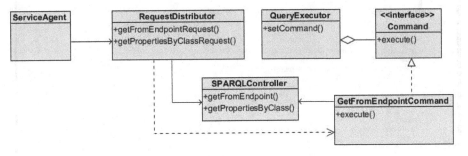

Fig. 2. Class Diagram of "Command" pattern for data collection

9   Preliminary Evaluation

The prototype was tested by a small group (7 people) of postgraduates and students enrolled in the master's program "Distributed Intelligent Systems".

Under this program the disciplines "Semantic Web" and "Multi-Agent Systems" are taught. Students would like to know more about these areas, e.g. about publications, conferences, ongoing projects, organizations and people who work in these areas, and get some data analysis (e.g., how many papers were published over the last few years on some particular topics, what are the dates to apply for a workshop, etc).

To do this, they should specify a list of data sources that can be set manually or selected from the list proposed by a service. After that the queries to structured data sources should be formed. As a result, on the main page of the application user sees aggregated data from predefined sources. The user may choose how to visualize the data: by informational blocks (publications, conferences, organizations, people, projects) with summaries (e.g. the number of found conferences) or an adapted RDF-graph. The user may choose the informational

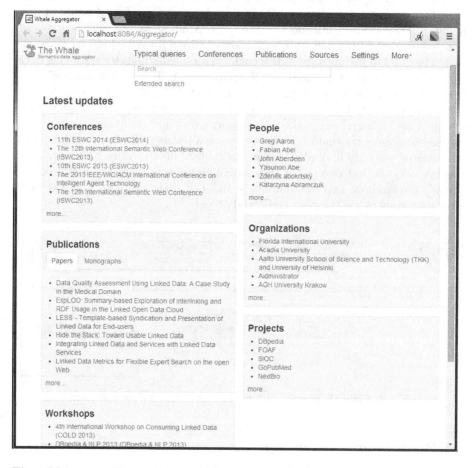

Fig. 3. Main page of the prototype which represents a few latest results of each category (conferences, publications, workshops, people, organizations and projects)

block he wants to know more about and get more detailed information on the page of the prototype dedicated to it. After aggregating data for the first time the user may set properties for updates aggregation to stay current.

As part of the test scenario the prototype was preconfigured to aggregate news about intelligent agents and the Semantic Web. Main page of the prototype, which represents a few latest results of each basic entity (conferences, publications, workshops, people, organizations and projects) collected using all predefined queries, is shown in Fig. 3. At the end of evaluation period (two weeks) the students confirmed that:

- the prototype saves time: all updates from sites without RSS-feeds were available without the need to visit them one by one;
- it is convenient to access RSS-feeds from the same interface;
- they were offered some publications on the predefined topics from SPARQL-endpoints which they had not previously considered as in-formation sources because of usage difficulties.

10   Conclusion and Future Work

To create a personalized service we have structured the information needs of specific categories of users and the information environment consisting of different types of sources. The prototype provides the ability to collect information in a variety of formats for the needs of a particular user and due to the ontological approach may be customized to the required information environment. However for now there are some difficulties in customization to the needs of a user. For that reason further development is needed, in particular in construction an interface for SPAQRL queries, more high level of automation of ontologies mapping, client agent configuration, etc).

In future we are planning to implement a conflict resolution module, an interface for SPAQRL queries construction for non-expert users and to add the ability to handle HTML microdata and microformats. The personalized service should also be tested over a wide range of users and its effectiveness should be evaluated with more rigorous metrics.

References

1. Ritz, T.: Personalized information services: An electronic information commodity and its production. In: Proceedings of the ICCC/IFIP Conference, pp. 48–59. IOS Press, Amsterdam (2001)
2. Academia.edu official site, https://www.academia.edu
3. ResearchGate official site, http://www.researchgate.net
4. Mendeley official site, http://www.mendeley.com
5. Sigma official site, http://sig.ma
6. Cyganiak, R., Catasta, M., Tummarello, G.: Towards ECSSE: live Web of Data search and integration. In: Semantic Search 2009 Workshop, Madrid (2009)

7. De Vocht, L., Selver, S., Ebner, M., Mhlburger, H.: Semantically driven Social Data Aggregation Interfaces for Research 2.0. In: 11th International Conference on Knowledge Management and Knowledge Technologies, pp. 43:1–43:10. ACM, New York (2011)

8. Al-Safadi, L., Alkhatib, N., Babaier, R., Assum, L.: Semantic Aggregator of Public Professional Events. J. of Applied Sciences 12(7), 653–660 (2012)

9. Panteleyev, M., Foteyeva, V.: Building aggregator of scientific and educational data for Semantic Web. In: 3rd Conference on Knowledge Engineering and Semantic Web, St. Petersburg, pp. 73–79 (2012)

10. Foteyeva, V., Panteleyev, M.: Agent-based semantic data aggregator. In: 4th Conference on Knowledge Engineering and Semantic Web, Book of abstracts, St.Petersburg, pp. 22–24 (2013)

11. Foteyeva, V.: Problems of building semantic aggregators. In: Proceeding of International Conference on soft Computing and Measurements, St.Petersburg, pp. 110–112 (2012)

12. Marchionini, G.: Information seeking in electronic environments. Cambridge University Press, Cambridge (1997)

13. Belkin, N.J., Oddy, R.N., Brooks, H.M.: ASK for information retrieval: Part I. Background and theory. J. of Documentation 38(2), 61–71 (1982)

14. Scopus official site, http://www.scopus.com

15. Google scholar official site, http://scholar.google.ru

16. WikiCFP official site, http://wikicfp.com/cfp

17. Jena framework official site, http://jena.apache.org

18. Jade framework official site, http://jade.tilab.com

19. Coma 3.0 - a schema matching system official site, http://dbs.uni-leipzig.de/Research/coma.html

20. Grau, B.C., Dragisic, Z., Ecker, K.: Results of the Ontology Alignment Evaluation Initiative. In: 12th International Semantic Web Conference, pp. 61–100 (2013)

21. Semargl official site, http://semarglproject.org

22. Structured Data Markup Helper, https://www.google.com/webmasters/markup-helper/

23. Freeman, E., Robson, E., Bates, B., Sierra, K.: Head First Design Patterns. O'Reilly Media (2004)

Towards Building Wordnet for the Tatar Language: A Semantic Model of the Verb System

Alfiya M. Galieva, Olga A. Nevzorova, and Ayrat R. Gatiatullin

Kazan Federal University
Research Institute of Applied Semiotics of the Tatarstan Academy of Sciences
{amgalieva,onevzoro}@gmail.com, agat1972@mail.ru
http://ips.antat.ru/

Abstract. Wordnet is a lexical database where nouns, verbs, adjectives, and adverbs are organized in a conceptual hierarchy linking semantically and lexically related concepts to each other. This paper reports on the prototype of the Tatar Wordnet which currently contains about 5,500 Tatar verbs. Within our project we are creating a model of the semantic system of Tatar verbs as a hierarchical structure considering specifics of the Tatar language. For this purpose we use the entries of available Tatar dictionaries (explanatory dictionaries and those of synonyms). As the first step the extraction of available verbal synonyms from the dictionary of synonyms of the Tatar language was carried out. Then the most frequent 5156 Tatar verbs were selected and classified into several groups (synsets) according to their dominant semantic components with the purpose of adding new synsets and enriching those already existing (currently about 1,500 core synsets were distinguished). Then semantic relations between synsets were mapped (the verbs were linked according to their troponymy, entailment, and causality). The paper presents the results obtained, and discusses some problems encountered along the way.

Keywords: Wordnet, synset, Tatar language, verb.

1 Introduction

Developing semantic networks of various types for different languages is an issue of current importance in Natural Language Processing. WordNet [1,2,3] is a lexical database where words marked as belonging to a certain part of speech are linked via semantic relationships. Wordnet-like thesauri are organized around the notion of synset (synonym set).

Wordnets for many languages vary in the degree of development. Wordnets for Turkic languages have not been developed yet. The Turkish wordnet project has been initiated by the Human Language and Speech Technologies Laboratory at the Sabanci University (Kemal Oflazer group) [4], but unfortunately it has not been completed. One of the undertakings in Turkic languages is building the Tatar Wordnet prototype, which is presented in this paper. This project

P. Klinov and D. Mouromtsev (Eds.): KESW 2014, CCIS 468, pp. 57–66, 2014.

is carried out at the Research Institute of Applied Semiotics of the Tatarstan Academy of Sciences. We are going to create a model of the semantic system of Tatar verbs, considering specifics of the Tatar language. Our aim is to build the Tatar Wordnet with modeling of the Tatar verb system using Princeton WordNet core synsets and EuroWordNet Basic Concepts [5].

The paper is organized as follows: Section 2 presents the morphological complexity of the Tatar language and the resources used. Section 3 discusses the process of creating the Tatar Wordnet, limitations of the approach, problems encountered along the way, and proposes some plans for further refinement of the Tatar Wordnet. Section 4 reflects the results of the preliminary research of the Tatar corpus data.

Tatar verbs are given in Turkish-oriented graphics.

2   Challenges

2.1   Morphological Complexity of the Tatar Language

The Tatar language belongs to the Turkic family; Tatar shares characteristic features of all Turkic languages, such as agglutination and progressive vowel harmony.

Of all parts of speech the verb stands as the most complex and comprehensive, and the Turkic verb system has particularly complex and branched forms. The Turkic verb is characterized by the following:

- a complicated negative form (often corresponding to English single word or collocation: *däşü* — to speak, *däşmäw* — to keep silence;
- a complex system of tenses and moods, including synthetic and analytical forms;
- a developed and polynomial system of verbal names: deverbal names (names of actions), adverbial verbs, adjectival and participle forms;
- a complex system of grammatical voices (active, passive, reciprocal (cooperative), causative, reflexive), the ability to combine voice affixes with each other within a word form (*yuu* — to wash, *yuılu* — to be washed, *yuışu* — to help wash, *yuınu* — to wash oneself, *yuındıru* — to make somebody wash; *kölü* — to laugh, *kölderü* — to make somebody laugh);
- various forms of expression of causative category; a word form may contain two, three or even more causative indices modifying the action expressed by the word stem to the left of the causative affixes (*qaytu* — to return, *qaytaru* — to bring, *qaytartu* — to make somebody return, to make somebody bring something).

In Tatar the same verb may denote:

- an action: *yatu* 'to lie down',
- a state of being: *yatu* 'to be down'.

As a result, it may enter multiple synsets.

2.2 Available Resources in Tatar Language

Let us give a brief description of the available linguistic resources appropriate for building the Tatar Wordnet.

In the wordnet building basically four kinds of resources have been used:

1. English WordNet as an initial skeleton (lexical database, types of synsets, super-subordinate relations of synsets),
2. already existing taxonomies of the language (both at word and sense level),
3. bilingual dictionaries (English and the target language),
4. monolingual dictionaries [6].

In the development of the Tatar Wordnet we used all these kinds of resources. Moreover, additional data was obtained from published online dictionaries and the Tatar National Corpus.

We have at our disposal only one specialized dictionary – the printed dictionary of synonyms of the Tatar language (1999), compiled by S. S. Khanbikova and F. S. Safiullina [7]. It contains 25,000 words of different parts of speech united in 4,500 entries. The portion of verbal lexis in the dictionary is not large. The main difficulty of working with the dictionary is that criteria for considering words to be synonyms are unclear, and as a consequence the dictionary synonyms series contain numerous descriptive expressions rather than synonyms, so dictionary entries for wordnet building require critical analysis and error correction. The dictionary does not reflect the diversity of the Tatar language, as it contains a small number of entries. A large part of synsets consists of basic vocabulary and they have to be enriched. Besides, being a classical dictionary of synonyms, the dictionary compiled by S. S. Khanbikova and F.S. Safiullina merely consists of a list of synonyms, and it does not contain information on semantic relations between the synonyms series and it does not include concepts that are expressed by single words.

Tatar lexicons in the form of explanatory disctionaries [8,9] provide entries and senses for synonyms extraction and synset construction. Such data are especially important for synsets that are not represented in the dictionary of synonyms or for synsets requiring enriching. The explanatory dictionaries contain data that have been selected for the purpose of representation of the Tatar language's inventory of lexemes; these dictionaries keep a small number of strings of synonyms only as a means of word definition mapping; nevertheless they can be a great help in clarifying concepts and filling synsets.

The entries of Russian-Tatar electronic bilingual dictionaries can also be used as a resource for synonyms extraction, since bilingual dictionaries offer a translation of a number of synonyms for basic meanings of words. The Russian-Tatar electronic dictionary ABBYY Lingvo X3 contains 47,000 words (7896 verbs) [10].

The Tatar National Corpus [11] includes writings of all sorts from literary novels and popular scientific literature and educational texts to everyday newspapers and magazines, texts of Internet publications on informative, social and political topics and official documents. The corpus is an open system, therefore it permits expansion of the annotation system (currently only grammatical annotation is used). In the current version of the corpus the texts are divided into two types: fiction (71,5 %) and non-fiction (28,5 % of the total volume). In future a more detailed classification of genres of texts will be introduced [12].

The system of morphological annotation of the National Corpus of the Tatar Language is mainly oriented at presenting all the existing grammatical word-forms. In the model used for formal representation of the Tatar agglutinative morphology a word-form is built by consecutive adding regular word-formative and inflectional affixes to the root. As a rule, each grammatical meaning is expressed by a separate affix, and the affixes are unambiguous and regular. Thereby, in order to mark up a word, it is necessary to analyze the structure of its affixal chain, using stems dictionaries. Grammatical annotation of a Tatar word includes the information about the part of speech of the word and a set of morphological features (parameters). The Corpus as the most reliable source of linguistic information is used for revealing frequency distributions of words and senses.

Thus we have lexicographical sources of different types and the corpus text collection for wordnet building. First we extract available verbal synonyms from the dictionary of synonyms of the Tatar language. Then we supplement manually derived synsets and add new ones using the words automatically extracted from other dictionaries and the corpus data.

3   Methodology

3.1   General Principles of Wordnet Development

Despite existing general principles of development of wordnets and Wordnet-like thesauri and depending on the fact that these thesauri may or may not be combined into a system of interconnected semantic networks as EuroWordNet or BalkaNet, a set of resources and methods of their usage varies greatly in different projects. The standard method of constructing national Wordnet-like thesauri includes a conceptual and definitional analysis, an analysis of collocations, corpus studies, processing statistic data, methods of formalization.

There are two basic approaches to the development of Wordwet-like thesauri [14]. The first—the widespread Expand Model—assumes that the selection is done in Princeton WordNet [1] and the WordNet synsets are translated automatically (using bilingual dictionaries) into equivalent synsets into the other language. The WordNet relations are taken over and where necessary adapted to the new wordnet. Possibly, monolingual resources are used to verify the wordnet relations imposed on non-English synsets. In such projects adding synsets which do not exist in Princeton WordNet is often considered as a future plan [13].

Another approach known as the Merge Model sets a task to define synsets and relations in particular language and then align new wordnet with the Princeton WordNet using equivalence relations. The Merge Model results in a wordnet that is independent of Princeton WordNet, which enables to represent and maintain the language-specific properties.

Relations of synonymy, linking words on similarity of the meaning, are basic to all types of Wordnet-like thesauri. By the synset we understand a string of words of the same part of speech that can be interchanged in a certain context.

In EuroWordNet, developers mark two words that denote the same range of entities as semantically equivalent, irrespective of the morpho-syntactic differences, differences in register, style or dialect or differences in pragmatic use of the words. Another, more practical, criterion which follows from the homogeneity principle is that two words which are synonymous cannot be related by any other semantic relation defined [14].

3.2 Language Specific Features of the Tatar Verbs in a Wordnet-Like Thesaurus

Our project's aim is to develop a semantic classification of Tatar verbal lexis and to create a complex semantic model of the verbal system of the Tatar language by means of the Wordnet technology (Merge Model). The Expand Model is impossible for us to use in default of an English-Tatar dictionary containing the real wealth of the Tatar language both at the word and sense level (available Tatar-English and English-Tatar dictionaries contain only basic vocabulary and can be used only for educational purposes).

The Tatar language has a complex morphology and one of the main reasons for this complexity is the wide use of various combinations (agglutination) of verbal inflectional affixes of different types.

Because of the specificity of the grammatical system of the Tatar language the same synset may contain verbs of the basic voice as well as of other voices (especially causative), for example:

The synset 'to throw': {*taşlau, atu, atıp bärü, ırgıtu*}.

The verbs *taşlau, atu, atıp bärü* are in the form of the basic voice, and the verb *ırgıtu* is in the form of the causative voice.

In many cases adding an affix and affixes combination to the verb stem modifies noticeably the verb meaning and even leads to a change in its semantic class. Some examples are given in Table 1.

A polysemantic word can belong to multiple synsets (Table 2).

Every synset contains a group of synonyms of different type: 1) one-word synthetic verbs (for example, *uqu* - to read, 2) analytical verbs consisting of a notional word expressing the lexical meaning and an auxiliary verb (for example, *yärdäm itü* - to help, *gıybädät kılu* - to pray, 3) word-combinations which include a word expressing the lexical meaning and a notional verb as an auxiliary verb (for example, collocations like *aşıysı kilü* — to feel hungry).

Monolingual wordnets had to have their synsets aligned with the translation equivalent synsets of the Princeton WordNet. We set a task to create our original model of semantic system of Tatar verbs as the hierarchical structure which would be relevant to the lexical system of the Tatar language. In doing that we rely upon Global Base Concepts [5].

Linguistic specificity of the lexical system causes some difficulties at the stage of alignment of synsets.

Table 1. Meanings of Tatar verbs with different voice affixes

Tatar verb (stem+ affixes)	Voice	English transla-tion	Verb class	transitivity
aldaw (alda+w)	basic	deceive, cheat; trick; swindle	behavior verb	transitive
aldanu (alda+n+u)	reflexive	to be deceived	behavior verb	intransitive
aldatu (alda+t+u)	causative	allow to deceive oneself	behavior verb	transitive
aldaşu (alda+ş+u)	reciprocal (coop-erative)	deceive, cheat; trick; swindle	behavior verb	intransitive
räncü (ränc[e]+ü)	basic	to take offense	emotion verb	intransitive
räncetü (ränc[e]+t+ü)	causative	to give umbrage to smb.	behavior verb	transitive

Table 2. Tatar polysemantic verb

Tatar polyse-mantic verb	sense	synonyms
karaw	to look	karaw, bagu
karaw	to look after	karau, küzätü, saklaw, küz-kolak bulu
karaw	to follow smb.'s example	karaw, ürnäk alu
karaw	to repair	karaw, remontlaw, remont yasaw, tözätü

One of the features of the Tatar language is a large number of lower-level synsets consisting of words of particular meaning, while more general higher-level concepts are often not lexicalized. For example, there are in abundance sound verbs characterizing sound in many particular aspects (type of sound source, timbre, pitch, homogeneousness or heterogeneousness of the sound, etc.), but there is a lacuna as to a verb denoting sound emission in general (no analogous to English verb *to sound* (Table 3)). Most Tatar sound emission verbs have no equivalents in English, for example, verbs in Table 3 may be translated roughly as 'crash; peal; rumble'.

A serious problem for us in the Tatar Wordnet building is the imperfection of word definitions given in the Tatar lexicons. For example, the descriptions of meanings of most sound verbs in the Tatar lexicon look like the following:

dañgıldaw 'to emit a sound resembling *dañg*';

dıñgırdaw 'to emit a sound resembling *dıñgır*'[9].

So the lexicon entries contain only imitative words, and no description of sound type and character. Such definitions are often unsuitable or deficient for synset construction, thus we intend to offer our original definition for concepts within the framework of our project.

Table 3. Example of sound emission verbs synsets

troponym 'to emit a sound (= to sound)' — non verbalized	troponym 'to cause sound emission' — non verbalized
basic voice	causative voice
specific manner of sound emission' {dañgıldaw, dañgırdaw, dıñgıldaw, dıñgırdaw}	'to cause specific manner of sound' {dañgıldatu, dañgırdatu, dıñgıldatu, dıñgırdatu }

A set of non-lexicalized concepts may be revealed in the course of a semantic analysis on the step of synset building as well as construction and alignment of the hierarchy of synsets.

The table of Verbal Base Concepts selected in the English, Dutch, Italian and Spanish Wordnets includes a concept *to have* as a basic concept of high level [5]. The Tatar language has no verbalized concept of '*to have*'; possessive relations in Turkic languages are expressed by means of the verb *to be*:

Minem maşinam bar.

My car is/exists (word by word translation).

I have a car.

Nonetheless many Tatar verbs contain the concept to have in a bound form:

— *Tamırlanu* 'to take roots',
— *Sabaqlanu* 'to form a stalk',
— *botaqlanu* 'to form branches',
— *börelänü* 'to form buds'.

The semantic structure of these verbs includes the following integral semes: 'beginning', 'proper possessivity', 'meronymy relations' and 'characterization'. So, a large number of Tatar possessive verbs with the meaning component 'part of plant', may be interpreted as 'starts to have what is named a deriving stem', i.e. the interpretation of such verbs can look like 'S starts to have Sm', where Sm is stem (motivating) word. The meaning component 'to have' in a bound form is contained in the semantic structure of many other groups of verbs.

The category of possessivity, as well as that of space and time, can be referred to as a universal category, reflecting typical extra-linguistic relations of possessivity. The basic universal category of possessivity has its real implementation in every language, its unique set of expressive means and its place in a special model of the world. In languages of different types, possessive verbs have different semantic organization, and they are characterized by different features of collocability. Besides, the structure of the category of possessivity is not homogeneous for different lexical classes, that is why in order to determine the boundaries, the composition and peculiarities of implementation of this category, it is necessary to analyze the conceptualization of possessive relations in different lexico-semantical groups.

The main characteristic of the Base Concepts is their importance in wordnets. From our point of view, the concept *to have* is very important in the semantic system of the Tatar language, and its importance is caused by the ability of this concept to function as an anchor in attaching other concepts with possessive meaning. Although the concept *to have* is not lexicalized in Tatar, nonetheless the meaning component 'to have' is to be distinguished in the semantic structure of some groups of verbs and to be used in the constructing hierarchy. So the structure of the thesaurus should take into account the lexicalized concepts as well as non lexicalized ones.

If entries of lexicographic resources seem arbitrary we search the corpus data for information. Let us take, for example, the synset *to help*; the dictionary compiled by Sh.S. Khanbikova and F.S. Safiullina represents it as {*yärdäm itü* (headword), *yärdämgä kilü*, *yärdäm kürsätü*, *bulışlık itü*, *bulışka kilü*} [7].

The corpus data give evidence that noun *bulışlık* 'help' combines with auxiliary verb *itü* as well as *kürsätü* (roughly 50% of documents contain *bulışlık itü*, 50% — *bulışlık kürsätü*), so the synset with headword *yärdäm itü* 'to help' must contain the collocation *bulışlık kürsätü*. Whereas the study of frequency distribution shows that the collocation *bulışka kilü* is characterized by low frequency (3 occurrences only) and may be excluded.

As a result the synset with headword *yärdäm itü* 'to help' looks like the following:

{*bulışu, yärdäm itü, yärdäm kürsätü, bulışlık itü, bulışlık kürsätü*}.

So our task consists of extracting synsets from available dictionaries, enriching these synsets, adding other semantic links to the taxonomic structure, and aligning this structure with other existing ontologies (Princeton WordNet and EuroWordNet).

One of the biggest problems facing the developers of the Tatar Wordnet is representing actual distribution of meanings of Tatar verbs. To achieve this goal the contexts of lexemes under consideration are extracted from the Tatar National Corpus. The set of extracted contexts for each lexeme is annotated regarding the scheme of meanings given in the explanatory dictionary.

In selecting the optimal number of corpus contexts for the analysis we have relied on the results obtained by I. Azarova and her colleagues during the creation of Russian Wordnet (RusNet)[15]. According to these data, the selective annotation of 100-150 contexts taken randomly from different works gives the same distribution scheme of contexts as a complete set, including 1500-2000 contexts. Thereby a set of meanings that should be represented in the thesaurus is established through the context analysis of the corpus data. The isolated (single) instances of realization of meanings are considered occasional. For delimitation of occasional and usual meanings we introduce a threshold in 1% of the total number of contexts. The experiments carried out on the corpus data demonstrate that this value is relevant for selecting common usage senses.

If necessary, headwords in synsets are also established by means of using the statistical method of research of the corpus data.

Thus we solve some key problems in the course of the Tatar Wordnet project:

- constructing new verbal synsets and enriching the existing ones;
- constructing the hierarchical network of Tatar verbal synsets;
- including analytical forms in synsets;
- correlating causative pairs;
- improving word definitions on the corpus data in cases where the definitions given in the vocabularies are incomplete;
- revealing non-lexicalized hyperonyms;
- considering corpus frequency information for synset construction.

The feasible application of the developed resource lies in the textual analysis of the Tatar language (i.e. disambiguation), machine translation, semantic annotation of the Tatar National Corpus, and systematization of Tatar verbal lexis in building new dictionaries, in particular, the semantic dictionary of the Tatar verbs.

4   Preliminary Evaluation

As the first step the extraction of available verbal synonyms from the dictionary of synonyms of the Tatar language was carried out (about 1,000 synsets). Then the most frequently used 5,156 Tatar synthetic (one-word) verbs were selected automatically from Tatar lexicon and Tatar-Russian dictionary and manually classified into several groups according to their dominant semantic components. Also the list of most frequently used (common) analytical verbs (compound verbs) in Tatar was compiled from the corpus data, and frequency distribution of these verbs was determined. We have obtained 250 compound verbs having the auxiliary component *itü* (to do, to make) and 100 compound verbs having the auxiliary component *kılu* (to do, to make), for example, *säyähät itü* – to travel, *häräkät itü* – to move, *hökem kılu* - to sentence, to condemn.

We enriched the verbal synsets from the dictionary of synonyms of the Tatar language by manually deriving synsets and adding the words automatically extracted from other dictionaries and the corpus data. The next step is the construction of the hierarchical semantic network of synsets as wordnet requires, which is done manually. Currently about 1,500 core synsets are compiled, with the semantic relations between them mapped according to the verbs' troponymy, entailment, and causality relations.

Preliminary experiments on the corpus data verify that the developed prototype of Tatar Wordnet represents the most significant structural relations of Tatar verbal vocabulary. We have selected 50 sound emission verbs of different types from 25 synsets, then extracted from the Tatar National Corpus and studied 1000 contexts containing these verbs. The context analysis prompts a conclusion that selected synonyms satisfy the criterion of interchangeability. Almost all of the sound verbs have causative correlates. Lexicalized and non-lexicalized concepts at the higher, more abstract levels of hierarchies correspond to their English analogues. Nevertheless, the synonyms of the low level reflect language-specific lexicalization patterns.

5   Conclusion

Our goal is to combine the experience of traditional Tatar lexicography, the reliable corpus data and the advantages of the Wordnet thesauri standard that will enable us to represent the Tatar language in a way that would meet the demands of contemporary computational linguistics.

The presented methods enable us to represent adequately the specific features of the Tatar lexicon, and to minimize the subjectivity of lexical data differentiation, thus to make them open for verification and to maintain language-specific relations in wordnets. The current Tatar Wordnet is still being actively developed so the numbers reported are expected to change soon.

Acknowledgments. The work is supported by the Russian Foundation for Humanities (project #14–14–16031).

References

1. WordNet. A lexical database for English, `http://wordnet.princeton.edu`
2. Miller, G.A.: WordNet: A Lexical Database for English. Communications of the ACM 3(11), 39–41 (1995)
3. Fellbaum, C.: WordNet: An Electronic Lexical Database. MIT Press, Cambridge (1998)
4. Bilgin, O., Özlem, C., Kemal, O.: Building a Wordnet for Turkish. Romanian Journal of Information Science and Technology 7(1-2), 163–172 (2004)
5. Piek, V., Bloksma, L., Rodriguez, H., Climent, S., Calzolari, N., Roventini, A., Bertagna, F., Bertagna, A., Peters, W.: The EuroWordNet Base Concepts and Top Ontology. Deliverable D017 D 34:D036 (1998)
6. Farreres, X., Rigau, G., Rodriguez, H.: Using WordNet for Building WordNets. In: COLING-ACL Workshop on Usage of Wordnet in Natural Language Processing Systems, Montreal, Canada (1998)
7. Khanbikova, S. S., Safiullina, F. S.: Dictionary of synonyms of Tatar language. Kazan (1999) (in Tatar)
8. The Tatar explanatory dictionary in 3 volumes. Kazan (1977-1981) (in Tatar)
9. The Tatar explanatory dictionary in 1 volume. Kazan (2005) (in Tatar)
10. ABBYY Lingvo, `http://www.abbyy.ru/lingvo`
11. Tatar National Corpus, `http://web-corpora.net/TatarCorpus/search/?interface_language=en`
12. Suleymanov, D., Nevzorova, O., Gatiatullin, A., Gilmullin, R., Khakimov, B.: National corpus of the Tatar language "Tugan Tel": Grammatical Annotation and Implementation. Procedia — Social and Behavioral Sciences 95, 68–74 (2013)
13. Isahara, H., Bond, F., Uchimoto, K.: Development of the Japanese WordNet. In: 6th International Conference on Language Resources and Evaluation, Marrakech (2008)
14. Vossen, P. (ed.): EuroWordNet General Document. Version 3 (2002), `http://vossen.info/docs/2002/EWNGeneral.pdf`
15. Azarova, I.V., Sinopalnikova, A.A., Yavorskaya, M.V.: Guidelines for Russ-Net structuring, `http://www.dialog-21.ru/Archive/2004/Sinopalnikova.htm` (in Russian)

Access Control, Triggers and Versioning over SPARQL Endpoint

Sergey Gorshkov

TriniData, Mashinnaya 40-21,
620089 Ekaterinburg, Russia
serge@trinidata.ru

Abstract. Industrial use of RDF triple stores is facing lack of supplementary functionality such as fine-grained access control, changes approval, triggers and versioning. We have faced industrial use case in which this functionality is essential. The solution is the transparent proxy middleware implemented over SPARQL endpoint. It allows usage of the standard application interface, not requiring any changes in third-party software working with the triple store. It provides all the required functionality by using metadata stored outside of the model, leaving triple store content intact. The general middleware algorithm and some particular workaround are described. Performance slowdown factor is reduced by implementing internal caching for frequently used queries.

Keywords: Access control, SPARQL endpoint, RDF triple store, triggers, versioning, collaborative authoring.

1 Introduction

Expressiveness of semantic models leads to an idea of replacement of relational databases (RDBMS) by RDF triple stores as the data storage for corporate software. One of the most promising areas for such upgrade is the Master Data Management (MDM). Semantically expressed master data, available through SPARQL endpoint, are significantly richer by classification features, attributes model (including multiple values for each object/attribute pair), and methods of use, than any RDBMS-based MDM solution could be.

However, most of the currently available RDF triple stores are lacking of functionality which is standard for RDBMS: access control and triggers. This causes difficulties in implementation of such features as versioning and changes approval, required for MDM. We've enriched advantages of RDF triple stores by implementing RDMBS-like features such as access control, triggers, changes approval and versioning, by building the middleware layer, serving as proxy for SPARQL queries.

To proceed with discussion of our solution, let's look first at the existing experience in triple store access control, triggers implementation and ontology versioning.

P. Klinov and D. Mouromtsev (Eds.): KESW 2014, CCIS 468, pp. 67–75, 2014.
© Springer International Publishing Switzerland 2014

2   Related Work

Since the functionality similar to GRANT/REVOKE SQL queries is not yet contained in SPARQL specification [15], we cannot expect the unified implementation of security control at the endpoint level. Existing particular implementations have very limited functionality. The very basic way of securing RDF triple stores is restricting access to specific named graphs [1].

The more flexible method, and as far as we know – the only native implementation, is used in Oracle Triple store. There are two ways of model security control. One of them is label-based: each triple is associated with security label. The same set of labels may be assigned to the user or session, and used for filtering ontology content. The other way of security control assigns security labels to the subjects and predicates, which allows more pragmatic use; however, using this way is not recommended by Oracle [2].

Some specific approaches are developed for particular applications of semantic computing. For example, LiMDAC framework provides complex access rights control mechanism for medical data organized in cubes. However, this platform is generating SPARQL queries by itself, while user requests are formulated by other ways [3]. RAP framework stores access rules using special ontology, which allows very flexible rules definition, but it is also implemented as Web service having its own set of methods [4].

Finally, some authors propose not to develop custom (and non-standard) query interface, but to perform security check over usual SPARQL queries and its results [5]. In this case, the proxy layer between end-user and actual SPARQL endpoint is implemented. The end-user works with it using standard SPARQL endpoint interface, but it requires transfer of some authorization and/or context information along with query. These identification markers are used to determine appropriate access level. It is usual to rely on external authorization methods in this case, such as WebID [6].

An especially interesting and promising approach is proposed by S. Kirrane in [16]. Extrapolating the DAC concept which is accepted as a standard for relational databases, author presents a framework providing similar functionality for RDF data storages, including query language extension with GRANT/REVOKE-like operations. However, at the current implementation stage this framework processes only simple queries (no subqueries and aggregates support); also, the rights definition mechanism is extensive, but is not exactly suitable for our practical task.

We might conclude that RDF/SPARQL access control engines could be classified by:

— The level of protection: only output filtration [7], output and INSERT/DELETE, or all methods including bulk graph import;
— Protection granularity: named graphs, whole triples, subjects, predicates;
— The way of implementation: built in SPARQL endpoint, framework with custom program interface (often Web-service), or SPARQL proxy;
— Rules evaluation type: use of ACL [8], or defining rules as SPARQL statements, evaluated using ASK query which involves user identification information [9].

The task of ontology versioning is also may be resolved by implementing middleware [10]. In the case mentioned above, middleware combines versioning with access control functionality. Kiryakov and Ognyanov propose to perceive ontology evolution as a set of states, each of them characterized by an identifier and the full ontology image. In their practical implementation of KCS (Knowledge Control System) they propose to extend the schema of underlying database, over which RDF store is implemented. We cannot act this way in our case, not being bound with any particular triple store implementation, and being unable to do any changes at triple store level.

It is useful to implement logical grouping of ontology changes, because a group of triple-level operations may refer to the single logical action, such as editing one object [11]. Some authors are considering Version Control system-like approach (SVN etc) applicable and useful for ontology versioning [12].

We should state that most researchers are focused on ontology comparison problem, rather of tracking versions of the one specific ontology.

Some implementations of trigger-like functionality over RDF stores are developed, although there are a significantly lesser number of such solutions comparing to access control and versioning. A good example is OUL, a standalone application which allows defining handlers for ontology update events [13]. However, in this case handlers can only perform cascading updates within the ontology. We are interested in handlers which could perform external actions, such as firing events to external applications.

We have concluded that there is no single solution that can fulfill all of our functional requirements "out of the box"; various implementations are having their strong and weak points, but none of them have the balance required for our use case. Especially, we've strongly needed the triggers implementation, while there is no single product offering this functionality at the satisfactory level, in conjunction with access control/versioning. The task of ontology changes approval/moderation isn't resolved in the solutions we've reviewed. So we've chosen the way of creating our own implementation from the scratch, keeping in mind the task of facilitating further development and providing necessary level of functional flexibility of the solution.

3   Motivation

Our task is to implement all-in-one middleware covering all the tasks mentioned above. The main ideas of this middleware are:

— It should allow third-party software to work with the endpoint not being aware of proxy existence – that is, it should implement standard SPARQL interface.
— It should not affect the model itself.

Our development has been conducted in the context of industrial Master Data Management system implementation. The Triple Store (Apache Jena / Fuseki) is considered as the master data storage. It is surrounded by a number of program components and interfaces providing master data query and update functionality. Ontology management software (Onto.pro, web-based ontology editor, which access ontology using SPARQL queries) is used by a number of users having different roles. Model update policies require that:

- Users could be granted access for read, propose updates, or update without confirmation instances of particular classes, and/or classes and attributes definitions.
- Some users may approve or reject changes proposed by another, in case if they have sufficient rights to perform proposed change.
- Every change in the model should be registered in the log, which is accessible by third-party software in a programmatic way.
- Even accepted changes could be reviewed later and rolled back if necessary.
- A wide number of external program components should access the model by performing SPARQL queries over the endpoint, or by using special wrapper implemented as SOAP web-service. These programs might be granted rights for requesting instances of particular classes, and their properties.
- The master data storage should immediately notify external applications on ontology elements update. Those applications might subscribe on notifications using list of classes of interest.

All these policies have produced the following functional requirements:

- A middleware should be created to wrap the standard endpoint SPARQL interface to provide all the required functionality.
- Master data storage (triple store) should allow access control both for read and update, depending on rights defined for accessing user or program component.
- If user trying to perform some update has the right only to propose changes – the actual model should not be modified, but proposed change should be placed in the queue for review by the users who have approval rights.
- All the changes made in the model should be written in the log, which will allow to review and rollback every change.
- Trigger-like notification mechanism should be implemented.
- External applications not aware of accessing secure parts of the master data, or performing updates, should work with the middleware without supplying any authorization information and work with it like with standard SPARQL endpoint interface.

4   Implementation

We see the only way of implementation of all the mentioned requirements by developing a middleware which will rewrite SPARQL queries. List of the actions need to be performed on each type of query should look as shown in the table 1.

Other query types were not considered due to conditions of particular use case.

As we have mentioned, we're assigning access rules for the user group / class pairs. It means that each rule is telling that the users of a particular group may (or may not) perform some operations with the objects belonging to some class. List of the operations is limited to: read, update with confirmation (moderation), update. As we have only one level of rights definition, the conflict resolution policy is simple: the strictest of the applicable rules is always selected. However, such a model of rights assignment is the result of our practical task conditions, not of some built-in restrictions, so it easily can be extended.

Table 1. Types of query

Query type	Query processing	Results processing
SELECT, ASK, CONSTRUCT		Filter results by removing information on all objects that cannot be accessed
INSERT, DELETE, UPLOAD	Check for URIs of objects that cannot be updated (at the subject position), reject query if found. Place proposed changes into queue for approval, if needed. Keep previous version of the data and log action. Send notifications on query complete.	Notify application if query was not executed due to access rights restrictions.

Filtering results of SELECT query is split into two parts: query and results processing. Query processing, at first glance, implies checking access rights to all the objects mentioned in it. The object rights checking, in its turn, is a process of finding all its classifications (including inferred ones), and checking limitations for the current user against these classes. If a prohibited object is found, the whole query has to be cancelled. Subqueries are processed separately at the query processing stage: they are extracted at the first step, and processed recursively.

Response processing includes filtering result set line-by-line, removing the objects which cannot be read, and then rebuilding the whole response structure.

In some cases, filtering requires a special workaround. For example, the query result might not contain URI of prohibited object, but contain its properties. Consider the following query:

```
SELECT ?prop WHERE { ?object <has_property_1> "some val-
ue".
        ?object <has_property_2> ?prop }
```

Imagine that this pattern will match some prohibited object for the "object" variable. But in this case, URI of the prohibited object will not be contained in query nor result. We are rewriting such queries by setting the projection to all variables – it means replacing variables list with the *, so object URI will be present in the result acquired by middleware. After results filtering, the set of returning variables is reduced to the one defined in the query (the projection requested by the initial query).

Similar workaround is applied for COUNT(*) queries. COUNT(*) is replaced with the *, returned rows are cleared, and the size of the resulting rows set is returned.

All these algorithms are increasing the retrieved result set and thus reducing performance, but this can be overrun in general only by simplifying the functional requirements, which was unacceptable in our case. So we were trying to find another solution to compensate performance loss, which we will describe further.

Almost the same logic is applied for DELETE WHERE queries: such queries are first rewritten to extract all the triples going to be deleted, and if access check control does not pass for any of affected triples – the whole operation is rejected. We should note that data retrieve operations might be performed partially (the returned results are filtered), but ontology update operations are approved or rejected only in whole. Moreover, due to absence of UPDATE query in SPARQL 1.1 standard, model updates are always performed by the pairs of consequent DELETE / INSERT queries. These queries should be approved, placed for moderation or rejected only in pairs. Such paired queried needs to be identified and processed by other way than pure INSERT or DELETE operations. All these algorithms have been implemented in our middleware.

To be able to control access rights, we need to identify user/application account. Non-identified user may access only elements of ontology for which access rules are not defined (non-secured objects). The application pretending to access secured objects should pass authentication information as session parameters. List of user accounts, groups and applicable restrictions is stored in the meta-data database.

Because middleware shouldn't store metadata in the model, it will need additional data storage for it. We have used relational database for this purpose. The interface of Onto.pro, which becomes administration application for the middleware, was modified to work with this metadata (access rights and notifications settings, model changes approval, change log review and rollback).

SPARQL queries rewrite is a challenging task in general [14], so it is useful to take some assumptions, which should decrease rewritten queries size and complexity, and simplify rewrite process to reduce computational cost. In our case, these assumptions are derived from the access rules definition logic.

As our primary task was to control access to the instances of particular classes, access level calculation may be represented as the following simple algorithm:

— Identify all the classes that the processed object belongs to, including standard-defined types such as owl:Class or owl:Property (restrictions might be defined for these types too). List of classes should be built taking into account indirect classifications caused by model rules (rdfs:subClassOf etc).
— Find the most strict access level for the classes of this list, and apply it to the requested operation.

One of pragmatic uses of notifications feature is connecting semantic MDM with the Enterprise Service Bus (ESB). In our use case, MDM should fire events to ESB on every update of the ontology, to notify applications that are possibly using changed objects. Implementation of this feature is rather obvious: when the INSERT or DELETE queue affecting the object of the monitored type is executed, the middleware is placing this event to the internal notifications queue. The paired DELETE+INSERT queries are recognized and merged into the single event. The separate notifications handler process is sending events from this queue as the data packages over the bus, or simply writes some information to the external RDBMS. The data package describing an event contains its type (create/update or delete), affected object identification and classification, assigned values of the attributes. The bus can then route this package according to the business rules.

The operations log is written to the RDBMS. It allows to quickly find out all the events affecting some object, and thus to display its changes history (including author of every change), and restore any of the previous states, if necessary.

5   Benchmark

Obviously, middleware layer is reducing performance. We have considered that slowdown of ontology update operations is not critical because of rare changes in the master data. But data retrieval speed, in general, should not be significantly affected by the middleware. To reduce middleware impact on the speed, we have performed frequency analysis of the queries performed over the model by the consuming applications. This analysis had shown that more than 50% of the queries are of two types: "A is subclass of B", and "C is a member of class A". This led us to the idea of implementing caching of those queries. Cache is used for both answering client application's queries, and for internal use by the access level computation algorithm. Necessary procedures for cache renewal on ontology or access rights update were developed. Caching has allowed to almost eliminate slowdown impact of the middleware. It is interesting to compare middleware impact on queries execution speed both with and without caching.

Because our middleware was created for the specific task and specific environment, our benchmarking program is closely related with the supposed way of its use. We have recorded actual query log for two most typical scenarios of our ontology usage: one for model update, and another for data retrieval by the average user session. The update operation have consisted of several DELETE+INSERT queue pairs, reflecting the object editing operation in the Onto.pro editor. The SELECT operations were taken from the Wiki page generation procedure, which queries all the properties and classifications of the displayed object, and all the objects it is related to. The mentioned logs then were passed through the middleware several times to record execution time.

The results are presented in the table 2. The cells are containing execution slowdown, in percent relative to the direct SPARQL endpoint request.

Table 2. Middleware layer performance

Operation	Using Middleware	Using Middleware (caching is off)
DELETE+INSERT	+595%	+750%
SELECT	+13%	+115%

We have not considered another query types in the experiment, but it is clear that ASK/CONSTRUCT queries will show the performance similar to the SELECT, as they are processed by the same code.

The relative slowdown factor we've showed above does not significantly depends on the data set size, at least in the conditions of our tests (up to 100 000 triples).

Update operations are expectedly slowed down in several times, due to necessity of extensive security checks, logging, triggers firing and cache update. The interesting fact, however, is that the SELECT query performance is reduced only by 13%. Comparison to the right table column proves that introducing cache has allowed us to almost compensate impact of security check algorithm which is performed over each SELECT query.

However, these results were obtained on the particular industrial ontology example with the use-case specific set of business rules. As the number and complexity of the rules are significant for security check duration, in the other cases performance may vary.

6 Conclusions

We have developed the middleware framework for transparent SPARQL queries processing. It provides functionality absent in current triple store implementations, but required by the business processes. The middleware does not place any metadata in the model storage, and does not require non-standard applications interface (if the application does not pretend accessing secured objects). Performance reduce for SELECT operations is almost eliminated by implementing caching of the most frequently used queries, and those required for the access rights computation algorithm.

Further work includes improving performance of INSERT/DELETE operations, and extending access rights rules definition logic.

References

1. Costabello, L., Villata, S., Gandon, F.: Context-Aware Access Control for RDF Graph Stores. In: 20th European Conference on Artificial Intelligence (2012)
2. Fine-Grained Access Control for RDF Data,
   http://docs.oracle.com/cd/E16655_01/appdev.121/e17895/fine_grained_acc.htm
3. Kamateri, E., Kalampokis, E., Tambouris, E., Tarabanis, K.: The Linked Data Access Control Framework. Journal of Biomedical Informatics. Special Issue on Informatics Methods in Medical Privacy (2014)
4. Reddivari, P., Finin, T., Joshi, A.: Policy-Based Access Control for an RDF Store. In: Proceedings of the Policy Management for the Web Workshop, A WWW 2005 Workshop (2005)
5. Abel, F., De Coi, J.L., Henze, N., Koesling, A.W., Krause, D., Olmedilla, D.: Enabling Advanced and Context-Dependent Access Control in RDF Stores. In: Aberer, K., et al. (eds.) ISWC/ASWC 2007. LNCS, vol. 4825, pp. 1–14. Springer, Heidelberg (2007)
6. Sacco, O., Passant, A., Decker, S.: An Access Control Framework for the Web of Data. In: International Joint Conference of IEEE TrustCom 2011/IEEE ICESS 2011/FCST 2011 (2011)
7. Flouris, G., Fundulaki, I., Michou, M., Antoniou, G.: Controlling Access to RDF Graphs. In: Proceedings of the Third Future Internet Conference on Future Internet, Berlin, Germany, pp. 107–117 (2010)

8. Hollenbach, J., Presbrey, J., Berners-Lee, T.: Using RDF Metadata to Enable Access Control on the Social Semantic Web. In: Workshop on Collaborative Construction, Management and Linking of Structured Knowledge (2009)
9. Costabello, L., Villata, S., Delaforge, N., Gandon, F.: Ubiquitous Access Control for SPARQL Endpoints: Lessons Learned and Future Challenges. In: Proceedings of the 21st International Conference Companion on World Wide Web, Lyon, France (2012)
10. Ognyanov, D., Kiryakov, A.: Tracking Changes in RDF(S) Repositories. In: Gómez-Pérez, A., Benjamins, V.R. (eds.) EKAW 2002. LNCS (LNAI), vol. 2473, pp. 373–378. Springer, Heidelberg (2002)
11. Auer, S., Herre, H.: A Versioning and Evolution Framework for RDF Knowledge Bases. In: Proceedings of the 6th International Andrei Ershov Memorial Conference on Perspectives of Systems Informatics, Novosibirsk, Russia (2006)
12. Noy, N., Musen, M.: Ontology Versioning in an Ontology Management Framework. IEEE Intelligent Systems 19(4), 6–13 (2004)
13. Sangers, J., Hogenboom, F., Frasincar, F.: Event-Driven Ontology Updating. In: Wang, X.S., Cruz, I., Delis, A., Huang, G. (eds.) WISE 2012. LNCS, vol. 7651, pp. 44–57. Springer, Heidelberg (2012)
14. Le, W., Duan, S., Kementsietsidis, A., Li, F., Wang, M.: Rewriting Queries on SPARQL Views. In: Proceedings of the 20th International Conference on World Wide Web, Hyderabad, India (2011)
15. Kirrane, S., Mileo, A., Decker, S.: Applying DAC Principles to the RDF Graph Data Model. In: 28th IFIP TC-11 SEC International Information Security and Privacy Conference (2013)
16. Kirrane, S., Abdelrahman, A., Mileo, A., Decker, S.: Secure Manipulation of Linked Data. In: Alani, H., et al. (eds.) ISWC 2013, Part I. LNCS, vol. 8218, pp. 248–263. Springer, Heidelberg (2013)

Return on Investment in Linking Content to CRM by Applying the Linked Data Stack

Daniel Hladky[1,2], Svetlana Maltseva[1], Dmitriy Ogorodniychuk[1],
Grigory Drobyazko[1], Martin Voigt[2], and Jon Jay Le Grange[2]

[1] National Research University Higher School of Economics (HSE), Moscow, Russia
{dhladky,smaltseva,ogorodniychuk,gdrobyazko}@hse.ru
[2] Ontos AG, Mittelstrasse 24, 2560 Nidau, Switzerland
{daniel.hladky,martin.voigt,jonjay.legrange}@ontos.com

Abstract. Today decision makers in enterprises have to rely more and more on a variety of data sets that are internally but also externally available in heterogeneous formats. Therefore, intelligent processes are required to build an integrated knowledge base. Unfortunately, the adoption of the Linked Data lifecycle within enterprises, which targets the extraction, interlinking, publishing, and analytics of distributed data, lags behind the public domain due to the lack of frameworks which are efficient to deploy and easy to use. In this paper we present our adoption of the lifecycle through our generic, enterprise-ready Linked Data workbench. To judge its benefits, we describe its application within a real-world Customer Relationship Management (CRM) scenario. It shows (1) that sales employees could significantly reduce their workload and (2) that the integration of sophisticated Linked Data tools come with an obvious positive Return on Investment (ROI).

Keywords: Linked Data, CRM, ROI, GeoKnow Workbench, information integration, Semantic Web.

1 Introduction

In the last years, the amount of available semantic data on the Web has increased and thanks to initiatives like Linked Open Data (LOD) many data sets are publicly available. In parallel the Semantic Web, especially the Linked Data (LD) community, has developed many LD tools that support various tasks within the LD life cycle [3]. Most of the LD initiatives have demonstrated its value through a variety of projects aiming at improving data accessibility for primarily public and academic users [4]. Success stories related to LD for enterprises are still rare.

Today, enterprises are more and more challenged by taking decisions based on a variety of data that is available on internal sources but also more and more on external sources [5]. As in the use case of this paper, the sales representative has to answer customer inquiries in a short time or has to prepare a business meeting. As usual in organizations, the employee has to optimize his time and react in a timely manner. Mixing data from internal and external sources within

P. Klinov and D. Mouromtsev (Eds.): KESW 2014, CCIS 468, pp. 76–89, 2014.
© Springer International Publishing Switzerland 2014

the LD process can bring immediate benefit. According the McKinsey report[1] such usage can unlock innovation and enhance performance.

Unfortunately, accessing data in an enterprise context is not a solved research challenge [10,12] as digital information in various data silos is growing. The LD initiative was proposed to deal with exactly this problem in the public domain, i.e. removing the barriers to data access and sharing, by developing and applying single tools. For their efficient adoption in enterprise scenarios, it would be too cumbersome to deal with every mechanism separately. For this reason, we developed an integrated workbench based on the GeoKnow Generator[2] supporting the LD lifecycle that is easy to setup, to maintain and to integrate into existing applications.

The contributions of this paper are twofold. First, we showcase the successful implementation of the LD stack in a generic, holistic workbench and its application in a real-world enterprise scenario. Second, we underpin the benefits of porting the LD technologies in the enterprise context regarding the more efficient work of the employees and also in respect of the Return on Investment.

The rest of the paper is structured as follows: In Section 2, we describe our customer relationship management use case by structuring the required information and by explaining users tasks to solve. In the following section, we elaborate on our adoption of the LD process based on our workbench and it application on the defined use case. In Section 4, we validate the usage of our approach by calculating the Return on Investment. Before we finally conclude our work and point to future improvements in Section 5, we briefly discuss the related work in Section 5.

2   CRM Use Case Scenario

Todays businesses need to resolve problems effectively, anticipate potential issues, and cultivate product and brand loyalty and gain additional business from customers. Unfortunately most fail due to lacking context integration. CRM systems have been the central application supporting the user through a centric view to all data.

2.1   The Problems Faced by the CRM User

In preparation for a meeting or in answering customer queries an employee from the sales department needs to collect for example information about open payments, customer revenue, actual news about the customer and the market, current stock data and additional background information about his customer. The knowledge gathering involves a variety of internal and external sources and often use of different front-end applications. Fig. 1 shows all potential sources that are related to a customer. In our use case we will deal with data related to revenue,

---

[1] http://goo.gl/T83cio
[2] http://geoknow.eu/

web information and activities. Web information is split to actual online news and to customer background information that can be found in Wikipedia[3].

Revenue data can be retrieved from the financial system or Enterprise Resource Planning System (ERP). Data about activities is stored in the Customer Relationship Management System (CRM), in our use case in the Sugar CRM[4] system. Web information, especially background data about the customer is retrieved from Wikipedia. Current news about the customer are searched using online sources such as Google News[5], Yahoo News[6], the New York Times[7] or any other online news provider.

The identification of the different sources provides just the starting point of the problem solving. Another issue is to verify if the data source exists as machine-readable data that can be consumed by the LD technology. For example DBpedia is a project that extracts certain data from Wikipedia on a regular base and provides the result as machine-readable data via a SPARQL endpoint. A major problem remains: time consuming media discontinuity. The user has switch from one system to another in order to aggregate the information. Last but least the sales person needs to store the collected data in a unified view so it can be consumed.

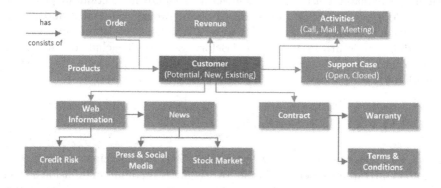

Fig. 1. Customer Information Model

2.2   Required Data Sets

Based on the problem described in the previous subsection we have identified the different data sets that are needed in order to build the aggregated view of information. Table 1 shows the summary of the data sets by information type, source and its accessibility, thus, if it is only internally or externally available.

---

[3] https://en.wikipedia.org/wiki/Main_Page
[4] http://www.sugarcrm.com/
[5] https://news.google.com/
[6] http://news.yahoo.com/
[7] http://www.nytimes.com/

Table 1. Identified data sets

Information Type	Data Source	Accessibility
Activity	SugarCRM relational database	Internal
Revenue	RDBMS Sage Sesame ERP	Internal
Stock Market	Yahoo Finance	External
Background Info	Wikipedia via DBpedia as RDF	External
Current News	NYT Article Search API v2	External
	Ontos News Data Set[8]	External

The internal data sets are all available via relational database management systems (RDBMS). The external data sets are mainly accessible via REST web services, which publish their data in JSON or CSV format, e. g., Yahoo Finance and NYT, or via SPARQL endpoints returning RDF like DBpedia[9]. The Ontos News data set is stored as RDF triples, too, but is only accessible via VSQL. A great benefit of LD becomes clearly visible as both news services link the entities within their data sets to DBpedia using *owl:sameAs*.

2.3   Average Time Required to Fulfill the Tasks without LD

To better understand users work but also to measure the improvement of his efficiency through applying our LD process model, we conducted a small user study with 5 advanced CRM users. To manage the reproducibility between the subjects we introduced and assigned six concrete tasks they had to fulfil. Their execution was observed silently and we tracked the required time for each task. Table 2 shows the key activities, some exemplary questions, and the average time spent in seconds in order to aggregate and summaries the information related to the queries.

Based on this simple scenario the sales user spends on average 7-8 minutes each time in order to gather a complete information view. We are aware off that news gathering could be better organized by using aggregation services which are collecting information automatically, e. g., by using RSS Feeds and a set of key words. A drawback this approach is the lack of personalization [14] that would provide the user with more flexibility and more content related information. From the observation it is also obvious that the CRM system is the central system for the sales representative. Therefore, it would be logical to have all the aggregated data inside the CRM system.

Many of those information-gathering processes are very manually driven and, thus, are ideal candidates for the LD process assuming the sources are machine-readable and the user gets granted access to the data. The following section describes the enterprise-driven LD process.

---

[9] http://wiki.dbpedia.org/Publications

Table 2. Average time spent on information collection

Key Activity	Example	Avg. time in s
Revenue (ERP)	Ask people in financial department to produce a recent revenues report for a given customer	92
Stock Market	Check current stock information on services like Yahoo or Google finance	65
Check Wikipedia	Browse to Wikipedia, search for customer and copy/paste the data needed	70
Activities	Logon to CRM and open activity list of customer	50
Actual Online News	Open news at google/yahoo and search by key word related to customer. Search at NYTIMES and Ontos News portal using key word search. Copy/paste the data and compile a summary	135
Create Summary/Digest	Copy/paste all from above into a single page	65

3   Adoption of the Linked Data Lifecycle

In reference to the LD lifecycle [2] we propose a guided approach. It is focusing on the conversion of internal and external data into RDF, the linking of the data sets, the storage of the aggregated information into a RDF graph database, and its consumption within the CRM. Fig. 2 illustrates the basic idea in order to solve the problem of the CRM use case (cf. Section 2). On the left, it shows various data sets that are either internal or external. In the middle, it exemplifies the LD lifecycle and, on the right, it represents the CRM and its user that consumes the interlinked data. In the following, we explain the process in more detail based on our implementation within the Ontos Linked Data Information Workbench (OntosLDIW).

3.1   Ontos Linked Data Information Workbench

The OntosLDIW is based on the GeoKnow Generator[10] and unifies different software tools that are needed to manage the LD process as described in Fig. 2. Through the navigation menu within OntosLDIW (Box 1 in Fig. 3) the user can easily start any of the tools that are then shown in the main administration frame (Box 2 inside Fig. 3). After specifying the configuration parameters the tools are executed. Next section briefly introduces the process steps that have been executed in order to satisfy the CRM use case.

---

[10] http://generator.geoknow.eu/

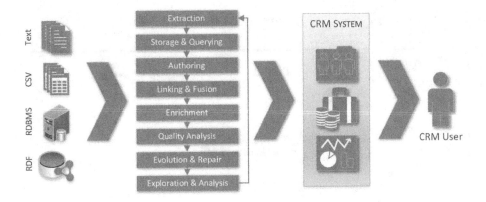

Fig. 2. LD process including the Linked Data Lifecycle for CRM use case

Extraction. The first step of the LD lifecycle Fig. 3-1 represents its implementation within our OntosLDIW deals with the extraction of data from different sources by a given vocabulary. Sources are RDBMS, RDF files, SPARQL endpoints, or also natural language text using natural language processing tools (NLP). In our use case, we facilitate the D2RQ[11] tool for the RDBMS and OntosMiner[12] NLP engine (commercial from Ontos AG) to extract named entities from text. For its initialization, the user selects ontology using OntoDix (Fig. 4) and binds it with the D2RQ (Fig. 3-2) or the OntosMiner system. The binding procedure for D2RQ involves the mapping between the ontology properties to table columns of the selected RDBMS file. Their executing provides data as RDF triples.

Storage and Querying. To store and query the new, integrated information we employ OntoQUAD[13] that is a lightweight, high-performance triple store implementation supporting RDF and SPARQL 1.1. The store supports a model of representing triples in a vector model based on quadruples [13].

Authoring. Fig. 4 shows OntoDix[14]. It is a proprietary tool from Ontos that allows for viewing and editing data stored in a graph-based system. Therefore, we just configured the SPARQL endpoint for the data access. It comes with a dedicated caching services acting as proxy between the frontend and the SPARQL endpoint. It fosters the high-speed data access (read and write) also for big data sets. The user can validate, edit, and enhance certain data regarding the structure and instances.

---

[11] http://d2rq.org/
[12] http://www.ontos.com/products/ontosminer/
[13] http://www.ontos.com/products/ontoquad/
[14] http://dix.ontos.ru/dix/?locale=en

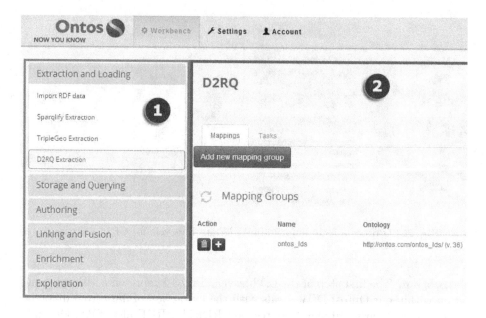

Fig. 3. Mapping of ontology with D2RQ

Linking and Fusion. Until this stage of the process, the data sets are available as RDF all the data is available but not yet interlinked. Based on the CRM use case we need to be able to discover and link entities like a company or a person between the data sets. In order to solve the problem of creating links between entities of different data sets we reuse the LIMES[15] tool that can be configured and started easily within our workbench.

Exploration and Analysis. Currently, a user has two possibilities to consume the aggregated data within OntosLDIW. First, he can use the OntoDix component to browse through the RDF store and visualize the data in a predefined table view. Second, an advanced user is able to facilitate the RDF store interface where he can write own SPARQL queries in order to retrieve and display the data. Since this kind of browsing is not very convenient, as it requires knowledge about graphs, the SPARQL language, concepts and properties, this tool is targeting data scientists and knowledge engineers.

Especially for our CRM use case, we developed further dedicated data views addressing domain experts. They are explained in more in detail in the next subsections.

3.2 Applying OntosLDIW to the CRM Use Case

As a first step, we used OntoDix to specify an ontology fitting to the needs of our customer information model (Fig. 1). In the next step, we applied D2RQ to

---
[15] https://github.com/aksw/limes

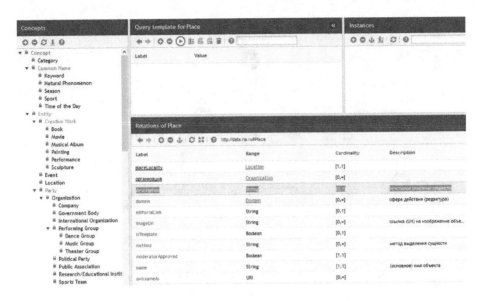

Fig. 4. OntoDix for representing and editing LD

map the data sets to our ontology. This included the creation of mappings from the Sage, SugarCRM and Stock Market databases. Subsequently, we were able to launch D2RQ server that provides a SPARQL endpoint for every database by performing SPARQL to SQL conversions and vice versa. This allows us to directly query the legacy databases via SPARQL and changes within the instance data are automatically reflected. This is especially crucial with regard to the financial information provided by the ERP system. The available RDF interfaces are the foundation to run LIMES in order to create *owl:sameAs* links between the internal data, DBpedia, and the NYT Linked Open Data. With the results, we were able to query the NYT Article Search API to retrieve relevant news articles for those entities. We also implemented SPARQL queries to retrieve current stock market data.

After the application of the LD process sketched above all the data is available within the triple store and could be consumed. Therefore, we have developed and integrated an additional Ontos Linked Data frame inside SugarCRM that is illustrated in Fig. 5. Within this view the user can easily switch between the information sources like the data from DBPedia (Fig. 5–2), News (Fig. 5–3), ERP Financials (Fig. 5–4), and stock information. The required data is queried through SPARQL from the OntoQUAD store, as well as the D2RQ SPARQL endpoints.

The new frame mashing up the information from the LD process brings great benefit to the sales users by enabling:

1. Integrated views of all relevant data inside the CRM system;
2. Time and cost efficiency, no need to access different sources;
3. Up-to-date information enables queries from customers to be answered ad-hoc.

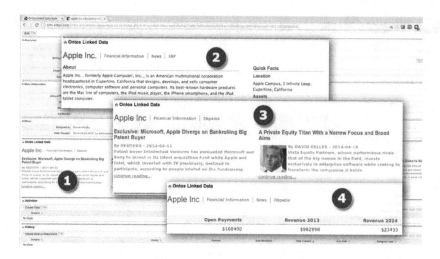

Fig. 5. Mashing up and presenting the LD in SugarCRM

In Table 2 we have shown the average time needed to collect all information before the implementation of the Linked Data process. With the integrated view the user does not need to switch to other systems but only clicks on the frame with the aggregated information. The average time is about 1 minute to answer the exemplary queries what reflects the significant improvement in efficiency.

3.3 Project Status and the Lessons Learned

Public news can lead to major decisions concerning customer relations and thus impinge on account activities. In this project, we collect and compile data from multiple sources and present it to domain experts in a coherent fashion. Harvesting of data is running in the background and feeds the RDF stores on a continuous basis.

The project was launched in February 2014 and went live in April 2014. A reasonable amount of time was used to configure the GeoKnow Workbench to the customer needs by adding OntoDix and the D2RQ. Those modules are components that do not belong to the GeoKnow project [1]. The remaining time was used to finalize the customer requirements and on designing the LD frame with the SugarCRM system. Customizing the tools like D2RQ and LIMES required one to two days work.

So far, the lessons learnt are related to mainly two aspects: missing parts of the implementation of the LD lifecycle and its general adoption in enterprises. With respect to the first, we need a component or framework like proposed in [15] that enables the end user of the LD process to efficiently create (composite) visualisations allowing for the exploration and analysis of RDF data. At best, it is easily to integrate in 3rd party web applications, e. g., by using IFrames. Furthermore, a workflow driven support process to explain which components of the LD process are needed at what time is required. We have determined that domain experts with little knowledge of LD are overwhelmed in the beginning and do not understand which part of the LD lifecycle is needed how it should be configured.

One of the major barriers to successfully exploiting the LD concepts in an enterprise environment is the general lack of knowledge of the technologies and the benefits they can bring. We have also encountered people who have heard the term Semantic Web but in reality do not know what it means and how the technology can be applied within an enterprise. Hence, a lot of marketing which clearly illustrates the benefits for organizations, e. g., cost savings or better decision making support, and for their employee, e. g., gathering information in higher quality in shorter time, but which also showcases the ease of integration by now is required. Providing better access to data has to be clearly linked to tangible benefits of business applications. Connecting data silos and exposing the data as SPARQL endpoints alone is not sufficient. Given the short time of the project setup and implementation we see a great potential in the usage of Linked Data technologies for enterprises. The next section is an attempt to justify the investment and calculating a Return on Investment that supports the finding of work efficiency.

4   ROI Validation

Supporting the implementation of LD within enterprises, we have taken the approach of measuring the efficiency with a Return on Investment (ROI) model. In the broad corpus of literature, there are many definitions [11] but for the CRM use case we will use the ROI algorithm shown in Fig.6 that determine when the investment could be paid back. The payback is evaluated making the intersection between the trend of costs and benefits in the time using the *TotCost* and *TotBenefit* in the months after the LD implementation for the CRM use case:

$$TotCost = IC + \sum_i \left(\frac{Cost}{Month} \right)$$

$$TotBenefit = \sum_i \left(\frac{Benefit}{Month} \right)$$

TotCost represents the total costs of the investment based on the initial investment (IC) and the day-to-day costs for keeping the system running. *TotBenefit* is the sum of the earning associated with the LD for CRM. The expectation is to gain a positive value from the IT project after a certain number of months. Table 3 and 4 show all relevant ROI components that are needed to calculate the ROI.

The following briefly describes the components used for the ROI calculation:

– IT infrastructure component includes the cost for renting the infrastructure in the cloud.

- LD software as a Service rent includes the subscription costs for the commercial components like OntosMiner, OntoQUAD and OntoDix.
- Labour and training costs for adapting the system and to develop the CRM integration.
- Based on the efficiency of reducing the average time needed to query the data the company estimates a cost saving of half a person in the sales team.
- Improved quality of data and more information about the sales opportunity the company estimates an increase in sales revenue.

In order to calculate the intersection by number of months (intersection of *TotCost* and *TotBenefit*) we will use the presented algorithm in Fig. 6. IC is calculated by addition of labor and training costs. IC = 18000 + 2000 = 20000 €. All other cost from Table 3 are divided by 12 to get the monthly costs. Monthly costs (*Cost Month*) equals to 4000 €and the monthly benefit (Benefit

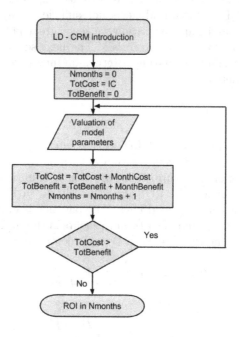

Fig. 6. The ROI algorithm

Table 3. Cost components for the LD project

Cost Component	Description	Amount in €/year
IT infrastructure	LD in the Cloud, renting a host	12000
LD software	LD software as SaaS (Software as a Service)	36000
Labor	Consulting services to install, customise the solution. Develop SugarCRM frame	18000
Training	End-User training and LD administrator	2000
Total costs		68000

Table 4. Return components for the LD project

Return Component	Description	Amount in €/year
Cost savings	Hiring additional sales employee(s) "$\frac{1}{2}$ person". Increase actual efficiency	45000
Increased revenue	Estimated increased revenue through efficiency and better information	60000
Total Financial Return		105000

Month) equals to 8750 €. Based on the given numbers and the ROI algorithm we get a ROI after 5 month. According this short period an investment into the LD technology is recommendable for our CRM use case.

5 Related Work

In 2007, [7] stated that the big ITC vendors, e. g., Oracle or Vodafone, started to apply Semantic Web and LD technologies but also that it need about 10 more years for a broader adoption within enterprises. On this way, for example, the big search machine ticked together and published schema.org and recent EU funded projects, such as DataLift , GeoKnow, and LOD2 have tackled the different stages of the LD process. They developed sophisticated tools underpinning the whole LD lifecycle, e. g., the extraction, transformation and loading (ETL), authoring, enrichment, interlinking, fusing, and storage [2]. Nowadays, the technologies and tools are applied in multiple scenarios and domains, e. g, in health or media [6], but also for knowledge management and intelligent search in the automotive sector [8]. Interestingly, only one publication exists which reports about the integration of Semantic Web technologies with CRM system [9] but without calculating a ROI for the use case. Finally, we need to state that there is currently no work discussing the ROI of applying the LD stack in enterprise scenarios and thus emphasize its benefit.

6 Conclusion and Further Work

In this in use paper we presented our technical adoption of the LD lifecycle through the generic OntosLDIW. Based on the GeoKnow Generator Workbench it eases the orchestration of various sophisticated components that are hard to handle on their own by data scientist or domain experts. For example, it allows for loading data sets, converting sources to RDF, linking and exposing them to a RDF store. Moreover, we showcased its successful application within a concrete scenario: the CRM. Therein, mashed up various, heterogeneous data sources to a homogenous knowledge base that could be consumed by domain experts having no Semantic Web, data crawling, or programming skills.

Through our work, we have reached two major advantages. First, the task of the domain experts, in our case the sales employees, could work more efficiently since they can identify, analyse, and summarize customer information up to six times faster. Second, we calculated a very positive ROI that creates a payback after 5 months.

A next step to improve our framework is to integrate advanced visualization and analytics capabilities. One of the key lessons from this work is that inter-linking data silos with the LD tools is supported very well but it is hard to find a generic out-of-the-box ready visualization framework that consume the RDF data. One of the ongoing Swiss CTI projects, DoW, is working on methods and tools to fill this gap.

Acknowledgements. This work is partially supported by the Swiss CTI (Grant No. 16057.1) fund related to the Linked Data Orchestration Workbench (DoW). Research leading to these results has received funding under the European Union Commissions Seventh Framework Programme from ICT grant agreement (No. 318159) for GeoKnow.

References

1. Athanasiou, S., Hladky, D., Giannopoulos, G., Garcia-Rojas, A., Lehmann, J.: Geo-Know: Making the web an exploratory place for geospatial knowledge. European Research Consortium in Informatics and Mathematics News (2014)
2. Auer, S., et al.: Managing the Life-Cycle of Linked Data with the LOD2 Stack. In: Cudré-Mauroux, P., Heflin, J., Sirin, E., Tudorache, T., Euzenat, J., Hauswirth, M., Parreira, J.X., Hendler, J., Schreiber, G., Bernstein, A., Blomqvist, E. (eds.) ISWC 2012, Part II. LNCS, vol. 7650, pp. 1–16. Springer, Heidelberg (2012), http://dx.doi.org/10.1007/978-3-642-35173-0_1
3. Auer, S., Lehmann, J., Ngonga Ngomo, A.-C., Zaveri, A.: Introduction to Linked Data and its lifecycle on the web. In: Rudolph, S., Gottlob, G., Horrocks, I., van Harmelen, F. (eds.) Reasoning Weg 2013. LNCS, vol. 8067, pp. 1–90. Springer, Heidelberg (2013), http://dx.doi.org/10.1007/978-3-642-39784-4_1
4. Bizer, C., Heath, T., Berners-Lee, T.: Linked Data - the story so far. International Journal on Semantic Web and Information Systems 5(3), 1–22 (2009), http://eprints.soton.ac.uk/271285/
5. Blomqvist, E.: The use of Semantic Web technologies for decision support - a survey. Semantic Web (October 2012), http://iospress.metapress.com/content/411L726N60G14032
6. Brewster, C.: Ready for change? transition through turbulence to reformation and transformation. In: Heimer-Rathbone, C. (ed.) Ready for Change? Transition Through Turbulence to Reformation and Transformation, pp. 73–90. Palgrave Macmillan (2012)
7. Cardoso, J.: The Semantic Web Vision: Where Are We? IEEE Intelligent Systems 22(5), 84–88 (2007)
8. Frischmuth, P., Auer, S., Tramp, S., Unbehauen, J., Holzweiig, K., Marquardt, C.M.: Towards Linked Data based Enterprise Information Integration. In: Procs. of the Workshop on Semantic Web Enterprise Adoption and Best Practice, WASABI 2013 (2013), http://www.wasabi-ws.org/papers/wasabi03/paper.pdf

9. Goy, A., Magro, D.: How semantic web technologies can support the mediation between supply and demand in the ict market: The case of customer relationship management. In: Kajan, E., Dorloff, F.D., Bedini, I. (eds.) Handbook of Research on E-Business Standards and Protocols: Documents, Data and Advanced Web Technologies, pp. 185–209. IGI Global (2012)

10. Hladky, D., Maltseva, S.: Linked Data paradigm for enterprises: information integration and value chain. Biznes-Informatika 24(2), 3–12 (2013), http://bijournal.hse.ru/en/2013--224/86477749.html (in Russian)

11. Mogollon, M., Raisinghani, M.: Measuring roi in e-business: A practical approach. Information Systems Management 20(2), 63–81 (2003), http://dx.doi.org/10.1201/1078/43204.20.2.20030301/41472.10

12. Munkvold, B.E., Päivärinta, T., Hodne, A.K., Stangeland, E.: Contemporary Issues of Enterprise Content Management: The Case of Statoil. Scand. J. Inf. Syst. 18(2), 69–100 (2006), http://dl.acm.org/citation.cfm?id=1317114.1317119

13. Potocki, A., Polukhin, A., Drobyazko, G., Hladky, D., Klintsov, V., Unbehauen, J.: OntoQuad: Native High-Speed RDF DBMS for Semantic Web. In: Klinov, P., Mouromtsev, D. (eds.) KESW 2013. CCIS, vol. 394, pp. 117–131. Springer, Heidelberg (2013), http://dx.doi.org/10.1007/978-3-642-41360-5_10

14. Rohr, C., Tjondronegoro, D.: Aggregated cross-media news visualization and personalization. In: Proceedings of the 1st ACM International Conference on Multimedia Information Retrieval, MIR 2008, pp. 371–378. ACM, New York (2008), http://doi.acm.org/10.1145/1460096.1460157

15. Voigt, M., Pietschmann, S., Meißner, K.: A Semantics-Based, End-User-Centered Information Visualization Process for Semantic Web Data. In: Hussein, T., Paulheim, H., Lukosch, S., Ziegler, J., Calvary, G. (eds.) Semantic Models for Adaptive Interactive Systems. Human Computer Interaction Series, pp. 83–107. Springer, Heidelberg (2013), http://dx.doi.org/10.1007/978-1-4471-5301-6_5

Creating Cognitive Frames Based on Ontology Design Patterns for Ontology Visualization

Pavel Lomov and Maxim Shishaev

Institute for Informatics and Mathematical Modeling of Technological Processes,
The Kola Science Center of the Russian Academy of Sciences
{lomov,shishaev}@iimm.ru

Abstract. In this paper we continue the study focused mainly on simplifying understanding of ontologies by the user. In our previous work it was proposed to create special structures, the so-called *cognitive frames* for concepts of the ontology. It is expected that using cognitive frames for concept visualization will increase effectiveness of ontology knowledge transmission to the user. In this paper, we propose to create cognitive frames based on popular ontology design patterns. We also provide some experimental evaluation of cognitive qualities of such frames created for the concepts of the application ontology.

Keywords: Ontology visualization, semantic web, ontology comprehension, cognitive frame, ontology design patterns.

1 Introduction

Visualization of ontologies is an integral part of their practical use. Nowadays a lot of technologies of ontology visualization has been developed. Their effectiveness depend essentially on the task to be solved. One such task is a *sensemaking* [19]. It is usually appeared in case of reusing ontologies. The process of sensemaking allows the user to decide whether a given ontology or its fragment is suitable for particular application. It provides understanding the common structure of the ontology leaving aside insignificant specific details. Approaches and software tools focused on this problem are presented in the papers [21,26,22,19]. Their main features include providing high level overviews of ontology, zooming and filtering the displayed items.

Another important issue in the context of formal ontology is visualization of logical inference. It is to make a visual representation that can illustrate the conclusion of logical statements, and justification of output results [2,3,14]. By means of such presentation developer can understand the ontology in more detail, as well as quickly find and correct the problem axioms that lead to semantic conflicts.

Also there is a task associated with using of ontologies for structuring, collecting and an exchanging of knowledge between users, which are not expert in the ontology engineering. Its solution involves presenting an ontology visualization, that would allow to the user understand a meaning of any concept with

P. Klinov and D. Mouromtsev (Eds.): KESW 2014, CCIS 468, pp. 90–104, 2014.

least effort. Existing tools focus on another aspects of ontology visualization. Therefore they often does not take into account the fact that some of the concepts can be defined by several axioms, which should be represented as one by a composite image. Also they pay less attention to the cognitive features of a visualization, which define complexity of its interpretation by a user. Taking into account these drawback we propose ontology visualization approach, that would provide efficient transmission of the knowledge contained in an ontology to user. To achieve this purpose it is offered to carry out visualization on the basis of special structures, the so-called *cognitive frames* (CF).

In general, the cognitive frame refers to the visualized fragment of ontology, which allows to adequately transmit the knowledge of a target concept to the user. Adequacy in this case implies a quick and accurate enough for interpretation of the concept meaning. By its cognitive function frame is close to the notion of viewpoint [1], but unlike the latter, it includes, besides a set of facts about the concept, the corresponding visual image.

When creating cognitive frames it is necessary to consider the psychological characteristics of the users and their general principles of structuring information. To this end we consider questions of CF's components creation on the base of ontology design patterns (ODP)[6] and the principles of Gestalt psychology [13,12]. We expect that this will allow to extract a holistic ontology fragment satisfying certain viewpoint[1] on the concept and build a visual image, which provides a simple and correct interpretation of concept meaning. This results to successful transmitting of knowledge contained in ontology to user.

The paper is organized as follows: Section 2 briefly describes our previous work on the subject. Section 3 discusses the usage of ODPs for the task of viewpoint extraction. In Section 4 the general principles and some examples of the pattern based CFs creation are presented. Section 5 describes the experimental evaluation of cognitive qualities of the proposed approach to visualization. The final section provides conclusions and directions for further research.

2   Background

Visualization of ontologies for their comprehension was considered in a series of previous studies by the authors. In [15] a technology for automatic generation of simplified modifications of OWL ontologies adopted for visualization was proposed. Such modification is described in terms of the SKOS model [23] and is named "User presentation ontology" (UPO). The SKOS model is simpler than the OWL model and allows for a visual representation as a node-link diagram. To generate UPO, initial axioms of the OWL ontology are represented using elements in the SKOS model: concepts, relations, and collections. The nodes of the obtained graph structure are concepts corresponding to the classes in the original OWL ontology. Links represent relationships between the OWL classes.

The next paper [16] was focused on visualization of UPO, corresponding to some domain ontology, based on CFs. According to definition, CF has two key components - the content corresponding to the ontological context of the target concept, and the visual image, which is presented to user. The first component provides an answer to the question what should be visualized for effective transmission of knowledge on the concept, while the second - how to do it. The following general definition of the cognitive frame was given:

$$CF\,(t) = \langle CT, VS \rangle, \tag{1}$$

where t - target concept of cognitive frame; CT - content of the frame; VS - the visual image created on the basis of the content. Content is a set of links of the form "concept-relation-concept", which are reflecting the meaning of the concept.

The paper also formulates a set of requirements for cognitive frames:

– **Compactness** - the cognitive frame should contain no more than 7-9 visual items (according to Miller's "magical number" [18]);
– **Completeness** - the cognitive frame should to present all the information about the concept;
– **Familiarity** - visual image of frame should be either familiar to the user, or represent the concept from a known viewpoint.

Observe that requirements of completeness and compactness are in general in contradiction. Simultaneous satisfaction of them is difficult in cases where the definition of a concept include a lot of components. To solve this problem, one may resort to alternative methods of forming content or visual image of CF[27], such as removing of unnecessary detail or considering "orthogonal" (non-overlapping) perspectives and producing a hierarchical structure of several CFs.

This work also considered the generation of CFs on the basis of invariant for subject domain relations - taxonomy, partonomy and dependence. To form their contents appropriate algorithms based on neighborhoods of the target concept have been proposed.

3   Considering Ontology Design Pattern as Viewpoints

In work [1] viewpoint is defined as coherent collections of facts that describe a concept from a particular perspective. Concept image creation based on viewpoint, given by the ontology developer ensures correctness of user interpretation of the meaning of concept. The main problem with operating viewpoints is an extracting of facts relevant to them from the knowledge base. For different knowledge bases it can be quite difficult because of viewpoint definitions abstractness that allows to implement them in an arbitrary way.

In recent years common technique in ontology engineering becomes the using of ontological design patterns (ODP)[6,7]. ODPs are a recommended solutions of ontology engineering problems, which often arise during knowledge representation in different domains. ODPs can be reused in most cases, thereby eliminating the need to look for solutions of modeling problems. On the one hand it saves time and simplifies the ontology development on the other hand it makes the structure of ontology more understandable to other ontology engineers familiar with the ODPs.

There are several types of ODPs [20], each of them is used to solve a some kind of ontology engineering tasks:

- **Structural ODPs** determine the overall structure of the ontology according to the required computational complexity, as well as solve design problems where the primitives of the representation language do not directly support certain logical constructs.
- **Correspondence ODPs** are used for describing the existing ontology by another language, as well as for ontologies integration to determine correspondences between their concepts;
- **Content ODPs** are small ontologies that address a specific modeling issue. They can be directly reused by applying specialization, extension, and composition to them in the ontology under development;
- **Reasoning ODPs** are applied to obtain certain reasoning results;
- **Presentation ODPs** are used to deal with usability and readability of ontologies from a user perspective;
- **Lexico-Syntactic ODPs** are linguistic structures or schemas that consist of certain types of words following a specific order, and that could be used to build ontology fragments from natural language texts.

In this paper we consider the ontology content design patterns (CDPs), because of their similarity with the notion "viewpoint". Both represent some ontology fragment(set of facts), defining a domain concept. Main differences of CDP are more detailed structure of the fragment and focusing on OWL-ontology. Thus, a CDP can be regarded as a formal definition of a viewpoint that could potentially be used to define the concepts in different domain ontologies. This fact allow us to to determine a common approach to CFs forming, based on CDPs that were used for concept definition.

To determine the patterns that could be used as the basis of CFs, the analysis of CDPs presented in ODP catalog [20] has been made. As the result the most general CDPs, that can be used for any domain were selected. Among them are "Agent-Role", "Participant role", "Task execution", "Description-Situation", "Time interval", "List", "Bag", "Sequence" and others. In most cases selected patterns are the fragments of well known upper-level ontologies such as: DOLCE [17], BFO [9], GFO [10]. This fact guarantees the using of patterns during domain ontology development.

4   Creating CDP-Based Cognitive Frames

The main CF components are the content and the visual image. The following sections describe creation of the components based on the CDPs and the principles of Gestalt psychology.

4.1   Creating the Content of Cognitive Frames

CF's content creation based on patterns involves at first a solution to the design patterns recognition problem [11,24]. This task is to detect pattern instantiations - concepts and relations, that correspond to the structure of CDPs:

$$P_k = \{\langle c_i, c_j \rangle\}, \tag{2}$$

where P_k - instantiations of a CDP in some ontology, (c_i, c_j) - relation existing in the ontology between the concepts c_i and c_j and corresponding to some CDP.

Then, detected pattern instantiations form the CF's content. Thus, one may consider the contents of a CF as set of pattern instantiations which include its target concept:

$$CT = \bigcup_{k \in I} P_k, \tag{3}$$

where $\forall P_k \exists (c_i, c_j) : (c_i, c_j) \in P_k \wedge (c_i = t \vee c_j = t)$, t - target concept of CF, $I \in \mathbb{Z}_+$.

Note that such approach to the CF's content creation makes possible to add the patterns with incompatible meaning to it. An example of such CDPs can be "N-ary participation", representing some concept as participant of an event occurring at a particular time and place and pattern "List", representing the same concept as an element of an ordered list. To prevent such situations during the procedure of content creation for each chosen CDP the set of the compatible patterns was defined. It gets rid of bugs in the case of composite viewpoints [1] and thereby allows for formation of a more detailed visualization of the concept.

To meet the requirements of completeness and compactness of a CF it is offered to add each pattern instantiation, corresponds to target concept, entirely (i.e. all of its elements) until the total number of concepts in the CF's content not reach the limit of 9 elements. The remaining instantiation will be included in the content of the next new CF.

4.2   Building Images of Cognitive Frames

CF's visual image should provide a fast and correct (from an ontology developer's perspective) interpretation of target concept meaning by the user. This is the main indicator of cognitive qualities of the resulting image.

We assume that a "good" visualization may based on principles of perception from Gestalt psychology. The basic idea of these principles is that the human perception of real-world objects is connected with spontaneous ordering of received sensations in mind. As a result of this ordering some integral structure called *gestalt* is formed. Thus consciousness imposes certain organizational principles on perceptions. The use of such principles during the building of a visual image of CF, allows us to pre-determine the creation of gestalt which corresponds to the meaning of some CDPs. As a result, users will spend less mental effort to analyze image. This is because intuitively formed gestalt will direct the user to the correct interpretation of image.

The proposed approach is confirmed by the results obtained in the work [8] devoted to the evaluation of cognitive ergonomics of ontologies. They show that the following Gestalt principles in the development of ontologies will facilitate their understanding by users.

The following perception principles are the most important and should be considered when one creates visual images:

1. **The Principle of Proximity**. Elements located close in time or space are perceived together;
2. **The Principle of Common Fate or Good Continuation**. It appears in binding of the observed elements in a continuous sequence, or in giving them a specific orientation.
3. **The Principle of Similarity**. Similar objects are perceived as a group.
4. **The Principle of Closure**. It shown in the effect of suggesting a visual connection or continuity between sets of elements which do not actually touch each other in a image.
5. **The Principle of Symmetry**. The mind perceives objects as being symmetrical and forming around a center point. It is perceptually pleasing to divide objects into an even number of symmetrical parts.
6. **The Principle of Inclusion**. It is tendency to perceive only image, which includes some other image and not one that is included.

More detailed description of the Gestalt principles and examples of their application in computer science are presented in works [4,5].

These principles underlie the creation in the mind of a "good gestalt" - the most simple, steady, symmetrical image of the observed real-world object. If such object will have the details, that do not fit into the "good gestalt", they may be perceived only through the following detailed object examination. Thus, when creating an CF's image, it is necessary that the components of CDPs underlying the CF fit in the "good gestalt".

From the perspective of the visualization complexity the considered CDPs can be divided into the following groups:

– **Simple CDPs.** These patterns consist of a pair of concepts linked by some relation invariant to subject domain. For example, such patterns include: "Agent-Role", "Participation", "Region", "Sequence" and others;
– **Composite CDPs.** Composite patterns consist of a set of concepts connected by different relations. This group includes varieties of patterns "Situation" and "Description and situation", as well as more specific patterns with a complex structure, such as "CommunicationEvent", "EventProcessing", "Standard Enforcer Pattern".

The main goal of visualization of simple patterns is to present the meaning of relations between their concepts. It is important to avoid the use of textual labels of relations. This is due to the fact that the simple CDPs often serve as components of more complex patterns, so it is necessary to make them compact. Accordingly, the basic Gestalt principle in forming the image of simple CDPs is the principle of proximity. The main aim here is to ensure that the concepts presented by simple pattern are percepted as a separate group.

Further the following designations will be used:

- $VC(c)$ - visual image of the concept c;
- $VR(\langle c, n \rangle)$ - visual image of the relation between concepts c and n;
- $LC(VC(c), VC(n))$ - visual image obtained by applying the principle of proximity to the images for the concepts c and n;
- $LS(VC(c), VC(n))$ - visual image obtained by applying the principle of symmetry to the images for the concepts c and n;
- $LF(VC(c), VC(n))$ - visual image obtained by applying the principle of common fate to the images for the concepts c and n;
- $LI(VC(c), VC(n))$ - visual image obtained by applying the principle of inclusion to the images for the concepts c and n;
- $LE(VC(c), VC(n))$ - visual image obtained by applying the principle of similarity to the images for the concepts c and n;
- $VP(P)$ - visual image of the pattern P.

For example, let's consider instantiation of the CDP "Agent-Role" and its visual image. Formal designations corresponding to them are as follows:

$$P_{AG} = \{\langle a, r \rangle\} \tag{4}$$

$$VP(P_{AG}) = \{LI(VC(a), VC(r))\} \tag{5}$$

where, P_{AG} - instantiation of the pattern "Agent-Role", $VP(P_{AG})$ - visual image of instantiation, a - concept-agent, r - concept-role, $\langle a, r \rangle$ - "playing role" relation.

A possible implementation of the considered image is presented on (Fig. 1)

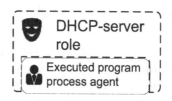

Fig. 1. Image of instantiation of the "Agent-role" pattern

In this case, instead of the principle of proximity the principle of inclusion was used. The visual image of the concept-role "absorbs" the image of the concept-agent. This allows us to emphasize the meaning of this pattern, which suggests to consider the agent as acting in the context of the role.

Note that there is no explicit representation of relationship on the visual image. In this case, meaning of relation implicitly follows from the superclasses names - "Role" and "Agent", which are the parts of concept's names. This fact in turn is an implementation of one of presentation ODP, requiring the use of the superclass name as fragment of subclass name. More preferred practice is to use pictogram instead of a superclass name. It will serve as the cognitive graphic metaphor [25], which allows the user to instantly understand a concept type and also overcome the language barrier. However, it should take care that the user always interprets it correctly.

An examples of a composite CDPs are "Situation based patterns", which represent some state of things in the subject domain (situation context) or reificate n-ary relationships. Thus, the main difference from the simple patterns is that they include more than two different concepts.

Within the situation-based patterns, the situation-concept is associated with its components-concepts. This is expressed by some kind of the "has-setting" relation between the components and the situation. The kind of such relationships depend on the meaning of components in context of situation. For example, in the pattern "BasicPlanExecution" [20] between the concept of situation "PlanExecution" and the concept-executor of actions under the plan, "includesAgent" relation is defined.

When visualizing situation-based pattern instantiation the meaning of each component-concept for situation should be expressed. At the same time images of concepts which have different meanings should be separated from each other. The principles of similarity, common fate and proximity could be applied in this case. For example, consider an visualization of instantiation of pattern "N-ary Participation". It allows to reflect the participation of several objects in an event occurring at a particular time.

The formal designations of this pattern instantiation and its visualization are as follow:

$$P_{NP} = \{\langle n, t \rangle \, \langle n, e \rangle, \langle n, o \rangle, \langle o_1, e \rangle, ..., \langle o_n, e \rangle\} \tag{6}$$

$$VP(P_{NP}) = \{LF(VC(e), VC(t)), LC(VC(e), VC(t)),$$
$$VR(\langle o_1, e \rangle, ..., \langle o_n, e \rangle)\} \tag{7}$$

where P_{NP} - instantiation of the pattern "N-ary Participation", n - concept-situation, t - concept of time interval, e - concept-event, $o_1, ..., o_n$- concepts-participants of an event, $\langle n, t \rangle, \langle n, e \rangle, \langle n, o \rangle$ - relations between the concept-situation and its components, $\langle o_1, e \rangle, ..., \langle o_n, e \rangle$ - "participant-in" relations connecting the concept of participants with the concept-event.

A possible implementation of the considered image is presented on (Fig. 2)

There is no separate visual image of concept-situation because it need only to define in ontology some context, which includes set of concepts. The meaning of concepts-components for a given situation implicitly follows from the location and the forms of their images. For example the concept "Event" and the corresponding concept "time interval" have a similar shape and direction. At the same time, the images of concepts of the event participants have different shape and directed perpendicularly to the image of concept-event. So they form another group of the images.

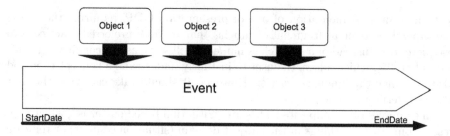

Fig. 2. Implementation of the image for "N-ary participation" pattern

Note that for most of simple patterns discussed earlier, there are analogues involving time indexing. In this case, their visual images are complemented by time line as an additional visual element.

The pattern "Description and situation" is used to conceptualize a situation by a specific conceptual language. For example, some action, produced by anyone, can be conceptualized as a crime. Concepts acting as components of the description are associated with the concepts of situation components by some kind of "classifies" relation. The concrete form of the relationships depends on the kinds of concepts they connect. For example, between the concept-role and the concept-agent "played-by" relation is setted, while the concept-parameter is connected with the concept-value by the "valued-by" relation. In case of correspondence of the situation to some description, the "satisfies" relation is established between them.

The main purpose of visualization of instantiations of this pattern kind is to present the meaning of concepts acting as components of the situation in the context of the concept of description. To do this, it is advisable to apply the principles of similarity and inclusion for presenting accordance of situation's and description's components .

Consider instantiation of the pattern "Description-Situation" and it's visualization. Their formal designation are as follows:

$$P_{DS} = \{\langle s,d \rangle \langle d,c_1 \rangle, ..., \langle d,c_n \rangle, \langle s,o_1 \rangle, ..., \langle s,o_n \rangle, \langle c_1,o_1 \rangle, ..., \langle c_n,o_m \rangle\} \quad (8)$$

$$VP(P_{DS}) = \{LI(VC(o_1),VC(c_1)), ..., LI(VC(o_n),VC(c_n)),$$
$$LE(VC(o_1),...,VC(o_n)), LE(VC(c_1),...,VC(c_n)),$$
$$VR(\langle s,o_1 \rangle), ..., VR(\langle s,o_n \rangle), VR(\langle d,c_1 \rangle), ..., VR(\langle d,c_n \rangle)\}, \quad (9)$$

where P_{DS} - instantiation of the pattern "Description-Situation", d - concept-description, s - concept-situation, $c_1, ..., c_n$ - concepts-description's components, $o_1, ..., o_m$ - concepts-situation's components, $\langle s,d \rangle$ - "satisfies" relation, $\langle d,c_1 \rangle, ..., \langle d,c_n \rangle$, - relation between the concept-description and its components, $\langle s,o_1 \rangle, ..., \langle s,o_n \rangle$ - relation between the concept-situation and its components,

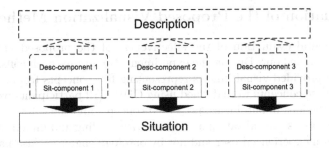

Fig. 3. Implementation of the image for "Description and situation" pattern

$\langle c_1, o_1 \rangle, ..., \langle c_n, o_m \rangle$ - "classifies" relation connecting concepts-description's components and appropriate concepts-situation's components.

A possible implementation of the considered image is presented on (Fig. 3)

In this visualization images of the description's components "absorb" images of situation's components. It allows to represent the pattern's meaning, which is making another conceptualization of concepts-components and situation as a whole.

Visualization of specific pattern instantiation, due to their lower prevalence, at this stage of the study was not considered.

A final visual image of the CF will consist of a combination of visual images created for the CDP's instantiations presented in the content:

$$VS = \{VP(P_i)\}, \tag{10}$$

where P_i - CDP's instantiation.

Example of a visual image of CF for the concept "Network routing task" of domain ontology developed by the authors is presented on (Fig. 4)

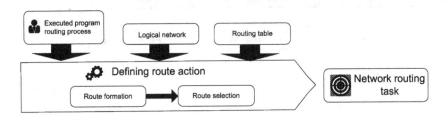

Fig. 4. Example of a visual image of CF for the concept "Network routing task"

This image includes the combined visualization of instantiations of the three patterns "Task execution", "Sequence" and "Participation".

5   Evaluation of the Proposed Visualization Method

An experimental evaluation of the effectiveness of the proposed visualization method was carried out. During the experiment, two groups each consisted of 10 people were provided visual images representing five concepts from the domain ontology. These concepts were defined using CDPs. All participants were not familiar with the idea of ontologies, presented concepts and the subject domain. It enabled us to assess visualization assistance with reading and understanding ontology by an inexperienced user and not by ontology engineer. Also participants had no experience in working with ontology editors like Protégé and TopBraid Composer and their visualization plugins. Therefore it was improper to use complicated visualization tools during comparison, because a user could spend a lot of time searching for a target concept and building its visualization.

For the first experimental group the concepts in node-link digram form were presented. Images were build by the Ontograph - Protégé ontology editor visualizer - as separate named tabs (Fig. 5).

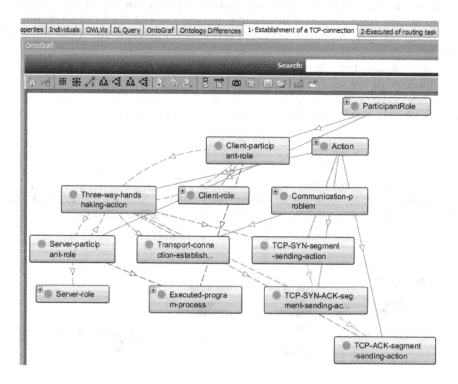

Fig. 5. Example of simple concepts visualization as node-link diagram

Second group was offered a set of CFs in printed form (Fig. 6).

Each group was proposed to answer the 10 questions relevant to competency questions of CDPs:

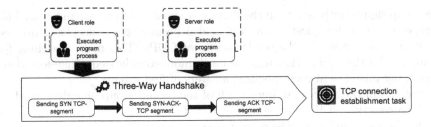

Fig. 6. Example of concepts visualization with the CF

1. What action is directed to carry out the task of transport connection establishment?
2. What tasks are performed as a result of the action "Three way handshake"?
3. What object performs an actions to carry out the transport connection establishment task? What role does it play in actions performing?
4. During execution of the three-way handshake will the action "Sending ACK-segment" be performed first or last?
5. What object performs actions to carry out network routing task?
6. What objects are involved in the actions to carry out the network routing task?
7. How many parts (levels) does the open systems interconnection model consist of?
8. Which component (level) is the first in open systems interconnection model?
9. What object can perform the the task of distributing network configuration parameters?
10. Which tasks are associated with role of "Primary DNS-server"?

The time to understand the concept meaning, as well as the accuracy and completeness of answers were marked. The results of the experiment are presented in Table 1.

Table 1. The Results of experiment of cognitive evaluation

Question number	1	2	3	4	5	6	7	8	9	10
Simple visualization										
- average elapsed time, sec	57	54	75	54	53	43	15	9	15	15
- errors, %	10	40	90	10	100	100	20	30	100	90
CF visualization										
- average elapsed time, sec	52	22	46	14	56	19	21	10	28	32
- errors, %	0	30	0	0	20	40	0	0	70	30

As the result of the experiment second group using CFs spent an average of 10 seconds less time to answer questions. The number of errors committed by the group significantly less than the first group used a simple visualization. This is especially true for questions 3, 5, 6 and 9 because the concepts mentioned in them were defined by the combinations of CDPs. This make searching for an answer by the simple visualization much more complicated. Therefore there were many mistakes in corresponding answers of first group.

Mistakes in the answers to question 9 of the second group, mainly caused by the incorrect title of the corresponding CF. This led to wrong selection of the CF by the users and made the correct answer impossible.

Note that to simplify the task for the first group the pre-built images potentially containing the correct answer were provided to them. Although user usually have to form such image by himself. However, despite this assumption the CF's visualization showed better results. Thus, we can conclude that the proposed visualization technology enables more efficient interpretation of visual images in terms of time and accuracy.

6   Conclusions and Future Work

In this article, we discussed the building of CDP-based CF and its visual presentation with taking into account the principles of Gestalt psychology. Using CDPs to generate content of CFs guarantees the integrity and completeness of their resulting visualization. Taking into account gestalt principles of human perception organization during forming the image of the CF makes it possible for the user to quickly and correctly interpret concept's meaning.

Proposed approach for visualization provides a more effective solution of the problem of ontological knowledge transmission to the user than with usings of a simple visualization of concept system in the form of node-link diagram. The wide using of ODPs for ontology development makes it possible to apply this approach for visualization in many cases.

Main directions of the future research are creation of a navigation system for a set of CFs. It's will allow to use proposed ontology visualization approach for building user interface of information systems, focused on learning and sharing of knowledge.

Acknowledgments. The work presented in this publication has been supported by the Russian Foundation for Basic Research (RFBR), the grant #13-07-01016.

References

1. Acker, L., Porter, B.: Extracting viewpoints from knowledge bases. In: 12th National Conference on Artificial Intelligence, pp. 547–552 (1994)
2. Bauer, J.: Model exploration to support understanding of ontologies. Master thesis, Technische Universität Dresden (2009)
3. Bergh, J.R.: Ontology comprehension, University of Stellenbosch, Master Thesis (2010)

4. Chang, D., Dooley, L., Tuovinen, J.E.: Gestalt Theory in Visual Screen Design — A New Look at an Old Subject. In: Australian Topics: Selected Papers from the Seventh World Conference on Computers in Education, Copenhagen, Denmark, pp. 5–12 (2002)

5. Desolneux, A., Moisan, L., Morel, J.-M.: From Gestalt Theory to Image Analysis: A Probabilistic Approach. In: Interdisciplinary Applied Mathematics, vol. 34. Springer (2008)

6. Gangemi, A.: Ontology Design Patterns for Semantic Web Content. In: 4th International Semantic Web Conference, Galway, Ireland, pp. 262–276 (2005)

7. Gangemi, A., Presutti, V.: Ontology design for interaction in a reasonable enterprise. In: Handbook of Ontologies for Business Interaction. IGI Global, Hershey (2007)

8. Gavrilova, T.A., Gorovoy, V.A., Bolotnikova, E.S.: Evaluation of the cognitive ergonomics of ontologies on the basis of graph analysis. Journal of Scientific and Technical Information Processing 37(6), 398–406 (2010)

9. Grenon, P.: Spatio-temporality in Basic Formal Ontology: SNAP and SPAN, Upper-Level Ontology, and Framework for Formalization: PART I. IFOMIS Report 05/2003, Institute for Formal Ontology and Medical Information Science (IFOMIS), University of Leipzig, Leipzig, Germany (2003)

10. Herre, H.: General Formal Ontology (GFO): A Foundational Ontology for Conceptual Modelling. In: Theory and Applications of Ontology: Computer Applications, pp. 297–345 (2010)

11. Khan, M., Blomqvist, E.: Ontology Design Pattern Detection — Initial Method and Usage Scenarios. In: 4th International Conference on Advances in Semantic Processing (SEMAPRO 2010), pp. 19–24 (2010)

12. Koffka, K.: Principles of Gestalt Psychology. Psychology Press (1999)

13. Kohler, W.: Gestalt Psychology: An Introduction to New Concepts in the Modern Psychology. Liveright Publishing Corporation (1947)

14. Liebig, T., Noppens, O.: OntoTrack: Combining browsing and editing with reasoning and explaining for OWL-lite ontologies. In: 3rd International Semantic Web Conference, Hiroshima, Japan, pp. 8–11 (2004)

15. Lomov, P.A., Shishaev, M.G., Dikovitskiy, V.V.: OWL ontology transformation for visualization and use as a basis of the user interface. In: Scientific Magazine "Design Ontology", pp. 49–61. Novaya Tehnika, Samara (2012) (in Russian)

16. Lomov, P., Shishaev, M.: Technology of Ontology Visualization Based on Cognitive Frames for Graphical User Interface. In: Klinov, P., Mouromtsev, D. (eds.) KESW 2013. CCIS, vol. 394, pp. 54–68. Springer, Heidelberg (2013)

17. Masolo, C., Borgo, S., Gangemi, A., Guarino, N., Oltramari, A., Shneider, L.: WonderWeb. Final Report. Deliverable D18 (2003)

18. Miller, G.A.: The magical number seven, plus or minus two: Some limits on our capacity for processing information. Psychological Review 63(2), 81–97 (1956)

19. Motta, E., Mulholland, P., Peroni, S., d'Aquin, M., Gomez-Perez, J.M., Mendez, V., Zablith, F.: A Novel Approach to Visualizing and Navigating Ontologies. In: Aroyo, L., Welty, C., Alani, H., Taylor, J., Bernstein, A., Kagal, L., Noy, N., Blomqvist, E. (eds.) ISWC 2011, Part I. LNCS, vol. 7031, pp. 470–486. Springer, Heidelberg (2011)

20. Ontology design patterns portal, http://www.ontologydesignpatterns.org

21. Plaisant, C., Grosjean, J., Bederson, B.: Spacetree: Supporting Exploration in Large Node Link Tree, Design Evolution and Empirical Evaluation. In: International Symposium on Information Visualization, pp. 57–64 (2002)

22. Shneiderman, B.: Tree Visualization with Tree-Maps: A 2D Space-Filling Approach. ACM Transactions on Graphics 11(1), 92–99 (1992)
23. SKOS Simple Knowledge Organization System Reference, W3C Recommendation (2009), http://www.w3.org/TR/skos-reference
24. Sváb-Zamazal, O., Scharffe, F., Svátek, V.: Preliminary results of logical ontology pattern detection using SPARQL and lexical heuristics. In: 1st Workshop on Ontology Patterns (WOP), pp. 139–146 (2009)
25. Valkman, J.R.: Cognitive graphic metaphors. In: International Conference "Znaniya-Dialog-Resheniye" (KDS 1995), Yalta, Crimea, pp. 261–272 (1995) (in Russian)
26. Wang, T.D., Parsia, B.: CropCircles: Topology Sensitive Visualization of OWL Class Hierarchies. In: Cruz, I., Decker, S., Allemang, D., Preist, C., Schwabe, D., Mika, P., Uschold, M., Aroyo, L.M. (eds.) ISWC 2006. LNCS, vol. 4273, pp. 695–708. Springer, Heidelberg (2006)
27. Zybin, V.E.: Graphic and text forms of the specification of difficult managing directors of algorithms: irreconcilable opposition or cooperation? In: 7th International Conference on Electronic Publications "EL-Pub2002", Novosibirsk, pp. 32–45 (2003) (in Russian)

$OntoMath^{PRO}$ Ontology:
A Linked Data Hub for Mathematics

Olga A. Nevzorova[1,2], Nikita Zhiltsov[1],
Alexander Kirillovich[1], and Evgeny Lipachev[1]

[1] Kazan Federal University, Russia
{onevzoro,nikita.zhiltsov,alik.kirillovich,elipachev}@gmail.com
[2] Research Institute of Applied Semiotics of Tatarstan Academy of Sciences,
Kazan, Russia

Abstract. In this paper, we present an ontology of mathematical knowledge concepts that covers a wide range of the fields of mathematics and introduces a balanced representation between comprehensive and sensible models. We demonstrate the applications of this representation in information extraction, semantic search, and education. We argue that the ontology can be a core of future integration of math-aware data sets in the Web of Data and, therefore, provide mappings onto relevant datasets, such as DBpedia and ScienceWISE.

Keywords: Ontology engineering, mathematical knowledge, Linked Open Data.

1 Introduction

Recent advances in computer mathematics [4] have made it possible to formalize particular mathematical areas including the proofs of some remarkable results (e.g. Four Color Theorem or Kepler's Conjecture). Nevertheless, the creation of computer mathematics models is a slow process, requiring the excellent skills both in mathematics and programming. In this paper, we follow a different paradigm to mathematical knowledge representation that is based on ontology engineering and the Linked Data principles [6]. $OntoMath^{PRO}$ ontology[1] introduces a reasonable trade-off between plain vocabularies and highly formalized models, aiming at computable proof-checking.

$OntoMath^{PRO}$ was first briefly presented as a part of our previous work [22]. Since then, we have elaborated the ontology structure, improved interlinking with external resources and developed new applications to support the utility of the ontology in various use cases. In summary, our key novel contributions in the current paper are:

- new links with external resources, such as DBpedia and ScienceWISE (Section 2.4);
- a concept-based mathematical formula search mashup (Section 3.2);
- experimental results on using the ontology in the learning process (Section 3.3).

---

[1] http://ontomathpro.org

P. Klinov and D. Mouromtsev (Eds.): KESW 2014, CCIS 468, pp. 105–119, 2014.
© Springer International Publishing Switzerland 2014

1.1   Motivation

The advent of the Web of Data [8] has opened many promising technologies to publish heterogeneous data from different content providers as a single inter-connected cloud of objects. We argue that the benefits of having an ontological model for mathematics and publishing mathematical knowledge as Linked Data include unification of the terminology for mathematicians, the convenient representation for applications in text mining and search, assistance in learning about mathematics, and the possibility of predicting unknown links between mathematical concepts.

Interoperability. Organizing scientific knowledge is utterly important for distributed teams working on large research projects. For example, it is illustrated by the emergence of ScienceWISE project [1] and its ontology[2] for physicists in CERN. Since $OntoMath^{PRO}$ has better coverage than Wikipedia regarding the developing vocabulary and particularly object properties, it can serve as the main repository for definitions of mathematical concepts in the Web of Data. It means that mathematicians may unambiguously refer to the ontology concepts via URIs on discussion groups, blogs, and trendy Q&A sites, such as Math-Overflow[3]. For this purpose, we provide a URI lookup service as well as a URI dereferencing service (Section 2.2).

Convenient Format for Mashups. The integrated representation of mathematical knowledge in a machine-readable format (RDF) may boost the development of new handy services, i.e., Semantic Web agents, for mathematicians. Such services could be run atop the ontology as well as datasets, modeled with the help of the ontology. In Section 3, we present our demo applications in text mining and mathematical formula search, which exploit the ontology as a rich linguistic resource.

Learning. From the learner's perspective, the ontology gives the helpful context for conceiving a mathematical term, including the definition, related concepts with respect to non-trivial relations, such as logical dependency and association. Besides, we argue that the ontology can facilitate educational assessment of students. In Section 3.3, we describe our experiments on using $OntoMath^{PRO}$ as a tool for measuring the effectiveness of the course on numerical analysis.

Discovering Hidden Links. The ontological model generally defines not only concepts from the domain of interest, but also relations between them and axioms (e.g. transitivity or cardinality of relations). Thus, ontologies may enable inference over knowledge bases of facts. $OntoMath^{PRO}$ has a rich set of relations between mathematical concepts. We expect that existing link prediction techniques (e.g. [9,23,28]) along with reasoning mechanisms (e.g. [24]) may reveal compelling hidden relationships between known concepts in mathematics. Such discovered highly probable relations may guide further research in the bleeding edge of mathematics, highlighting the most prospective directions.

---

[2] http://sciencewise.info/ontology/
[3] http://mathoverflow.net/

1.2   Related Work

To put our research into the context, we summarize the most relevant previous works for representing mathematical knowledge in this section. For a more comprehensive overview of services, ontological models and languages for mathematical knowledge management on the Semantic Web and beyond, we refer the interested reader to C. Lange's survey [19].

Symbolic Notation. The semantic layer of Mathematical Markup Language (MathML) [3,14] – Content MathML – as well as OpenMath Content Dictionaries [10] are extensible collections of definitions of symbols. Basically, they suffice high school and sophomore level education: arithmetics, set theory, calculus, algebra, etc. Each symbol has its own URI. In comparison, *OntoMath^{PRO}* does not contain definitions of symbols and could be easily integrated with Content MathML/OpenMath dictionaries.

High-Level Ontologies. Next, we overview ontologies for representing high-level structures in the mathematical knowledge: OMDoc [17,18], MathLang's Document Rhetorical aspect (DRa) Ontology [16], Mocassin Ontology [26]. These models enable making closely related assertions for the particular fields of mathematics, i.e., theories. Comparing to them, *OntoMath^{PRO}* rather specifies theories themselves.

Open Mathematical Documents (OMDoc), an XML-based language, is integrated with MathML/OpenMath and adds support of statements, theories, and rhetorical structures to formalize mathematical documents. OMDoc has been used for interaction between structured specification systems and automated theorem provers. The OMDoc OWL Ontology[4] is based on the notion of statements. Sub-statement structures include definitions, theorems, lemmas, corollaries, proof steps. The relation set comprises of partonomic (whole-part), logical dependency, and verbalizing properties. The paper [11] presents an OMDoc-based approach to author mathematical lecture notes and expose them as Linked Data.

The MathLang DRa Ontology characterizes document structure elements according to their mathematical rhetorical roles that are similar to the ones defined in the statement level of OMDoc. This semantics focuses on formalizing proof skeletons for generation proof checker templates.

The Mocassin Ontology encompasses many structural elements of the state-of-the-art models. However, this model is more oriented on representing structural elements that occur in real scholarly papers on mathematics. Our previous work [26] demonstrates its utility in the information extraction scenario.

Terminological Vocabularies. The general-purpose DBpedia dataset [2] contains, according to our estimates, about 7,800 concepts (including 1,500 concepts with labels in Russian) from algebra, 46,000 (9,200) concepts from geometry, 30,000 (4,300) concepts from mathematical logic, 150,000 (28,000) from mathematical analysis, and 165,000 (39,000) concepts on theory of probability and statistics.

---

[4] Available at `http://kwarc.info/projects/docOnto/omdoc.html`

Concepts are linked to DBpedia categories representing the fields of mathematics. Although there is a *skos:broader* relation between categories, there is no taxonomic (ISA) relationship between the concepts themselves.

A SKOS-based adaptation of Mathematics Subject Classification[5] is exposed as a linked dataset [20]. *OntoMath^{PRO}* ontology overlaps with this dataset in case of modeling hierarchy of fields, but it is significantly richer for representing terms and their interactions.

The Online Encyclopedia of Integer Sequences [25] is a knowledge base of facts about numbers. Given a sequence of integers, this service[6] returns the information about its name, general formula, implementation in programming languages, successive numbers, references, and other relevant links.

Thesauri and Ontologies. Hence, let us consider domain-specific resources, providing a more rich set of relations. [15] presents a formal ontology of mathematics for engineers that covers abstract algebra and metrology. Cambridge Mathematical Thesaurus [29] contains a taxonomy of about 4,500 entities in 9 languages from the undergraduate level mathematics, connected with logical dependency *referencedBy* and associative relationships *seeAlso*. This resource has been developed in education purposes and covers only bachelor level mathematics.

The ScienceWISE project ontology [1] gives over 2,500 mathematical definitions connected with ISA-, whole-part, associative, and importance relationships. The sources of definitions are Wikipedia, Encyclopedia of Science, and the engaged research community. The project focuses on achieving a consensus of opinion among mathematicians about given definitions.

The Ontology on Natural Sciences and Technology [12] contains 55,000 descriptions of scientific terms in Russian, covering the mathematical terminology on high school and freshman-sophomore university levels. The ontology is meant for applications of text analysis, and defines thesaurus-like relations, such as ISA, whole-part, asymmetric association, and symmetric association.

Due to the lack of space, we do not cover related works on semantic data analysis for mathematical texts, which are given in [7,21].

2 *OntoMath^{PRO}* Structure

In this section, we elaborate the modeling principles, the development workflow, the ontology structure, and links to external terminological resources.

2.1 Modeling Principles

Even though mathematics is the most exact science, modeling this domain is hard, due to:

- *abstractness*, i.e., many definitions are conventionally given in mathematical notation elements or formulas;

---

[5] http://www.ams.org/msc/
[6] http://oeis.org

- *duality*, i.e., there might be equivalent definitions for terms depending on which foundations of mathematics are used (set theory or geometry) – this aggravates asserting logical dependency relations between concepts;
- *emergence of novel terms*, i.e., developing, not commonly used parts of the vocabulary in the professional community.

To tackle these issues, we come up with the following modeling principles.

1. **Only Classes, No Individuals.** First, *OntoMath^{PRO}* is geared to be a linguistic resource for text processing. Therefore, the ontology does not contain individuals. The latter can be found in applications, e.g. concrete occurrences of named entities in texts. For example, while modeling mathematical numbers like π or e as individuals is natural, we model them as classes, because, in our case, individuals can be occurrences of these numbers in texts.

2. **ISA vs. Whole-Part.** Existing classification schemes, such as MSC or UDC[7], models hierarchies with respect to whole-part relation. Unlike them, our ontology posits the ISA semantics for hierarchies of mathematical knowledge objects, and preserves the same for fields and sub-fields. The reason is that there are only classes instead of individuals in *OntoMath^{PRO}*, we express the whole-part semantics through ISA relation taking into account its interpretability in terms of the set theory. Thus, we assume that a field of mathematics is a set of closely related statements. For example, fractal geometry is a sub-set of geometry.

3. **Validating Classes.** We deal with the developing vocabulary. To avoid coining a rare terminology, we require a reference from a refereed publication (i.e., an article or a textbook) for a term to be added to the ontology.

4. **Validating Relations.** Establishing correct relation instances is hard and requires high-level competence. Therefore, we basically rely on the opinions of experienced experts involved in the development. The exceptions include the logical dependency and *solves* relations that can be validated using references to refereed sources (see our explanation in Section 2.3).

5. **URI Naming Convention.** Since the ontology is bilingual (Russian/English) and our experts had started adding terms with Russian labels and translated them to English afterwards, we choose using surrogate URIs, e.g. `http://ontomathpro.org/ontology/E1` for a concept "Field of mathematics"[8];

6. **Multiple Inheritance.** Multiple inheritance with respect to ISA-relationships is permitted. For example, class E1892 Differential Equation is a sub-class of both E1891 Equation and E2688 Element of Differential Equations.

7. **Synset as Labels.** Synonyms are represented by labels of the same class. For example, E1226 Cauchy's Inequality has labels "Cauchy's inequality" and "Inequality of arithmetic and geometric means".

---

[7] `http://www.udcc.org/`

[8] The similar convention was adopted in CIDOC CRM Ontology [13].

We have worked with seven practicing mathematicians as domain experts for four months. The terminological sources include freely available materials, such as classical textbooks, Wikipedia articles, and real scholarly papers, along with personal experience of the experts. During the development, we used a collaborative tool WebProtege[9] [31].

2.2   Concepts

Each concept is represented as an OWL class in the ontology. Each class has a textual explanation or hyperlink to its external definition, Russian and English labels. All the metadata information, including adjacent properties, per each class can be seen on our URI dereferencing service[10]. To facilitate finding the URI for a given class (e.g. for adding a link to it on a webpage), this service features a URI lookup function. In future, we are going to add collecting backlinks per each class from HTTP referrers. It will allow us to display relevant webpages and discussions about the concept.

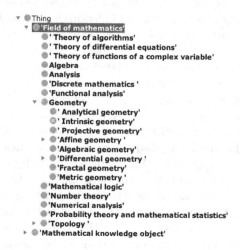

Fig. 1. A taxonomy of the fields of mathematics in $OntoMath^{PRO}$

We distinguish two hierarchies of classes with respect to ISA-relationship: a taxonomy of the fields of mathematics (Fig. 1) and a taxonomy of mathematical knowledge objects, i.e., elements of particular theories (Fig. 2). In the taxonomy of fields, most fundamental fields, such as geometry and analysis, have been elaborated thoroughly. For example, there have been defined specific subfields of geometry: analytic geometry, differential geometry, fractal geomentry

---

[9] http://webprotege.stanford.edu/
[10] According to the Linked Data principles, it is available on the ontology's URI: http://ontomathpro.org/ontology

and others. The ontology covers a wide range of the fields of mathematics, such as number theory, set theory, algebra, analysis, geometry, mathematical logic, discrete mathematics, theory of computation, differential equations, numerical analysis, probability theory, and statistics.

There are three types of top level concepts in the taxonomy of mathematical knowledge objects: i) basic metamathematical concepts, e.g. E847 Set, E1227 Operator, E1324 Map, etc; ii) root elements of the concepts related to the particular fields of mathematics, e.g. E2406 Element of Probability Theory or E3140 Element of Numerical Analysis; iii) common scientific concepts: E339 Problem, E449 Method, E1936 Statement, E1988 Formula, etc. Most concepts are inherited from the root elements of the fields of mathematics (type ii).

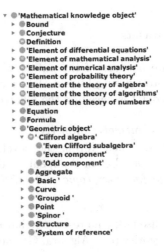

Fig. 2. A taxonomy of mathematical knowledge objects in $OntoMath^{PRO}$

In total, $OntoMath^{PRO}$ contains 3,449 classes.

2.3 Relations

$OntoMath^{PRO}$ defines four types of object properties:

- a directed relation between a mathematical knowledge object (E24) and a field of mathematics (E1) (*P3 belongs to* and its inverse *P4 contains*), e.g. E68 Barycentric Coordinates *P3 belongs to* E14 Metric Geometry;
- a directed relation of logical dependency between mathematical knowledge objects (*P1 defines* and its inverse *P2 is defined by*), e.g. E39 Christoffel Symbol *P2 is defined by* E213 Connectedness. This relation can be validated with providing a reference to the relevant definition in a refereed publication. The *P2 is defined by* relation instance is established, if the definition of the first concept ("subject" in the triple) explicitly refers to the second concept ("object");

- a symmetric transitive associative relation between mathematical knowledge objects (*P5 see also*), e.g. E660 Chebyshev Iterative Method *P5 see also* E444 Numerical Solution of Linear Equation Systems. The semantics of this relation is equivalent to *rdfs:seeAlso*, which is widely used in the LOD datasets for individuals;
- a directed relation between a method and a task (*P6 solves* and its inverse *P7 is solved by*), these properties are defined on E449 Method and E339 Problem classes. This relation can also be validated using references to refereed articles or textbooks.

In total, $OntoMath^{PRO}$ contains 3,627 ISA property instances, and 1,139 other property instances.

2.4 Links to Other Datasets

Although external links are no part of the ontology, we describe the subsets that have been mapped onto existing Linked Data resources. An alignment of $OntoMath^{PRO}$ with DBpedia[11] is based on the following features:

- class and resource labels (*rdfs:label* property);
- explicit links to Wikipedia, i.e., during the development of the ontology, some definitions were imported from Wikipedia and refer to it. We compare these references with *foaf:primaryTopic* and *rdfs:labels* property values in DBpedia.

For interlinking, we only use DBpedia resources that belong to the Mathematics category and its subcategories (e.g. Algebra, Geometry, Mathematical logic, Dynamical Systems) up to 5 levels with respect to *skos:broader* property. After the linking has been accomplished, we generate triples connecting the classes of the $OntoMath^{PRO}$ with the resources from DBpedia by using *skos:closeMatch* property. The alignment with DBpedia has resulted in 947 connections with 907 the ontology classes (some classes were linked with several DBpedia resources).

An alignment with ScienceWISE Ontology[12] only used class labels. As a result, this mapping comprises 347 connections. The mapping files are available on GitHub[13].

3 Applications

In this section, we describe the applications, which exploit different aspects of $OntoMath^{PRO}$.

---

[11] SPARQL endpoint: http://dbpedia.org/sparql
[12] http://data.sciencewise.info/openrdf-sesame/repositories/SW
[13] https://github.com/CLLKazan/OntoMathPro

3.1 Information Extraction

In our previous work [22], we have developed a semantic publishing platform for scientific collections in mathematics that analyzes the underlying semantics in mathematical scholarly papers and effectively builds their consolidated ontology-based representation.

Thus, every paper in the collection is dissected into a semantic graph of instances of the supported domain models with the help of NLP techniques, such as noun phrase recognition and entity resolution. Along with textual fragments, the platform is capable to understand the meanings of mathematical notation symbols and interpret them as ontology instances.

The corpus of publications we experimented with consists of 1,330 articles of the "Proceedings of Higher Education Institutions: Mathematics" (PHEIM) journal in Russian. The current RDF dataset[14] – PHEIM dataset – contains more than 850,000 triples including the descriptions of 1,330 articles, 17,397 formulas, 43,963 variables, and 66,434 textual occurrences of mathematical entities from the ontology.

3.2 Concept-Based Formula Search

Approach. Our demo application[15] supports a use case of searching mathematical formulas in the published PHEIM dataset that are relevant to a given entity. The user input supported by the application is close to a keyword search: our system is agnostic to a particular symbolic notation used in the papers to denote mathematical concepts, and the user is able to filter query suggestions by keywords. This feature makes our application different from a wide range of mathematical retrieval systems that require the input in the LATEX syntax (e.g. [27,33,35]). Such approaches usually suffer from ambiguous mathematical notations. However, it's worth mentioning *(uni)quation* [32], a formula search system that is robust to basic formula transformations including changes of variables.

Another rationale behind the concept-based search input interface is its cross-language capabilities, i.e., even though the indexed document collection is in Russian, the user still can search using keywords in English.

There have been a few efforts to enable a keyword search for retrieving mathematical content. A computational engine WolframAlpha [34] can handle keyword queries, generating a summary for a mathematical concept. However, the engine does not provide the similar functionality for documents in scientific collections. MCAT Math Retrieval System [30] applies an SVM classifier to detect descriptions of mathematical expressions and extends the TF-IDF ranking baseline for formula search in MathML documents. Unlike this tool, our solution is more powerful, because it resolves the lexical meanings of symbols in terms of *OntoMath*^{PRO} ontology, and, therefore, enabling reasoning with respect to the

---

[14] Is exposed via our SPARQL endpoint: `http://cll.niimm.ksu.ru:8890/sparql`, the graph IRI is `http://cll.niimm.ksu.ru/pheim`

[15] `http://cll.niimm.ksu.ru/mathsearch`

ontology relations (e.g. ISA). Additionally, our search interface supports filtering by the document structure context, i.e., a particular segment of the document (e.g. a theorem or a definition) that contains the relevant formula.

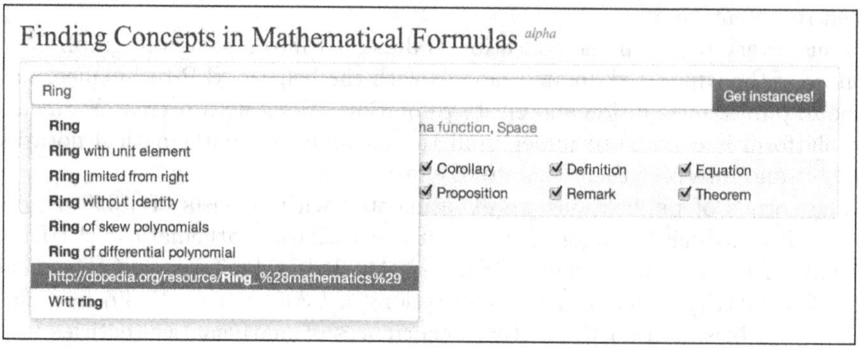

Fig. 3. Query interface of the mathematical formula search demo application

Demo. The application supplies the following search scenario. The user enters keywords in the search box (Fig. 3) and may choose a related concept suggestion. The suggestions are loaded from $OntoMath^{PRO}$ ontology as well as the DBpedia part aligned with the ontology.

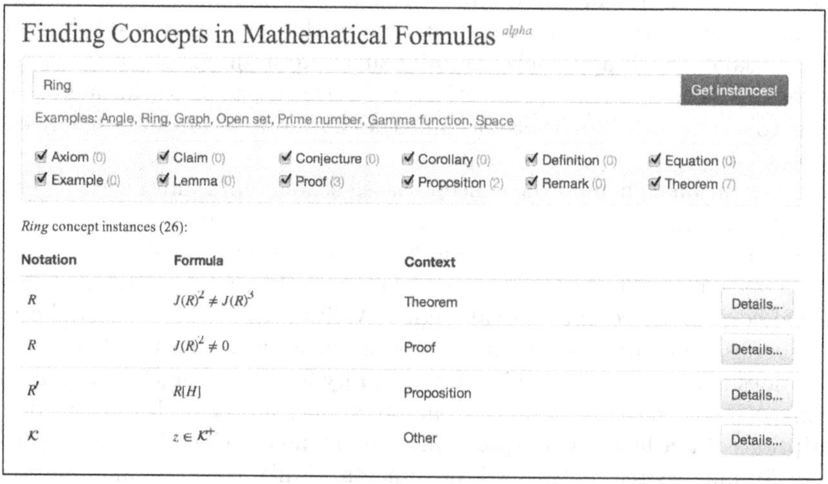

Fig. 4. A search result page

Then, the user clicks the "Get instances" button and gets a list of search results (Fig. 4). The hit descriptions are represented as table rows with the contextual information. Specifically, the application provides a symbolic interpretation of the chosen concept, the relevant formula, in which the notation element occurs, and the context, i.e., the document part, which contains the formula. Providing notation examples is instructive, because the same concept may be expressed in different documents using different symbols depending on the authors' writing style. Additionally, the user can refine the context of search results selecting proper checkboxes standing for particular document parts.

Finally, the user can examine the paper, which contains the relevant formula after clicking on the "Details" button (Fig. 5). This screen provides the relevant formula, the matched concepts as well as the related article information including links to its metadata page and PDF.

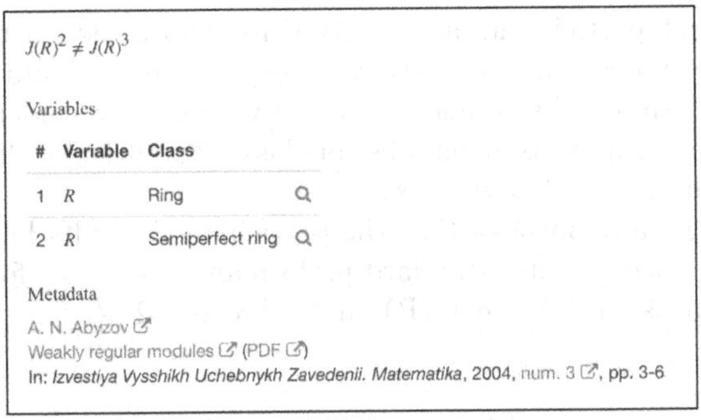

Fig. 5. A search result details page

We would like to note that the current search result set does not cover all the concepts defined in *OntoMath^{PRO}* ontology. The reason is twofold: i) the data set is quite limited; ii) many named entities are usually not expressed in a symbolic notation (e.g. theorems or the fields of mathematics).

From the engineering perspective, our demo application is a lightweight mashup that consumes the published RDF data set. It is written in JavaScript and queries our SPARQL endpoint.

3.3 Education

In this subsection, we describe our experiments on ontology-based assessment of the competence of students, who attended a course on numerical analysis instructed by one of the authors for 3-year undergraduate students at our university.

Most conventional approaches to assessment of students still tend to evaluate how much a student knows about the subject. However, problem-based learning is proven to be a more effective approach [5]. For a practicing mathematician, an ability of finding a method for solving a concrete task is crucial. The proficient solver must realize relationships between particular methods, tasks and other mathematical concepts, i.e., "know how to conceive a holistic image of the discipline"[16]. We propose to consider an ontology as a close approximation to such an image.

For our experiments, we extracted a small fragment of $OntoMath^{PRO}$ ontology (Fig. 6). It contains taxonomies of tasks and solving methods for systems of linear equations (numerical analysis) as well as relationships between them. We added a few relevant concepts that were not defined in the ontology due to questionable definitions, e.g. "a task of solving a system of linear equations with the coefficient matrix of order m*m, case $m > 100$". However, such concepts are useful for testing pragmatic competence.

Concerning the course coverage, only a few methods from the fragment were out of its scope. There is an assumption that students may have studied them during their research work.

The experiment participants are 25 students who attended the course and had high overall grades. They are 3-year undergraduate students (who have not yet passed the exam on the course), 1- and 2-year master students, and Ph.D. students. Each participant is given a list of classes and asked to link them using only two relationships (ISA and *P6 solves*).

Then, we stated a hypothesis that the participants' results have to correlate with their experience. We use standard performance measures for classification tasks, such as precision (P), recall (R), and F-score $= 2 \cdot \frac{P*R}{P+R}$.

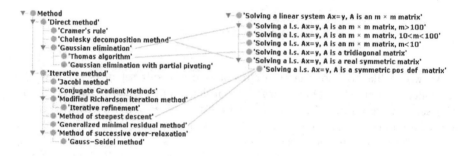

Fig. 6. A part of the correct solution for the interlinking task, the arrows mean *P6 solves* relation instances

We emphasize the importance of applying a reasoning mechanism during the calculation of experimental results. For the evaluation, we materialize all facts that might be acquired after reasoning. For example, a relationship *P6 solves* is inherited through both the taxonomies of methods and task. Thus, if the participant links correctly more specific classes, it results in lower recall, but does not affect precision.

---

[16] Translated from the Russian Federal Standard for Higher Education on mathematics for master students, Section 5.2:
http://www.edu.ru/db-mon/mo/Data/d_10/prm40-1.pdf

Table 1. Average results of interlinking ontology concepts from a course on numerical analysis for different groups of students. P means precision, R – recall, F – F-score.

Group of students	ISA Tasks			ISA Methods			P6 solves			Total		
	P	R	F	P	R	F	P	R	F	P	R	F
3-year undergraduates	1.00	1.00	1.00	0.76	0.59	0.67	0.46	0.27	0.34	0.69	0.50	0.58
1-year masters	1.00	1.00	1.00	0.79	**0.63**	0.70	0.43	0.26	0.32	0.70	**0.52**	0.59
2-year masters	1.00	1.00	1.00	0.65	0.55	0.59	0.51	**0.37**	**0.41**	0.63	**0.52**	0.56
Ph.D. candidates	1.00	1.00	1.00	**0.86**	**0.63**	**0.71**	**0.61**	0.23	0.33	**0.82**	0.50	**0.62**

Table 1 shows the results of the interlinking done by the participants. As expected, establishing links in the simplistic taxonomy of tasks have been done well by all participants. The reconstruction of a slightly complex taxonomy of methods has significantly lower performance values and correlates with the background of participants. Again as expected, classification of *P6 solves* relations turn out to be the hardest part. Interestingly, the performance values for this subtask correlate less with the level of participants: Ph.D. students give less complete results, than not so experienced participants. A possible explanation comes from the fact that Ph.D. students have chosen their specific directions of research, which might not overlap with systems of linear equations as a sub-field of numerical analysis. That's why they classify tasks and methods very well, but prefer to keep in mind relationships about solution methods that are only relevant to their area of expertise.

Finally, we may conclude that the proposed approach could be used for evaluation of the competence of students.

4 Conclusion

We present $OntoMath^{PRO}$, an OWL ontology that is geared to be the hub of mathematical knowledge in the Web of Data. Relying on this representation model, we are going to create an ecosystem of datasets and mashups around the ontology to benefit mathematicians from different backgrounds – from undergraduate students to experts. In this paper, we describe the first steps towards it. In particular, interlinking with other Linked Data datasets, the applications in information extraction, semantic search of mathematical formulas, learning are discussed.

We emphasize that although the ontology has achieved maturity, it is the result of ongoing work. We share the sources with the Semantic Web community and organize the further collaborative development of the ontology and its applications on the project page `ontomathpro.org` to engage our colleagues and mathematicians from elsewhere.

As a future research work, we plan to study topic fusion in educational mathematical documents, such as lecture notes and textbooks, through occurrences of concepts from different taxonomies of the ontology. Additionally, we will address applications of ontology reconstruction in learning purposes (as described in Section 3.3), and are going to extend this approach other areas.

Acknowledgments. This work was funded by the subsidy allocated to Kazan Federal University for the state assignment in the sphere of scientific activities. The authors would like to thank V. Solovyev, A. Kayumova, I. Kayumov, P. Ivanshin, E. Utkina, and M. Matvejchuk, who have contributed to the ontology, as well as the students at Kazan Federal University, who took part in the experiments. The authors are also very grateful to A. Elizarov for his support, E. Khakimova (University of Virginia) for the assistance in writing the related work section, and the three anonymous reviewers for their valuable suggestions.

References

1. Aberer, K., Boyarsky, A., Cudr-Mauroux, P., Demartini, G., Ruchayskiy, O.: ScienceWISE: A Web-based Interactive Semantic Platform for Scientific Collaboration. In: 10th International Semantic Web Conference, (ISWC 2011 - Demo) (2011)
2. Auer, S., Bizer, C., Kobilarov, G., Lehmann, J., Cyganiak, R., Ives, Z.G.: Dbpedia: A Nucleus for a Web of Open Data. In: Aberer, K., et al. (eds.) ISWC/ASWC 2007. LNCS, vol. 4825, pp. 722–735. Springer, Heidelberg (2007)
3. Carlisle, D., Ion, P., Miner, R. (eds.): Mathematical Markup Language (MathML) Version 3.0.2 W3C Recommendation of 10 April 2014. World Wide Web Consortium (2010)
4. Barendregt, H., Wiedijk, F.: The Challenge of Computer Mathematics. Philosophical Transactions of the Royal Society A: Mathematical. Physical and Engineering Sciences 363(1835), 2351–2375 (2005)
5. Barrows, H.S.: A Taxonomy of Problembased Learning Methods. Medical Education 20(6), 481–486 (1986)
6. Berners-Lee, T.: Linked Data – Design Issues (2006),
http://www.w3.org/DesignIssues/LinkedData.html
7. Biryaltsev, E.V., Elizarov, A.M., Zhiltsov, N.G., Lipachev, E.K., Nevzorova, O.A., Solovyev, V.D.: Methods for analyzing semantic data of electronic collections in mathematics. Automatic Documentation and Mathematical Linguistics 48(2), 81–85 (2014)
8. Bizer, C., Heath, T., Berners-Lee, T.: Linked Data – The Story So Far. International Journal on Semantic Web and Information Systems 5(3), 1–22 (2009)
9. Bordes, A., Usunier, N., García-Durán, A., Weston, J., Yakhnenko, O.: Translating Embeddings for Modeling Multi-relational Data. In: Advances in Neural Information Processing Systems, pp. 2787–2795 (2013)
10. Buswell, S., Caprotti, O., Carlisle, D.P., Dewar, M.C., Gaëtano, M., Kohlhase, M.: The Open Math Standard. Version 2.0. Technical report, The Open Math Society (2004), http://www.openmath.org/standard/om20
11. David, C., Kohlhase, M., Lange, C., Rabe, F., Zhiltsov, N., Zholudev, V.: Publishing Math Lecture Notes as Linked Data. In: Aroyo, L., Antoniou, G., Hyvönen, E., ten Teije, A., Stuckenschmidt, H., Cabral, L., Tudorache, T. (eds.) ESWC 2010, Part II. LNCS, vol. 6089, pp. 370–375. Springer, Heidelberg (2010)
12. Dobrov, B., Loukachevitch, N.: Development of Linguistic Ontology on Natural Sciences and Technology. In: Proceedings of Linguistic Resources and Evaluation Conference, pp. 1077–1082 (2006)

13. Doerr, M.: The CIDOC conceptual reference module: an ontological approach to semantic interoperability of metadata. AI Magazine 24(3), 75–92 (2003)
14. Elizarov, A.M., Lipachev, E.L., Malakhaltsev, M.A.: Web Technologies for Mathematicians: The Basics of MathML. A Practical Guide. Fizmatlit, Moscow (2010) (in Russian)
15. Gruber, T., Olsen, G.: An Ontology for Engineering Mathematics. In: Principles of Knowledge Representation and Reasoning, pp. 258–269 (1994)
16. Kamareddine, F., Wells, J.B.: Computerizing Mathematical Text with MathLang. Electronic Notes in Theoretical Computer Science 205, 5–30 (2008)
17. Kohlhase, M.: OMDoc – An Open Markup Format for Mathematical Documents [version 1.2]. LNCS (LNAI), vol. 4180. Springer, Heidelberg (2006)
18. Lange, C.: Enabling Collaboration on Semiformal Mathematical Knowledge by Semantic Web Integration. Studies on the Semantic Web, vol. 11, pp. 1–592. IOS Press (2011)
19. Lange, C.: Ontologies and Languages for Representing Mathematical Knowledge on the Semantic Web. Semantic Web 4(2), 119–158 (2013)
20. Lange, C., Ion, P., Dimou, A., Bratsas, C., Sperber, W., Kohlhase, M., Antoniou, I.: Bringing Mathematics to the Web of Data: The Case of the Mathematics Subject Classification. In: Simperl, E., Cimiano, P., Polleres, A., Corcho, O., Presutti, V. (eds.) ESWC 2012. LNCS, vol. 7295, pp. 763–777. Springer, Heidelberg (2012)
21. Nevzorova, O.A., Birialtcev, E.V., Zhiltsov, N.G.: Mathematical text collections: Annotation and Application for Search Tasks. Scientific and Technical Information Processing 40(6), 386–395 (2013)
22. Nevzorova, O., Zhiltsov, N., Zaikin, D., Zhibrik, O., Kirillovich, A., Nevzorov, V., Birialtsev, E.: Bringing Math to LOD: A Semantic Publishing Platform Prototype for Scientific Collections in Mathematics. In: Alani, H., et al. (eds.) ISWC 2013, Part I. LNCS, vol. 8218, pp. 379–394. Springer, Heidelberg (2013)
23. Nickel, M., Tresp, V., Kriegel, H.P.: A Three-way Model for Collective Learning on Multi-relational Data. In: 28th International Conference on Machine Learning, pp. 809–816 (2011)
24. Sirin, E., Parsia, B., Cuenca Grau, B., Kalyanpur, A., Katz, Y.: Pellet: A Practical OWL-DL Reasoner. J. Web Sem. 5(2), 51–53 (2007)
25. Sloane, N.: The On-line Encyclopedia of integer sequences. Notices of the AMS 50(8), 912 (2003)
26. Solovyev, V., Zhiltsov, N.: Logical Structure Analysis of Scientific Publications in Mathematics. In: The International Conference on Web Intelligence, Mining and Semantics, pp. 21:1–21:9 (2011)
27. Springer LaTeX Search, http://www.latexsearch.com
28. Sutskever, I., Salakhutdinov, R., Tenenbaum, J.B.: Modelling Relational Data using Bayesian Clustered Tensor Factorization. In: NIPS, pp. 1821–1828 (2009)
29. Thomas, R.: Millenium Mathematics Project—Bringing Mathematics to Life. MSOR Connections 4(3) (2004)
30. Topic, G., Kristianto, G.Y., Nghiem, M.-Q., Aizawa, A.: The MCAT Math Retrieval System for NTCIR-10 Math Track. In: The 10th NTCIR Conference (2013)
31. Tudorache, T., Vendetti, J., Noy, N.F.: Web-Protege: A Lightweight OWL Ontology Editor for the Web. In: OWLED (2008)
32. (uni)quation, http://uniquation.com
33. Wikipedia Formula Search, http://shinh.org/wfs
34. Wolfram Alpha, http://www.wolframalpha.com
35. Wolfram Formula Search, http://functions.wolfram.com/formulasearch

Semantic Analysis and Prediction of Various Risks of Diabetic Patients

Sherimon P.C.[1], Vinu P.V.[1] Reshmy Krishnan[2], and Youssef Takroni[3]

[1] M.S.University, India
sherimon@aou.edu.om
[2] Muscat College, Muscat, Sultanate of Oman
[3] Arab Open University, Muscat, Sultanate of Oman
vinusherimon yahoo.com, {reshmy_krishnan}@yahoo.co.in,
yst@aou.edu.om

Abstract. Any health care system will be effective only if relevant patient information is available to make specific diagnosis. Many health centers employ different strategies to collect the medical history of patients, of which face-to-face interaction is the common technique. But in most of the cases, the concerned medical staff is not able to collect relevant medical history of a patient and this may affect the process of further medical analysis of the patient. This paper proposes semantic analysis and prediction of various risks in Diabetic patients. We have used ontology driven approach to perform the analysis and to predict the risk. We assess the diabetic patient risk factors due to smoking, alcohol intake, erectile dysfunction, and cardiovascular problems. According to the patient history, a total score is calculated for each of the above factors. According to the score, the ontology performs the risk assessment on a patient profile and predicts the potential risks and complications of the patient.

Keywords: Patient profile, risk assessment, ontology, clinical guidelines, diabetic treatment, knowledge base.

1 Introduction

Diabetes has been recognized by World Health Organization as a chronic, debilitating and costly disease associated with major complications that pose severe risks for families, countries and the entire world. Globally, as of 2013, an estimated 382 million people have diabetes worldwide, with type 2 diabetes making up about 90% of the cases [9]. This is equal to 3.3% of the population, with equal rates in both women and men [22]. In 2011 diabetes resulted in 1.4 million deaths worldwide, making it the 8th leading cause of death [10]. Developing countries, where resources are scarce, are expected to witness a 170% increase in the number of people with diabetes compared to 41% in developed countries [7]. The number of people with diabetes is expected to rise to 592 million by 2035 [9]. The risk associated with diabetic patients varies according to factors such as age, gender, family history etc. It is a challenge to diagnose diabetic patients particularly if patient medical history is unknown. Patient's medical history is an important component in any health care system. At the time of emergency,

P. Klinov and D. Mouromtsev (Eds.): KESW 2014, CCIS 468, pp. 120–127, 2014.

the previous medical history of the patient is crucial, so that appropriate attention and treatment can be given immediately on any place at any time [16]. Currently, patient medical history is collected mainly through static questionnaires, patient information collection systems (hard coded systems) or through face-to-face interaction when patient visits the hospital. Normally, when a patient visits a hospital, a nurse will first diagnose the patient and will record the preliminary observations such as readings of blood pressure, height, weight, body temperature, etc. [1]. Then doctors carry out physical examination and gather further information about the patient. Here, in most of the cases, the patient medical history will be incomplete. There are many reasons for this incompleteness such as lack of experience of the medical staff in collecting relevant patient details, patient does not want to disclose certain sensitive and personal health problems, patient is not able to communicate many medical details related to family (family history) because of shortage of time, etc. Also in some cases, doctors may not be able to ask the exact questions to each and every patient. In effect, effective risk analysis cannot be done in most of the cases.

So in order to avoid these shortcomings, we had proposed an ontology driven system to predict the risk associated with diabetic patients. A patient semantic profile, the ontology is automatically generated from questionnaire ontology [16]. This profile will be given as input to an ontology reasoner to calculate and predict the risk using the guidelines. The intelligence of the system depends on its knowledge base and reasoning algorithm. This paper presents a part of our proposed system: analysis and prediction of risk factors of diabetic patients based on ontology. Instead of a normal database system, a knowledge based approach is used. In traditional medical systems, when a diabetic patient comes for treatment, risk predictions are rarely done. Doctors analyze the case and suggest appropriate treatment. But the risks are not foreseen. Here we use an artificial intelligence approach to predict the risk. Ontology based systems are easy to update without any additional cost or software engineering work. Ontology languages allow users to write explicit, formal conceptualizations of domain models [21]. They help to explicitly define the existing information about the domain and formally encode that information.

2   Background

Ontology is a formal specification of the concepts within a domain and their interrelationships [15]. It is a methodology which describes the domain knowledge structure in the area of specialty, which promotes its various kinds of data processing intended to provide systematic, semantic links among groups of related concepts [12]. They are well known for many years in the Artificial Intelligence and Knowledge representation communities [13]. Ontologies are used to represent knowledge. Domain knowledge is contained in the form of concepts, individuals belonging to these concepts and relationships between the concepts and, between concepts and individuals [18]. It was initially proposed to model declarative knowledge for knowledge-based systems [4].

It is an abstract model which represents a common and shared understanding of a domain [18]. Gruber proposed the most popular definition of ontology [3] which is defined as "...a formal, explicit specification of a shared conceptualization." The W3C has developed a language, called OWL that can be used to describe the ontology [6]. It is built on W3C standards XML, RDF/RDFS and extends these languages with richer modelling primitives [21].

An ontology driven approach is utilized here to model the medical history of the patient and to assess the patient risk. If relevant patient history is not collected, it will result in fault calculation of risks associated with diabetes. The ontology's structure facilitates the organization, retrieval, and analysis of the encoded knowledge, including database design and merging of databases [2]. Ontology Reasoners are used to checking the consistency of the ontology and to automatically compute the ontology class hierarchy [17]. The reasoner will find out any hidden relationship in the ontology [19]. The use of ontologies is well suited for applications in medicine. When certain relations are asserted in the ontology, an ontology reasoner can infer more relations, which is not explicitly asserted in the ontology [20]. They are renowned for their flexible architectures, easy to share and reuse knowledge modelling structures and inexpensive maintenance operations [11].

3   Methodology

The work presented in this paper is part of our funded project to develop an ontology driven system for the diabetic health centers of Oman. So initially, a questionnaire was designed to gather the medical history of diabetic patients with the help of doctors in our team and validated by experts from OMSB [Oman Medical Speciality Board]. This dynamic questionnaire was converted to OWL [Web Ontology Language]. The questions related to patient's family history, diabetic history, smoking history, etc. are included as ontological classes. Accordingly sub-classes, data properties and object properties were also defined. The user interfaces are created in Java. Jena API is used to read the questions from the ontology. Patient is required to answer a set of questions on diabetic history, family history, smoking history, alcohol history, physical-activity history, etc. Nurse will enter some vital information about the patient such as body temperature, blood pressure, height, etc. The dietician enters information about the nutritional history of the patient. The lab technician enters the results of different lab tests conducted and finally the doctor examines the patient and enters his/her observations. Finally the user input is analysed and the patient semantic profile is generated. It includes all information about diabetic patients. Diabetic Clinical Guidelines followed in Ministry of Health, Oman [5] is used to analyze the patient risk. It was decided to calculate and predict the risk associated with five relevant factors that affect diabetic patients, such as smoking, alcohol, cardiovascular, sexual and physical activity. For example, how the above factors will affect a diabetic patient is predicted.

4   Implementation

Stanford Protégé and OWL Java API are the tools used in implementing the analysis and risk prediction of diabetic patients. The dynamic questionnaire, Diabetes-Treatment ontology is created in Protégé. Using OWL APIs, the questions are read from the ontology and displays to the user. The different users of the questionnaire are Patient, Doctor, Nurse, Lab Technician etc. when the users complete the entry of the questionnaire, a patient instance (semantic profile) is generated automatically with *patientID* as the instance name. The values entered by the users are asserted into different data properties of the ontology. By performing the risk assessment on semantic profile, the potential risks and complications of the patient are predicted.

		Point(s)
1.	How many cigarettes do you smoke per day?	
	a) 10 or less	0
	b) 11 – 20	1
	c) 21 – 30	2
	d) 31 or more	3
2.	How soon after you wake up do you smoke your first cigarette?	
	a) 0 – 5 min	3
	b) 30 min	2
	c) 31 – 60 min	1
	d) After 60 min	0
3.	Do you find it difficult to refrain from smoking in places where smoking is not allowed (e.g. hospitals, government offices, cinemas, libraries etc)?	
	a) Yes	1
	b) No	0
4.	Do you smoke more during the first hours after waking than during the rest of the day?	
	a) Yes	1
	b) No	0
5.	Which cigarette would you be the most unwilling to give up?	
	a) First in the morning	1
	b) Any of the others	0
6.	Do you smoke even when you are very ill?	
	a) Yes	1
	b) No	0

Fig. 1. Questionnaire – Smoking history

Figure 1 represents the part of questionnaire related to smoking history. These questions are used to assess and predict the risk associated with smoking habit of the patient. A score is associated with each answer choice. When the user enters the answers to these questions, the answers are read by OWL API and asserted into the ontology. So accordingly, a total score is calculated for the smoking history of the patient.

The risk/risk level as per the score for each category is available in the clinical guidelines. The guidelines related to the smoking history are given in Table 1. The score is divided into three levels, Low, Medium and High Nicotine Dependence. The total score obtained for a particular diabetic patient, is checked with the concerned guidelines. Accordingly, the score, risk/ risk level, and suitable treatment are suggested by the system. Similarly the risk and suitable treatment is suggested for four other factors such as alcohol, cardiovascular, sexual and physical activity that mainly affects diabetic patients.

Table 1. Smoking Guidelines

TOTAL SCORE		
0-3: Low nicotine dependence	**4-6: Low nicotine dependence**	**7-13: High nicotine dependence**
1. Will benefit from professional counseling. 2. Pharmacotherapy not recommended at initial assessment. If patient has difficulty dealing with withdrawal symptoms, further assessment for pharmacotherapy to be carried out to be ascertain suitability. 3. Willpower and support from family and friends are important.	1. Require professional counseling. 2. May recommend pharmacotherapy if patient is assessed to be suitable. Pharmacist and/or doctor to provide more advice on pharmacotherapy. 3. Willpower and support from family and friends are important.	1. Require professional counseling. 2. Recommend pharmacotherapy if patient is assessed to be suitable. Pharmacist and/or doctor to provide more advice on pharmacotherapy. 3. Willpower and support from family and friends are important.

5   Results and Discussions

Data properties are used to store the scores, risk level and the treatment of each of the above factors. For example, smoking-score, smoking-risk-level and smoking-Treatment are the data properties related to smoking history. As per the clinical guidelines, the score, risk and treatment are calculated, an instance of Patient class is asserted in the ontology and the above calculated values are stored as data property values of the instance. Fig 2 shows the score, risk and treatment of a patient with ID P_789, for each of the parameters discussed earlier.

```
■ cardio-Score  "0"^^nonNegativeInteger
■ cardio-Treatment  "Aspirin should not be recommended."^^string
■ smoking-Score  "4"^^nonNegativeInteger
■ smoking-Risk-Level  "Medium nicotine dependence"^^string
■ physical-Treatment  "Counsel about the importance of being active, in
    follow up"^^string
■ sexual-Score  "18"^^nonNegativeInteger
■ sexual-Risk-Level  "Mild erectile dysfunction"^^string
■ cardio-Risk  1.5f
■ physical-Score  "8"^^nonNegativeInteger
■ alcohol-Risk-Level  "ZONE III"^^string
■ physical-Risk-Level  "Moderately Inactive"^^string
■ alcohol-Score  "16"^^nonNegativeInteger
```

Fig. 2. Patient Score, Risk and Treatment asserted as Data Property values

The patient risk analysis is also displayed in the form of a table for doctors to decide about further specific treatment of the patients. The system suggests treatment as per the risk associated with each factor. It is represented in Table 2.

Table 2. Patient Risk Analysis

PATIENT RISK ANALYSIS			
Parameter	Score	Risk	Treatment
Smoking	4	Medium Nicotine Dependence	Require Professional Counselling. May recommend pharmacotherapy if patient is assessed to be suitable. Pharmacist and/ or doctor to provide more advice on Pharmacotherapy. Provide will power and support from family and friends.
Alcohol	16	Zone III	Simple advice plus brief counseling and continued monitoring.
Sexual	18	Mile erectile dysfunction	Discuss with the patient the option of starting him on Sildenafil.
Cardiovascular	0	1.5	Aspirin should not be recommended.
Physical	8	Moderately Inactive	Counsel about the importance of being active, increase activity level and follow up.

6   Conclusion and Future Work

We have presented an ontology driven approach to analyze and predict the risk associated with five important factors that affects diabetic patients. Diabetes-Treatment ontology is used to represent the questionnaire used to collect the patient information. The questions are read from the ontology and presented to the users through relevant user interfaces. As per the input, the patient semantic profile [OWL file] is generated automatically from Diabetes-Treatment ontology which is used as the input to analyze the risk. Diabetic Clinical Guidelines followed in Ministry of Health, Oman is used to analyze the patient risk. These risk values (score) will help the doctor to understand about the current situation of a patient. The questionnaire can be updated anytime by just updating the Diabetes-Treatment ontology. Ontology based reasoning makes a way to discover new knowledge, which can lead to new directions in research. The future scope of our research is to represent the diabetic guidelines in SWRL (Semantic Web Rule Language).

Acknowledgement. This work is published as part of a project funded by The Research Council [TRC], Oman under Agreement No. ORG/ AOU/ ICT/ 11/ 015, Proposal No ORG/ICT/11/004 and Arab Open University, Oman Branch.

References

1. Ahmadian, L., Cornet, R., de Keizer, N.F.: Facilitating Pre-operative Assessment Guidelines Representation Using SNOMED CT. Journal of Biomedical Informatics 43(6), 883–890 (2010)
2. Mauer, A., et al.: Creating an Ontology-Based Human Phenotyping System: The Rockefeller University Bleeding History Experience, Technical Report (2009), doi: 10.1111/j.1752-8062.2009.00147.x
3. Gruber: A Translation Approach to Portable Ontologies. Knowledge Acquisition 5(2), 199–220 (1993)
4. El-Ghalayini, H.: E-Course Ontology for Developing E-Learning Courses. In: Developments in E-Systems Engineering(DeSE), pp. 245–249 (2011)
5. Heatherton, T., Kozlowski, L., Frecker, R., Fagerström, K.: The Fagerström Test for Nicotine Dependence: A Revision of the Fagerström Tolerance Questionnaire. Br. J. Addict. 86, 1119–1127 (1991)
6. Zhao, H., Zhang, S., Zhao, J.: Research of Using Protégé to Build Ontology. In: Proceeding(s) of the IEEE/ACIS 11th International Conference in Computer and Information Science, pp. 697–700 (2012)
7. http://www.moh.gov.om/en/mgl/Manual/diabetesmoh.pdf   (accessed January 11, 2013)
8. http://www.who.int/substance_abuse/activities/sbi/en/index.html (accessed January 8, 2013)
9. http://www.idf.org/diabetesatlas (accessed January 11, 2013)
10. http://www.who.int/mediacentre/factsheets/fs312/en/   (accessed January 11, 2013)
11. Farooq, K., Hussain, A., Leslie, S., Eckl, C., MacRae, C., Slack, W.: An Ontology Driven and Bayesian Network Based Cardiovascular Decision Support Framework. In: Zhang, H., Hussain, A., Liu, D., Wang, Z. (eds.) BICS 2012. LNCS (LNAI), vol. 7366, pp. 31–41. Springer, Heidelberg (2012)
12. Haghighi, M., Koeda, M., Takai, T., Tanaka, H.: Development of Clinical Ontology for Mood Disorder with Combination of Psychomedical Information. Journal of Medical and Dental Sciences 56(1), 1–15 (2009)
13. Akerkar, R.: Foundations of the Semantic Web. Narosha Publishing House (2009)
14. Rosen, R., Cappelleri, J., Smith, M., Lipsky, J., Peña, B.: Development and Evaluation of an Abridged, 5-item Version of the International Index of Erectile Function (IIEF-5) as a diagnostic tool for erectile dysfunction. Int. J. Impot. Res. 11, 322 (1999)
15. Subhashini, R., Akilandeswar, J.: A Survey on Ontology Construction Methodologies. International Journal of Enterprise Computing and Business Systems 1(1), 60–72 (2011)
16. Anand, S., Verma, A.: Development of Ontology for Smart Hospital and Implementation using UML and RDF. IJCSI International Journal of Computer Science Issues 7(5) (September 2010)
17. Sherimon, P.C., Vinu, P.V.: Reshmy Krishnan, Youssef Takroni.: Developing Survey Questionnaire Ontology for the Decision Support System in the Domain of Hypertension. In: IEEE South East Conference, Florida, April 4-7 (2013)
18. Sherimon, P.C., Reshmy, K., Vinu, P.V., Youssef, T.: Ontology Based System Architecture to Predict the Risk of Hypertension in Related Diseases. International Journal of Information Processing and Management 4(4) (June 2013), doi:10.4156/ijipm.vol4.issue4.5.

19. Sherimon, P.C., Reshmy, K., Vinu, P.V., Youssef, T.: Exhibiting Context Sensitive Behavior in Gathering Patient Medical History in Diabetes Domain using Ontology. International Journal of Advancements in Computing Technology, IJACT 5(13), 41–47 (2013), ISSN : 2005-8039 (Print) ISSN : 2233-9337 (Online) (2013)
20. Sherimon, P.C., Vinu, P.V., Reshmy, K.: Development Phases of Ontology for an Intelligent Search System for Oman National Transport Company. International Journal of Research and Reviews in Artificial Intelligence IJRRAI 1(4), 97–101 (2011)
21. Vinu, P.V., Sherimon, P.C., Reshmy, K.: Development of Ontology for Seafood Quality Assurance System. Journal of Convergence Information Technology 9(1), 25–32 (2014)
22. Vos, T., Flaxman, A., et al.: Years Lived with Disability (YLDs) for 1160 Sequelae of 289 Diseases and Injuries 1990-2010: A Systematic Analysis for the Global Burden of Disease Study 2010. Lancet 380(9859), 2163–2196 (2012), PMID 23245607

Interaction History Based Answer Formulation for Question Answering

Rivindu Perera and Parma Nand

School of Computer and Mathematical Sciences
Auckland University of Technology
Auckland, New Zealand
{rivindu.perera,parma.nand}@aut.ac.nz

Abstract. With the rapid growth in information access methodologies, question answering has drawn considerable attention among others. Though question answering has emerged as an interesting new research domain, still it is vastly concentrated on question processing and answer extraction approaches. Latter steps like answer ranking, formulation and presentations are not treated in depth. Weakness we found in this arena is that answers that a particular user has acquired are not considered, when processing new questions. As a result, current systems are not capable of linking two questions such as "When is the Apple founded?" with a previously processed question "When is the Microsoft founded?" generating an answer in the form of "Apple is founded one year later Microsoft founded, in 1976". In this paper we present an approach towards question answering to devise an answer based on the questions already processed by the system for a particular user which is termed as interaction history for the user. Our approach is a combination of question processing, relation extraction and knowledge representation with inference models. During the process we primarily focus on acquiring knowledge and building up a scalable user model to formulate future answers based on current answers that same user has processed. According to evaluation we carried out based on the TREC resources shows that proposed technology is promising and effective in question answering.

Keywords: Question answering, Answer formulation, Interaction history, Natural Language Processing.

1 Introduction

Question answering systems are designed to present an answer for a given question composed in natural language. Due to this fact, from existing question answering systems such as AnswerBus [1], START [2] and WolframAlpha [3] to early question answering systems like LUNAR and BASEBALL [4] shared the same objective of generating the answer through diverse research attempts. All aforementioned question answering systems considered questions as independent units and generated answers based on the information retrieval and

P. Klinov and D. Mouromtsev (Eds.): KESW 2014, CCIS 468, pp. 128–139, 2014.
© Springer International Publishing Switzerland 2014

extraction modules that are integrated. Recently, when attempting to investigate new dimensions in question answering, answer formulation and presentation also became a featuring factor [5].

Answer formulation is considered to be the final step in question answering systems which is responsible for presenting the answer to the user. As most of the early researches extensively focused on question processing and candidate answer extraction approaches, this unit kept relatively untouched. However, competition which is arisen among question answering systems, opened the path to discover novel ways of answer formulation which can immensely contribute for the uniqueness of a question answering system.

In this paper, we investigate a technique called Interaction History based Answer Formulation (IHAF) to build a user model to generate more personalized answers for users based on the past interactions for that particular user. We conduct experiments based on TREC question set and with different variations. However, it should be emphasised that in this implementation of question answering system, we are not going to mine the answers from the web or from a corpus. Instead we have provided the ranked sentence list from TREC to extract answers. This is carried out basically because of our attention is not on question answering itself but on answer formulation where underlying question answering system is not relevant for the process.

The remainder of the paper is organized as follows. The next section is committed to related work. In Section 3, we discuss about our approach towards the issue we have identified and provide complete overview of the technique. Section 4 is concentrated on results and evaluation schema we have used to assess our novel approach. In Section 5, discussion on the technique in relation to results is presented covering different perspectives. Finally, in Section 6, we conclude showing future directions of this new method towards question answering.

2   Related Work

Answer formulation for question answering systems is first brought into broad discussion by Hirschman and Gaizauskas [6] through an analysis of current question answering strategies. However, there are significant research attempts taken towards presenting and formulating an answer in question answering.

Wang et al. [7] present an interesting idea of generating answer based on relations mined based on focus information. Though, it does not express personalized answer generation method, employing pre-mined relations to generate answers draws the attention as a new method. Moving to an innovative direction authors of [8] propose a slightly different method. They utilize past answers to generate answers for new questions where they employ Yahoo! Answers track. This research is based on surface level feature extraction of top candidate and then classification through a random forest classifier. As answer generation is applied with the vision of social engagement, personalization of a particular answer based on the user is not treated. Evaluation shows that it has achieved good result in answer generation, but content applicability for the new question is not measured in a qualitative approach. Similar technique used in [8] is noticed in [9] and [10] as well with slight changes in the process.

Ni et al. [11] build a topic based user interest model to integrate with question answering. Though this research sounds well in the area of user based question answering, the model they propose is used only to recommend appropriate questions. Also it is observed that this proposed model is using latent topic model which limit the model to top level topic based user model. In contrast to this method, seminal work presented by Nyberg et al. [12] show an approach inspired by methodology showcased by Hovy [13]. Utilization of user discourse to boost the question answering based on the classified question types signals that this research is focusing on the question processing based on the user supplied concepts. But the lack of user centred question processing is still not achieved efficiently here. Advanced approach towards question processing with existing knowledge is demonstrated in system proposed by Harabagiu and Hickl [14]. In this novel attempt, Harabagiu and Hickl endeavour the gap between existing knowledge utilization and answer formulation through a promising application. Though this research significantly lies in the shallow text processing area, the concept unveiled and model built are extremely useful when mining answers for questions based on the existing knowledge that is already acquired.

Moving few steps further, Higashinaka and Isozaki [15] encompass the usage of casual expression patterns for answer extraction. Grounded on a corpus based technique to mine features to build the casual expression patterns, researchers attempt to apply the resulting model in a open domain question answering system. Different dimensions in the evaluation carried out by this research shows that their model outperforms in most of the scenarios. Basically, employing a WHY-type question set in the training and attempting to build a typological answer extraction model seems to be promising. Several early attempts such as [16], [17] and [18] also express similar candidate answer formulation models. When it comes to the feature selection and applicability in the question processing steps, model developed by Higashinaka and Isozaki can be considered as a more improved procedure.

3   Interaction History Based Answer Formulation (IHAF)

We have separated the contexts of user model building and answer formulation to two sections in order to focus on them more thoroughly. In next sections we delineate the framework of complete process resulted through our research. Before moving into the complete process, we first examine basic utilities that are built to serve the high level goal of the system.

3.1   Basic Utilities Incorporated

In this section we define some basic functionalities that we employ during user model building and answer formulation.

Generating Typed Dependency Parses. Typed dependency parsing is a way of representing dependencies between words given in a sentence structure with labelled grammatical relations [19] [20]. We employed dependency parsing mainly because of compared to a phrase structure with constituency, dependency parsing can easily transformed in to relation schema. Another, noteworthy point to notice here is that as labelled grammatical relations are present it can later be modified and normalized into more accurate relation if resulting typed dependency is not suitable to generate a relation. For the dependency parsing we utilize the Stanford parser based on 50 grammatical relations [20] [19]. Dependency Parse (DP) generated for a selected question from TREC development set is shown in Fig. 1.

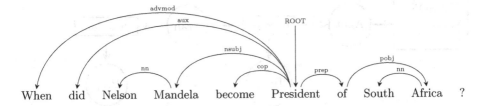

Fig. 1. Example of dependency parse of a question

From Dependency Parses to Conceptual Graph. Conversion from typed dependency parse to the Conceptual Graph (CG) is also considered as a principal process in representation workflow. Conceptual graphs introduced by Sowa [21] is considered as the basis of ontology and related knowledge representation strategies. An example CG we expect from question considered in Fig. 1 is shown in Fig. 2. As conversion of a language structure to a knowledge structure requires considerable effort, we have defined a set of rule set for 8 different case relations based on thematic roles, named entities and user defined types which are shown in Table 1. In all other cases where we are unable to label with appropriate case role of CG relation, by default typed dependency label is used.

We employed conceptual graphs after consideration several representation strategies such as lexical ontologies [22], frames [23] and semi-structured language fragments [24]. Factor that influenced us to choose CG, is the opportunity it provides to infer based on the model developed using Common Logic (CL) and six canonical formation rules [21] which supports us to perform projection operators which will be discussed in following section.

Key factor we noticed during preliminary analysis on conversion process is that DP structure is not identically mapped with CG. Therefore, simple conversion from one to one mapping converting DP root to CG root can lead us to severe errors in structure. Due to this major emphasis is placed on identifying a generalizable rule set to convert DP structure to a CG representation. Algorithm. 1 depicts the flow of applying rules during the conversion phase.

Table 1. Defined case relations

Case Relation	Abbreviation	Description
Agent	Agnt	Main actor of the event
Transition	Tran	Transition from one state to another
Attribute	Attr	Property of a object
Patient	Ptnt	Object which is subjected to an action
Experiencer	Expr	Object that experience the event
Recipient	Rcpt	Object that receive something
Temporal	Temp	Time related factor
State	Stat	Current state of the object

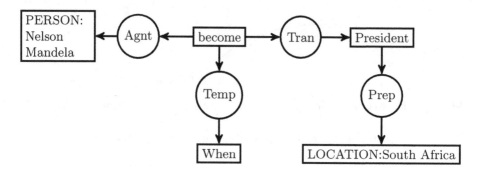

Fig. 2. Example of conceptual graph of a question

For the phrase extraction, we employ a three step process of *a*) stop word removal of the question *b*) stemming using Porter stemmer [25] *c*) calculation of Term Frequency and Inverse Sentence Frequency (TF-ISF) for the decomposed question terms.

As an initial step, Named Entity Recognition (NER) is also engaged using Conditional Random Field based NER tool - Stanford NER. The idea of NER is to output more semantically rich CG constructs labelled with entity type, which is again useful in searching based on type. Following initial steps, we then check the best candidate for the root of the CG (CG_{Root}). This is based on the condition that if DP is consisted of a copular verb (DP_{cop_v}), then it is selected by default and if not we continue with root of DP (DP_{Root}). Then after removal of all WH-pronouns, root of CG, root of DP and remaining auxiliary verbs and prepositions, we start relation generation where 9 different relation types are considered based on 9 different rule sets ($ruleSet_{<TYPE>}$). Each relation is labelled with the matching relation found ($< TYPE >_p$) based on the considered phrase (p). In case if matching relation is not found based on the predefined rule set, relation present in the DP is used to label the generated relation. Result of this flow is a CG which we later can be used with projection operators.

Algorithm 1. Flow of converting DP to mapping CG

Data: DP: Typed dependency representation, P:Extracted phrases of question
Result: CG:Conceptual Graph
begin

> $E \longleftarrow RecognizeNamedEntities(Q)$;
> **if** $DP_{cop_v} \neq NULL$ **and** $DP_{Root} \neq DP_{cop_v}$ **then**
> > $CG_{Root} \longleftarrow DP_{cop_v}$;
>
> **else**
> > $CG_{Root} \longleftarrow DP_{Root}$;
>
> $P \leftarrow P - \{WH_{pronoun}, CG_{Root}, DP_{prep}, DP_{aux}\}$;
> **for** $p \in P$ **do**
> > **switch** p **do**
> > > // Only one case is shown for 8 cases needed for 8
> > > different relation types - replacing <TYPE> generic
> > > type with Agnt, Ptnt, Expr, etc.
> > >
> > > **case** $relation_p \in ruleSet_{<TYPE>}$
> > > > **if** p $hasRelationWith$ CG_{Root} **then**
> > > > > generateRelation($< TYPE >_{p,CG_{Root}}$);
> > > >
> > > > **else**
> > > > > generateRelation($< TYPE >_{p,DP_{relatedPhrase}}$);
> > >
> > > // ...... remaining cases
> > > **otherwise**
> > > > generateRelation($DP - Type_{p,DP_{relatedPhrase}}$);
> >
> > **if** $p \in E$ **then**
> > > labelWithEntityType(p);

Conceptual Graph Projection. CG projection is the process of extracting or generating advanced knowledge based on two or more CGs. In our case, we utilize a simple projection operator based on nodes in the CG. Properties that are considered in projection are, named entities, root of CG and the specified CG relation (ex: agent, patient, etc.). Example projection based on our previous example in Fig. 2 is shown in Fig. 3. In this example we assume that CG for "Jacob Suma became president of South Africa in 2009" exists in the knowledge base.

According to the projection shown in Fig. 3, it can be noticed that named entities and temporal event annotations (When and 2009) are projected providing opportunity to extract necessary knowledge. Building the required natural language answer will be discussed in Section 3.3.

3.2   Building the User Model

Most significant element that is presented by this research can be considered as the user model that we have designed to build in order to link questions with

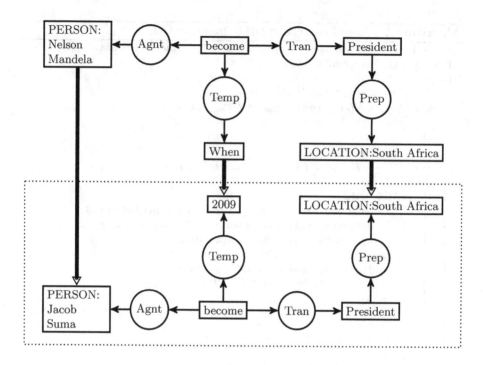

Fig. 3. Example of conceptual graph projection

previously processed questions by the same user.However, it is heavily dependant on basic utilities we described in Section 3.1.

Below we have defined the basic work flow of the user model creation based on the utilities discussed above.

1. Generate the Typed Dependency Parses (DP) of the question
2. Map the parsed question to Conceptual Graph (CG)
3. Save the CG to the knowledge base

The knowledge base constructed at this point will be unique and will be considered as the user model for that particular user.

For the initial training 120 questions are suggested to commence the model building process as it it needs considerable amount of question classes and answer candidates to link with next questions. This 120 questions, defined as the start-up items are selected based on 3 factors from TREC-9 data set, *a*) question type (WH-type) *b*) question target (person, location, date/time, etc.) *c*) named entities mentioned (ex: South Africa, Nelson Mandela,Jacob Suma, etc). Basis of selecting these 3 factors is adopted from several past research attempts which have highlighted the importance of them running empirical methods towards question answering [26,27,28].

3.3   Answer Formulation

In this section, we describe the approach taken towards generating answer for a given question employing an existing user model.

1. Generate the Typed Dependency Parses (DP) of the question
2. Map the parsed question to Conceptual Graph (CG)
3. Project CG to user model elements and extract similar structures
4. Generate language structures based on inferences and previous interactions acquired from user model

Answer formulation also utilize the basic utilities discussed, but move further with extracted knowledge from user model by building natural language. For the purpose of building naturally looking answer, we employ a surface realization engine where we get the final answer based on the structures defined. SimpleNLG [29] has shown high flexibility during our analysis for suitable realization engines. Structuring templates are defined by authors for the SimpleNLG to output the final natural language text for the given answer.

4   Results

For the evaluation, we employed TREC-8 [30] question set containing 200 questions. Main reason behind this section is that unlike TREC-9 and later TREC data sets, TREC-9 specifically focus on entity based answer extraction. As the approach discussed here is also based on entity types, TREC-8 provided us the most appropriate selection for the context.

To get a better understanding of the process, we carried out the evaluation in 5 different steps which is depicted in Table 2 with different number of questions for both training and testing.

Table 2. Evaluation setup

Type	Traning setup (#questions [TREC-type])	Testing setup (#questions [TREC-type])
T-1	120 [TREC-9]	200 [TREC-8]
T-2	240 [TREC-9]	200 [TREC-8]
T-3	360 [TREC-9]	200 [TREC-8]
T-4	480 [TREC-9]	200 [TREC-8]
T-5	200 [TREC-8]	200 [TREC-8]

During evaluation, we noticed that user model built based on initial training phase is used for four different target types, date/time, number, currency and distance are not fairly distributed in two different TREC datasets. It is also valuable to mention that while the execution, our system was able to link questions from testing set as well , but which we neglected as we strictly believed that answers must be drawn only from training set. To provide a baseline for the evaluation, we consulted Cosine Similarity (CS) between new question and previously processed question. If two questions (stop words removed) are shown in vectors A and B, then CS between A and B can be calculated as,

$$CS(A, B) = \frac{\sum_{i=1}^{n} t_{Ai} \times t_{Bi}}{\sqrt{\sum_{i=1}^{n}(t_{Ai})^2} \times \sqrt{\sum_{i=1}^{n}(t_{Bi})^2}} \tag{1}$$

where, t_i is the term weight for a word w_i, for which TF-ISF (Term Frequency, Inverse Sentence Frequency) value is used.

Table 3. Evaluation results

Test type	Precision	Recall	F-measure (IHBQA)	F-measure (baseline)
T-1	0.38	0.5	0.43	0.34
T-2	0.53	0.6	0.56	0.42
T-3	0.42	0.53	0.46	0.41
T-4	0.39	0.52	0.44	0.29
T-5	0.53	0.8	0.63	0.55

Table 3 shows the results we acquired during our evaluation phase. While testing with TREC-8 question sets, we noticed that some questions exists with answers having different measurement units. For example, miles and kilometres both are used (ex: Question 9 and Question 150) when providing answers for questions. To provide equal treatment during answer search, we manually converted them to metric units. It is also noteworthy to mention that as we are not involving with a question processing and answer extraction unit as in most question answering systems, results we achieved are completely focused on answer formulation. Therefore, error rate occurs in actual answer extraction with incorrect answers is not included here, as we are already having the exact answer for every question processed.

5   Discussion

According to the evaluation we carried out in 5 stage process, it can be noticed that random incrementation of number of question has no effect in accuracy of answer formulation. Through examination of this issue, highlighted two main factors to further investigate. Firstly, as we are incrementing questions in random fashion, number of recognized named entities has not proportionally incremented. This is partially due to the weakness of the NER tool that we employed to this research. Secondly, when number of questions increase, it is observed that CG projection operator has more choices based on inference rules used. This has lead the system to retrieve some of the less significant items due to overlapping inference rules.

Generally, our approach has produced errors when processing context sensitive questions which are difficult to determine the type by WH-pronoun. One such erroneous observation is following two questions which are linked during evaluation without having similar context or target type:

- What is the fare cost for the round trip between New York and London on Concorde?
- What is the duration of the trip from Bristol to London by rail?

During the evaluation, it has reached to its highest accuracy in test type-5, when same test collection is used for the training phase. As we investigated this is mainly due to the style of TREC-8 questions, which are more focused on entity types and much simpler than TREC-9 questions considering context and target identification.

Though these experiments provides standard levels to compare with, the most appropriate evaluation that can be applied for a question answering system in this nature is the real world evaluation. As there are multiple entities incorporated and question types are difficult to determine, answer formulation for real world question answering can place a benchmark on evaluation in a more precise manner. However, at this stage, no real world evaluation is done with human involvement which lies as a future goal.

Overall, though our approach has not achieved high accuracy in evaluation, it can be noticed that approach is still feasible and promising in answer formulation. As mentioned earlier, observed issues are mainly due to the process we have engaged for the CG construction and processing which can be considered as a main unit that contributes for user model building.

6 Conclusion and Future Work

We presented a novel, answer formulation approach for question answering based on the concept of interaction history of a user. In contrast to previous approaches, this new model targeted on more personalized answer - considering that linking with earlier acquired knowledge can dramatically increase the usefulness of an answer. User model and CG generation methods presented through this research can be seen as first step towards answer formulation for question answering with emphasis on interaction history. However, it should not be seen as a complete model. Through, observations during the evaluation, we noticed severe issues that lead our system to erroneous results as mentioned in previous section. Addressing these issues is necessary and important when attempting to build more personalized answer formulation for open domain question answering.

References

1. Zheng, Z.: AnswerBus question answering system. In: Second International Conference on Human Language Technology Research, pp. 399–404. Morgan Kaufmann Publishers Inc. (2002)

2. Katz, B., Borchardt, G., Felshin, S.: Natural Language Annotations for Question Answering. In: 19th International FLAIRS Conference, Melbourne Beach, Florida (2006)
3. Research, W.: WolframAlpha API (2011)
4. Woods, W.A.: Semantics and quantification in natural language question answering, 205–248 (1986)
5. Maybury, M.: New Directions In Question Answering. In: Strzalkowski, T., Harabagiu, S.M. (eds.) Advances in Open Domain Question Answering. Text, Speech and Language Technology, vol. 32. Springer, Netherlands (2008)
6. Hirschman, L., Gaizauskas, R.: Natural language question answering: The view from here. Natural Language Engineering 7(04), 275–300 (2002)
7. Wang, R., Ning, C., Lu, B., Huang, X.: Research on answer generation method based on focus information extraction. In: 2012 IEEE International Conference on Computer Science and Automation Engineering (CSAE), vol. 2, pp. 724–728. IEEE (2012)
8. Shtok, A., Dror, G., Maarek, Y., Szpektor, I.: Learning from the past. In: Proceedings of the 21st International Conference on World Wide Web, WWW 2012. ACM Press, New York (2012)
9. Wang, G., Gill, K., Mohanlal, M., Zheng, H., Zhao, B.Y.: Wisdom in the social crowd: An analysis of quora, pp. 1341–1352 (2013)
10. Liu, D.R., Chen, Y.H., Kao, W.C., Wang, H.W.: Integrating expert profile, reputation and link analysis for expert finding in question-answering websites. Information Processing & Management 49(1), 312–329 (2013)
11. Ni, X., Lu, Y., Quan, X., Wenyin, L., Hua, B.: User interest modeling and its application for question recommendation in user-interactive question answering systems. Information Processing & Management 48(2), 218–233 (2012)
12. Nyberg, E., Frederking, R.: JAVELIN. In: Proceedings of the 2003 Conference of the North American Chapter of the Association for Computational Linguistics on Human Language Technology Demonstrations, NAACL 2003, vol. 4, pp. 19–20. Association for Computational Linguistics, Morristown (2003)
13. Hovy, E., Hermjakob, U., Ravichandran, D.: A question/answer typology with surface text patterns, pp. 247–251 (2002)
14. Harabagiu, S., Hickl, A.: Using scenario knowledge in automatic question answering, pp. 32–39 (2006)
15. Higashinaka, R., Isozaki, H.: Automatically Acquiring Causal Expression Patterns from Relation-annotated Corpora to Improve Question Answering for why-Questions. ACM Transactions on Asian Language Information Processing 7(2), 1–29 (2008)
16. Yang, F., Feng, J., Di Fabbrizio, G.: A data driven approach to relevancy recognition for contextual question answering, pp. 33–40 (2006)
17. Li, B., Jin, T., Lyu, M.R., King, I., Mak, B.: Analyzing and predicting question quality in community question answering services. In: Proceedings of the 21st International Conference Companion on World Wide Web, WWW 2012, p. 775. ACM Press, New York (2012)
18. Stoyanchev, S., Song, Y.C., Lahti, W.: Exact phrases in information retrieval for question answering, pp. 9–16 (2008)
19. de Marneffe, M.-C., MacCartney, B., Manning, C.D.: Generating typed dependency parses from phrase structure parses. In: International Conference on Language Resources and Evaluation (2006)

20. de Marneffe, M.C., Manning, C.D.: The Stanford typed dependencies representation. In: Workshop on Cross-Framework and Cross-Domain Parser Evaluation, Association for Computational Linguistics, pp. 1–8 (2008)
21. Sowa, J.F.: Conceptual graphs as a universal knowledge representation. Computers & Mathematics with Applications 23(2-5), 75–93 (1992)
22. Veale, T., Hao, Y.: A context-sensitive framework for lexical ontologies. The Knowledge Engineering Review 23(01), 101–115 (2008)
23. Martin, P.: Knowledge Representation in CGLF, CGIF, KIF, Frame-CG and Formalized-English, pp. 77–91 (2002)
24. Liu, H., Singh, P.: ConceptNet A Practical Commonsense Reasoning Tool-Kit. BT Technology Journal 22(4), 211–226 (2004)
25. Porter, M.: An algorithm for suffix stripping. Program 14(3), 130–137 (1980)
26. Hartrumpf, S.: Adapting a semantic question answering system to the web, pp. 61–68 (2006)
27. Grappy, A., Grau, B., Rosset, S.: Methods combination and ML-based re-ranking of multiple hypothesis for question-answering systems, pp. 87–96 (2012)
28. Clarke, C.L.A., Terra, E.L.: Approximating the top-m passages in a parallel question answering system. In: Proceedings of the Thirteenth ACM Conference on Information and knowledge Management CIKM 2004, p. 454. ACM Press, New York (2004)
29. Gatt, A., Reiter, E.: SimpleNLG: a realisation engine for practical applications, pp. 90–93 (2009)
30. Voorhees, E.: Overview of TREC 1999. In: TREC 8, National Institute of Standards and Technology, Gaithersburg (1999)

Automatic Term Extraction for Sentiment Classification of Dynamically Updated Text Collections into Three Classes

Yuliya Rubtsova

The A.P. Ershov Institute of Informatics Systems (IIS),
Siberian Branch of the Russian Academy of Sciences
yu.rubtsova@gmail.com

Abstract. This paper presents an automatic term extraction approach for building a vocabulary that is constantly updated. A prepared dictionary is used for sentiment classification into three classes (positive, neutral, negative). In addition, the results of sentiment classification are described and the accuracy of methods based on various weighting schemes is compared. The paper also demonstrates the computational complexity of generating representations for N dynamic documents depending on the weighting scheme used.

Keywords: Corpus linguistics, sentiment analysis, information extraction, text classification and categorization, social networks data analysis.

1   Introduction

We live in a constantly changing world. Peoples' style and way of life, behaviors and speech are all changing. Natural language is constantly transforming and developing together with conversational speech: new words are included in active vocabulary, while old ones cease to be used. New words are born every day, and about half of them are slang. Slang responds to changes in all spheres more quickly than other types of language and is so important to modern society that last year 40 neologisms, some of which are slang words, were added to the Oxford English Dictionary. Slang is actively used in colloquial speech and written communication on social networking sites, as well as to express an emotional attitude towards a particular issue. Users of social networks are among the first to start using new terms in everyday language. Among about 1000 new words included in the Oxford English Dictionary near 40 were terms that came from social networks, such as "srsly", "me time" and "selfie". Accordingly, it is necessary to consider slang when developing sentiment classifiers, in particular when creating vocabularies of emotional language. Moreover, since active vocabulary is regularly updated with new terms, vocabularies of emotional language should also be updated regularly, and the weights of the terms in these vocabularies must be recalculated.

This paper presents an approach to extracting terms and assigning them weights in order to build a vocabulary of emotional language that is constantly updated.

P. Klinov and D. Mouromtsev (Eds.): KESW 2014, CCIS 468, pp. 140–149, 2014.

There will be a comparison of methods based on various weighting schemes and the computational complexity of recalculating the weights of terms in the vocabulary depending on the methods used will be demonstrated. All experiments to classify texts into three sentiment classes (positive, neutral, negative) were performed on two collections:

- Collection of short posts from microblogs [1];
- News collection.

2   Overview of Term Weighting Schemes

There are different approaches to the extraction of evaluative words from texts and the determination of their weight in the collection. In [2], the authors use a thesaurus to expand a vocabulary of evaluative words that had been collected manually. In corpus linguistics, methods of extracting terms based on measuring the relevance of a term to a collection are widely used, for example, the well-known methods based on the TF-IDF weighting scheme [3]. In [4], the authors show that variants of the classic TF-IDF scheme adapted to sentiment analysis task provide significant increases in accuracy in comparison to binary unigram weights. They tested their approach on a wide selection of data sets and demonstrated that classification accuracy enhanced.

The functioning of most existing methods of automatic and semi-automatic word extraction from texts are based on the assumption that all the data are known in advance, accessible and static. For example, to use a method based on the TF-IDF scheme [3], it is necessary to know the frequency each term occurs in the document, which means that the data set should not be changed during calculation. This greatly complicates computation is required for data calculation in real time. For example, when adding a new text to the collection, it is necessary to recalculate the weights for all terms in the collection. The computational complexity of recalculating all the weights in the collection is $O(N^2)$.

The Term Frequency – Inverse Corpus Frequency (TF-ICF) measure has been proposed [5, 6] in order to solve the problem of searching for terms and calculating their weights in real time. Information on the usage frequency of a term in other documents of the collection is not required in order to calculate TF-ICF, so the computational complexity is linear. The results of methods based on TF-ICF and TF-IDF have been compared [3] in order to evaluate the effectiveness of a method based on the TF-ICF weighting scheme for the task of extracting evaluative terms for a vocabulary of emotional language.

The formula for calculating the TF-IDF measure is as follows:

$$tfidf = tf \times log \frac{T}{T(t_i)} \tag{1}$$

Where tf is the frequency with which the term occurs in the collection (of positive or negative tweets), T is total number of texts in the positive and negative collections, and $T(t_i)$ is the number of texts in the positive and negative collections containing the term.

The formula for calculating the TF-ICF measure is as follows:

$$tf.icf = tf \times \log\left(1 + \frac{|C|}{cf(t_i)}\right) \tag{2}$$

Where C is the number of categories and cf is the number of categories in which the term to be weighed occurs.

In the TF-IDF scheme, both weighing factors assess the term at the document level. The proposed TF-ICF scheme is mixed: TF evaluates the term at the document level, ICF at the category level. Another approach for TF-ICF was suggested by Lertnatteed [7, 8], he proposed the use of a TF-ICF scheme in which the TF factor evaluates term frequencies at the category level, as would the ICF factor [6].

To test the effectiveness of approaches based on the selected weighting schemes, we proceed as in [9], taking 5 terms from a real corpus and evaluating the calculation of the term's weight depending on the collection it belongs to (positive, negative, neutral). The selected terms are as follows: "obidno" (it's a shame), "plokho" (bad), "lyublyu" (I love), "konechno" (of course) and "vremya" (time). Based on the frequency of the term usage in a collections suppose that first two terms belong to the class of negative posts, the following two – the positive class; the latter term is neutral and occurs equally often in the positive and negative collections. Tables 1-3 indicate the weight of each term depending on the method used and the collection it belongs to.

Table 1. A practical example of applying the methods for the category of positive tweets

Term	Frequency	tf-idf	tf-icf
Obidno (it's a shame)	55	0.000109944	0.00000871077
Plokho (bad)	424	0.000772331	0.0000671521
Lyublyu (I love)	2517	0.004197502	0.000398636
Konechno (of course)	1070	0.001950132	0.000169464
Vremya (time)	1313	0.002186481	0.00020795

Table 2. A practical example of applying the methods for the category of negative tweets

Term	Frequency	tf-idf	tf-icf
Obidno (it's a shame)	844	0.001687134	0.000133671
Plokho (bad)	1448	0.002637583	0.000229331
Lyublyu (I love)	1391	0.002319716	0.000220303
Konechno (of course)	665	0.001211998	0.000105321
Vremya (time)	1377	0.002293057	0.000218086

Table 3. A practical example of applying the methods for the category of neutral tweets

Term	Frequency	tf-idf	tf-icf
Obidno (it's a shame)	32	0.0000639672	0.00000506808
Plokho (bad)	152	0.000276873	0.0000240734
Lyublyu (I love)	61	0.000101727	0.00000966103
Konechno (of course)	280	0.000510315	0.0000443457
Vremya (time)	1321	0.002199803	0.000209217

Although the method based on the idf scheme ignores the category a term belongs to, and the weight values for positive, neutral and negative terms in the idf column should be identical, adding tf causes there to be a difference in this column.

As a result, the test sample shows that methods based on TF-IDF and TF-ICF schemes give similar results on static collections. This means that both methods attribute the word "bad" to the negative category, and the word "love" to the positive category, not vice versa. An analogous experiment, which showed similar results, was conducted to calculate and compare the weight of parts of speech for the three collections. That means we can expect accuracy result using methods based on TF-ICF for sentiment classification.

3   Corpora Characteristics

3.1   Short Text Corpus

In a previous paper [1], the author describes an approach to building a Russian-language corpus of short texts based on posts from social network Twitter. Twitter is a social networking and microblogging service that allows users to write messages in real time. Often, tweets are directly posted from a mobile device at the place where the event is taking place, which adds emotion to posts. Due to the platform's limit, the length of a post on Twitter may not exceed 140 characters. In connection with this aspect of the service (short posts, which are published in real time, possibly using mobile devices), people use abbreviations, shorten words, use emoticons, and make spelling mistakes and typing errors. As Twitter has the features of a social network, users are able to express their opinion on a variety of issues, ranging from the quality of cellphones to international economic and political developments. This is why the Twitter platform has attracted the attention of researchers.

There are no publicly available prepared general-topic corpora of short texts in Russian, which is why the stream Twitter API was used to assemble a collection consisting of about 15 million short posts. The corpus was put together over several weeks in late 2013 and early 2014.

The method described in [10] showed the effectiveness of using emoticons (special symbols denoting emotions in written communications), for the automatic text classification into positive and negative classes. The emotion of the post can be determined with high accuracy if the author included a symbol that designates emotion.

For this reason, vocabularies of characters representing the positive or negative attitude of the author were constructed. For example, the icon :) stands for a positive emotion, :(a negative one. Since the length of a post is limited to 140 characters, it was assumed that an emoticon used to express emotion refers to the whole post, and not just a part of it.

Posts with positive and negative sentiments were searched for in accordance with the written symbols for emotions and two collections were formed. These collections will be used for further analysis of posts with positive and negative sentiments and the identification of patterns in positive and negative posts.

To form a collection of neutral posts were taken text from news microblogging accounts.

Filtering [1] was carried out to maintain experimental integrity:

- Texts containing both positive and negative emotions were deleted from the collection. Such texts cannot be automatically attributed to either collection of posts (positive or negative).
- Not informative tweets (less than 40 characters long) were deleted.

On the basis of raw collection using a method [10] and the filtration proposed by the author [1] was formed a balanced corpus, comprising the following collections:

- collection of positive posts – 114 991 entries;
- collection of negative posts – 111 923 entries;
- collection of neutral posts – 107 990 entries.

The ratio of word forms and unigrams in the collections is shown in Table 4. The corpus is publicly available [11].

Table 4. The ratio of unigrams and unique unigrams in the short text collections

Type of collection	Number of unigrams in the collection	Number of unique unigrams in the collection
Positive posts	1 559 176	150 720
Negative posts	1 445 517	191 677
Neutral posts	1 852 995	105 239

3.2   News Corpus

News collections were assembled on news websites. Experts manually tagged the corpus by positive, neutral and negative collections. The difference between the news collection and the short texts collection are that news items are less emotional, their vocabulary is more neutral and there are few slang words, abbreviations and obscene expressions. Typically, news texts do not contain spelling errors. News texts do not contain symbols that denote emotions in a written form (emoticons). News texts are significantly longer than 140 characters.

The corpus of news texts consists of the following collections:

- collection of positive documents that consists of 22 976 news items;
- collection of negative documents that consists of 21 592 news items;
- collection of neutral documents that consists of 22 381 news items.

The ratio of word forms and unigrams in the collections is presented in Table 5.

Table 5. The ratio of unigrams and unique unigrams in the news collections

Type of collection	Number of unigrams in the collection	Number of unique unigrams in the collection
Positive news items	4 553 010	104 001
Negative news items	10 400 699	202 354
Neutral news items	7 667 441	155 538

4 Preparation for the Experiment

4.1 Preparation Texts for the Classifier

Before using the text classifier, the texts must be converted to vector format. That's why the collection of short texts, as described in 3.1, was subjected to filtration. In order to produce an emotive vocabulary, the following were filtered out from the collection:

- Punctuation – commas, colons, quotation marks (exclamation marks, question marks and ellipses were retained);
- References to significant personalities and events – the attitude towards them may vary over time, but a classifier trained on "old texts" will not be able to adapt quickly;
- Proper names;
- Numerals (references to years and time were retained);
- All links were replaced with the word "Link" and were taken into consideration as a whole.

The final vocabulary contains 21 481 words.

Using formulas 1 and 2, the weights of each word in the vocabulary were calculated and stored for the corpus of short texts.

4.2 The Classifier

The proven [12, 13] support vector method was used to classify text into three classes. Since computational complexity of LibSVM [14] is rather high on large amount of sparse vectors, the LibLinear library [15] – a modification of the LibSVM algorithm with a linear kernel – was used for classification.

4.3 Quality Assessment

Accuracy, precision, recall and F-measure were selected as measures to evaluate the classification of texts into three classes.

Accuracy rate is the percentage of test set samples that are correctly classified.

Precision and recall were calculated using a confusion matrix. For example, the confusion matrix for the collection of short texts using a weight calculation method based on TF-IDF is represented in Figure 1. The dimension of the matrix corresponds to the number of classes for classification – and is equal to three. The columns of the matrix are reserved for expert solutions, the rows for the classifier's solutions. When we classify a document from the test sample, we increment the number at the intersection of the row of the class returned by the classifier and the column of the class to which the document really belongs.

Twitter TF-IDF				
	0.958	0.965	0.987	0.923
0.955		-1	0	1
0.976	-1	21855	71	455
0.908	0	547	19616	1429
0.981	1	251	194	22531

Fig. 1. Confusion matrix for the collection of short texts. The weights of words were calculated using the method based on the TF-IDF scheme.

Precision (3) is equal to the ratio of the corresponding diagonal element in the matrix and the sum of the entire row of the class. Recall (4) is the ratio of the diagonal element in the matrix and the sum of the entire column of the class. Formally:

$$Precision_x = \frac{A_{x,x}}{\sum_{i=1}^{n} A_{x,i}} \tag{3}$$

$$Recall_x = \frac{A_{x,x}}{\sum_{i=1}^{n} A_{i,x}} \tag{4}$$

The F-measure is the harmonic mean of precision and recall. If the precision or recall tend to zero, it tends to zero. F-measure is calculated according to the formula (5):

$$F = 2\frac{Precision \times Recall}{Precision + Recall} \tag{5}$$

5 Results of the Experiment

Several experiments were conducted on two different datasets in order to compare the precision of the classifier depending on the selected method to determine the weight of a term in a collection. Text collections are constantly updated therefore it is necessary to constantly update the dictionary, and recalculate the weights of the terms in the dictionary.

The first experiment was conducted on the short text corpus, for which it was randomly divided into training and test collection. The ratio of positive, neutral and negative texts was preserved in the training (267 924 documents) and test collections (66 980 documents). The results are shown in Table 6.

Table 6. Comparison of TF-IDF and TF-RF for a collection of short texts

	TF-IDF	TF-ICF
accuracy	95.5981	95.0664
Precision	0.955204837	0.94984672
Recall	0.958092631	0.953112184
F-measure	0.956646554	0.95147665

There is insignificance of the difference between the two methods' results when applied to the short text corpus due to the data sparseness. Despite the fact that the precision of the method based on the TF-ICF scheme is lower, it is evident from the table that this error is negligible. Therefore, methods based on the TF-ICF scheme may be applied to calculate weights in dynamically updated collections of short texts.

A similar experiment was carried out on longer texts – the collection of news items. The news collection was also divided into training (111 214 documents) and test collections (27 802 documents). The experiment showed that methods based on the TF-ICF scheme show significantly worse results on long texts than those based on TF-IDF. The results are shown in Table 7.

Table 7. Comparison of TF-IDF and TF-RF for the collection of news items

	TF-IDF	TF-ICF
accuracy	69.8619	58.1397
Precision	0.698624505	0.581402868
Recall	0.709246342	0.61278022
F-measure	0.703895355	0.596679322

6   Conclusion

This paper shows an approach to automatically constructing vocabularies of emotional language. A vocabulary is based on prepared collections and is general-topic, i.e. does not belong to any predetermined domain. The weights in the vocabularies are calculated using methods based on two weighting schemes. The computational complexity of the methods for updating a collection by adding new posts has been determined. In contrast to methods based on recalculating the weights of every term in the collection, the computational complexity of the method based on TF-ICF is linear.

Despite the fact that the precision of classifying long texts into three classes is significantly reduced when using methods based on TF-ICF, the precision of short text classification is only slightly reduced.

The software module obtained as a result of this paper makes it possible to dynamically update a vocabulary of emotive language, monitor and record lexical changes over time, and add new terms to the active vocabulary and recalculate the weight of these terms depending on the collection that they belong to.

The further prospect of this paper include the use of N-grams and morphological tagging on the collection of news items in order to reduce the difference between methods based on the TF-IDF and TF-ICF schemes, as well as to increase the accuracy of text classification into three classes: positive, neutral, negative.

References

1. Rubtsova, Y.: A method for development and analysis of short text corpus for the review classification task. In: Proceedings of Conferences Digital Libraries: Advanced Methods and Technologies, Digital Collections, RCDL 2013, pp. 269–275 (2013)
2. Hu, M., Liu, B.: Mining and Summarizing Customer Reviews. In: KDD 2004, Seattle, pp. 168–177 (2004)
3. Salton, G., Buckley, C.: Term-weighting approaches in automatic text retrieval. Journal of Information Processing and management 24(5), 513–523 (1988)
4. Paltoglou, G., Thelwall, M.: A study of information retrieval weighting schemes for sentiment analysis. In: Proceedings of the 48th Annual Meeting of the Association for Computational Linguistics, Uppsala, Sweden, July 11-16, pp. 1386–1395 (2010)
5. Jones, K.S.: A Statistical Interpretation of Term Specificity and Its Application in Retrieval. J. Documentation 28(1), 11–21 (1972)
6. Reed, J., Jiao, Y., Potok, T.: TF-ICF: A new term weighting scheme for clustering dynamic data streams. In: Proceedings of the 5th International Conference on Machine Learning and Applications, USA, pp. 258–263 (2006)
7. Lertnattee, V., Theeramunkong, T.: Analysis of inverse class frequency in centroid-based text classification. In: Proceedings of the 4th International Symposium on Communication and Information Technology, Japan, pp. 1171–1176 (2004)
8. Lertnattee, V., Theeramunkong, T.: Improving Thai academic web page classification using inverse class frequency and web link information. In: Proceedings of the 22nd International Conference on Advanced Information Networking and Applications Workshops, Japan, pp. 1144–1149 (2008)
9. Jones, K.S.: A Statistical Interpretation of Term Specificity and Its Application in Retrieval. J. Documentation 60(5), 493–502 (2004)
10. Read, J.: Using Emoticons to Reduce Dependency in Machine Learning Techniques for Sentiment Classification. In: Proceedings of the Student Research Workshop at the 2005 Annual Meeting of the Association for Computational Linguistics, pp. 43–48. Ann Arbor, Michigan (2005)
11. Short text collection, http://study.mokoron.com
12. Lan, M., Tan, C.L., Su, J., Lu, Y.: Supervised and Traditional Term Weighting Methods for Automatic Text Categorization. IEEE Transactions on Pattern Analysis and Machine Intelligence 31(4), 721–735 (2009)

13. Sebastiani, F.: Machine learning in automated text categorization. ACM Computing Surveys 34, 1–47 (2002)
14. Chang, C.C., Lin, C.J.: LIBSVM: A library for support vector machines (2001), http://www.csie.ntu.edu.tw/cjlin/libsvm
15. LIBSVM – A Library for Support Vector Machines, http://www.csie.ntu.edu.tw/~cjlin/libsvm/ (retrieved on July 02, 2014)

Distributed Knowledge Acquisition Control with Use of the Intelligent Program Environment of the AT-TECHNOLOGY Workbench

Galina V. Rybina and Yury M. Blokhin

National Research Nuclear University MEPhI
(Moscow Engineering Physics Institute), Russia
galina@ailab.mephi.ru

Abstract. The paper discusses the problem of distributed knowledge acquisition for the construction of complete and consistent knowledge bases in integrated expert systems via the sharing of knowledge sources of different topologies (the focused in this work databases as electronic media, experts and problem-oriented texts). The work is focused on models and methods of distributed knowledge acquisition from databases as additional knowledge sources and automation of the process by using an intelligent program environment. Special typical design procedure, called "Distributed knowledge acquisition" is reviewed, which provides synchronization ofdistributed knowledge acquisition processes. This procedure uses the technological knowledge base of the intelligent planner of the AT-TECHNOLOGY workbench and special program tools.

Keywords: Distributed knowledge acquisition, task-oriented methodology, AT-TECHNOLOGY workbench, intelligent program environment, intelligent planner, typical design procedures, reusable components, integrated expert system, IES, knowledge base.

1 Introduction

The problem of knowledge acquisition has been the focus of attention for the devel-opers of current intelligent systems, among them traditional expert systems (ESs) and more complicated integrated expert systems (IESs) with scalable architecture and expandable functionalities [1]. The main subject of this work is this prime course of artificial intelligence.

The results have been widely presented in both foreign papers [2] and domestic ones [1,3,4,5]. Nevertheless, the problems of the practical use of traditional methods for knowledge acquisition and the development of automated technology of knowledge acquisition are currently topical. This is because of the severe lack of experts and custom computer systems that simulate expert skills. The research into cognitive psychology shows that the newcomer to expert path takes over 10 years, due to the long professional practice required for adaptation to successful problem solving [6].

P. Klinov and D. Mouromtsev (Eds.): KESW 2014, CCIS 468, pp. 150–159, 2014.

In solving complicated practical problems, the most critical problems of knowledge acquisition arise in medicine, power energetics, space, ecology, and so on, where the opinion of one expert is not enough.

Therefore, to construct the most complete and consistent models of problem do-mains (PDs) and to reduce the risks of expert errors, a group of experts needs to be attracted, which significantly increases the cost and time parameters of IES design [1]. Thus the urgency and the role of expert labor automation, as well as the development of custom software increases. There is also increasing role of different "acquisition shells" directed to the support of knowledge acquisition from the experts or an expert groups. This knowledge is the basic source (first type knowledge source [5]).

However, there have been few investigations into grouped knowledge acquisition from experts. Among the best known of these are papers of a theoretical and meth-odological nature [6,7] and the foreign project that describes the facilities of graphical representation of distributed knowledge [8] and papers from the French ACACIA group who are developing the KATEMES tool (Knowledge Acquisition Tool for Explainable Multi-Expert Systems) for the partial automation of engineering work based on the evidence of knowledge at the group acquisition stage [9].

On the other hand, it is not only experts who affect the topology of knowledge sources. Significant volumes of expert knowledge have been accumulated in the natural language texts (second-type knowledge sources). In the few last years, third type knowledge sources appeared. This is the knowledge from the current information systems, which are complicated technical-organizational systems with network devices, servers, DBs (DBMSs), and so on.

The problem of knowledge acquisition (detection) from second-type sources relates to the rapidly progressing Text Mining technology [10], in which the problem of automated acquisition of knowledge from DBs in artificial intelligence is related to Data Mining and the Knowledge Discovery in databases (KDD) [11]. The Text Mining technology is successful due to the application of textual methods of knowledge acquisition from natural language texts (NL-texts), which are widespread in three types of current web-oriented NL systems: Information Retrieval, Information Extraction, and Text/Message Understanding [12].

Data Mining is applied in PDs, such as scientific research (into medicine, biology, bioinformatics, and so on); the solution of business problems (banking, finances, insurance, CMR, and so on); governmental problems (protection from terrorism, searching for wanted people, and so on), and the solution of problems of web resources analysis with basic courses, such as Web Content Mining (intelligence crawlers, as well as the classification and filtration of information) and Web Usage Mining (which implies the detection of laws in the actions of a web node user or group of users); and so on.

Each of these technology have been developing independently of one another, and, now, such autonomy and distribution do not allow effective monitoring of all information resources (knowledge bases, databases, and the ontologies that were developed in recent years) belonging to the intelligence systems, especially IESs.

The investigations into the construction of tools and the development of distributed knowledge acquisition from a variety of sources of different topologies currently do not exist.

The experience of the practical use of an entire set of applied IESs developed in terms of the problem-oriented methodology (POM) and with the AT-TECHNOLOGY workbench [1,13] (including the express diagnostics of blood, diagnostics of complicated engineering systems, design of unique engineering objects, complex ecological problems, and so on) has shown the necessity of monitoring, which lies in the checking and conforming of accumulated and formalizable knowledge in corresponding knowledge bases (KBs). The AT-TECHNOLOGY workbench was developed in our laboratory, thus we use it as a program base for further researches. Comparison of AT-TECHNOLOGY with similar tools is beyond this work.

In addition to the detection of errors (defects), duplication, inconsistency and incompleteness of information in the KBs of already developed applied systems, the above mentioned problems are of great importance during the modeling of PDs and design of KBs and DBs (the control of limited integrity, consistency, agreements between the terms used in PDs, and so on). For example, to overcome the problem of the incompleteness of a developed KB (i.e., the expert does not know of and/or forgets to note some fact required for problem solving), we can invite a specific expert at times or an expert group, as well as using an independent electronic knowledge source in the form of a DB [1]. The first two ways can lead to difficulties in the modeling PDs, both due to a significant increase of labor costs and due to the "noisy" personal features of experts (misunderstandings, failures to mention, conformism, cognitive protection, self interest, the lack of semantic unification of used terms of PDs, and so on [5]). The authors of [3] also noted such factors as "cognitive self-protection", "discreteness", the lack of human knowledge, and so on.

The most neutral and independent knowledge sources are DBs. Analysis of experimental data obtained during the creation of an entire set of applied IESs showed that the local use of DBs as an additional knowledge source can fill up the volume of KBs by 1020% according to the PD assignment [1].

Thus, the development of a new automated technology of knowledge acquisition distributed by different sources occurred. We can formulate the following conceptual basis of the present work [14,15]:

1. The notion of the "distributed acquisition" of knowledge is introduced to fit the integrated information from knowledge sources with different topologies;
2. The first-type and second-type knowledge sources in the combined method of knowledge acquisition (CMKA) implemented in the framework of the POM [1] are considered to be combined, since there is a collection of well-tested technological processes in the CMKA, which allow replenishing the information from experts using information detected from problem-oriented NL-texts (this information includes the processing of protocols for interviewing experts, the acquisition of the vocabulary of a knowledge engineer/system analyst, analysis of signal lexemes in the input NL-texts, and so on);

3. The problem of integration with information obtained from a DB as a third type source for the automated construction of the most complete and consistent models of a PD.

4. Since no universal methods for solving the problem of DB completeness exist, the development and application of the technology of knowledge acquisition from DBs as additional source of knowledge are a rather new application of the Data Mining and KDD concepts for the solution of this problem.

In the present paper, the authors discuss the general characteristic of the of the combined method for knowledge acquisition and describe the typical design procedure for the application of KDD and Data Mining at different stages of its life cycle related to the automated construction of the KB of IES prototypes. The features of distributed knowledge acquisition from the databases are described in details. The implementation of typical design procedure for knowledge acquisition from databases is reviewed.

2   General Characteristics of the Combined Method for Knowledge Acquisition

According to the conceptual bases of the POM of IES construction, the most important part of this methodology is the POM of knowledge acquisition the collection of the CMKA and the technology of its use at different stages of the life cycle of an IES and web-IES construction [1]. Within the limits of basic CMKA and the media of its realization, the so-called local variant of knowledge acquisition is under consideration.

However, the "distributed" variant of knowledge acquisition, which is based on the CMKA became possible upon use of the web version of the AT-TECHNOLOGY workbench. On the one hand, this variant provides the integration of all the above mentioned types of knowledge sources and, on the other hand, it allows one to take its geographical arrangement into account, as well as to deal with the groups of remote knowledge sources in the framework of client-server architecture.

In general, the generalized model of CMKA [1,14] that takes the features of distributed knowledge acquisition into account can be written in the form:

$$MKM = \left\langle \widetilde{N}, \widetilde{S}, \widetilde{F}, K, Z \right\rangle \tag{1}$$

where $\widetilde{N} = N_{locn}$, $n = 1, \ldots, m_n$ is the set of unstructured descriptions of a PD;

$$N_{locn} = \langle IN, TN, SN, CN \rangle \tag{2}$$

where IN is the serial number of the description; TN is the type of description; SN is the source from which the description is obtained; CN is the description; $\widetilde{S} = \widetilde{S}_m$, $m = 1, \ldots, mn$ is the set of structured descriptions of a PD; F is the set of procedures for the mapping of $\widetilde{N}$ in $\widetilde{S}$; K denotes the procedures for the conversion of the formed knowledge field (KF) into the formats of knowledge representation languages (KRL) of different tools for the ES construction (in the AT-TECHNOLOGY complex); and Z denotes the fragments of the DB in KRL formats of other tools for ES construction.

Therefore, in the course of interviewing an expert, the structuring of the information obtained in the form of a KF occurs, which is significant in the structuring of the information of the PD obtained from the expert. It provides the integrated representation and unification of basic concepts and ratios of the PD that were detected from different knowledge sources as a first step to the formalization in the concrete KRL.

According to the features of distributed knowledge acquisition, the generalized model of a KA can be presented as follows [14,15]:

$$Sm = \langle IS_m, TS_m, SS_m, O_m, R_m \rangle \tag{3}$$

where IS_m is the serial number of the structured description of PD; TS_m is the type of structured description of PD; SS_m is the source from which the description is obtained; $O_m = \{O_{mj}\}, j = 1, ; n$ is the set of objects; $Rm = \{R_{mk}\}, k = 1, ; p$ is the set of rules.

Thus, in going from the local variant of knowledge acquisition to the distributed one, the set of basic procedures of the CMKA is filled with the following procedures: acquisition of description from the distributed sources; correlation of different type acquired knowledge; refinement of the descriptions with detected inconsistencies; and grouped knowledge acquisition.

3   Applications of Distributed Knowledge Acquisition

As noted above, for the acquisition of knowledge from a DB in the framework of the CMKA, the KDD and Data Mining technologies used as an additional knowledge source to overcome DB incompleteness, because this provides the intelligent analysis of large volumes of information and the detection of the hidden laws within IESs developed in terms of the POM.

We emphasize that these terms are interpreted in the POM as follows: KDD denotes the entire process of knowledge acquisition from the DB to the representation of the obtained results, of which Data Mining is only some stage of the general process of the KDD.

According to the knowledge acquisition processes, the Data Mining concept is implemented in the CMKA in the three following ways [1]: the generation of an initial KF from a DB with further modification by an expert; the verification of a KF obtained by interviewing the expert, as well as the partial modification related to the finding of assurance coefficients for detected knowledge and the merging of the KF as a result of application of two methodologies.

One feature of KDD and Data Mining application in the framework of CMKA is the necessity of arranging access to a specific DB containing the information of the analyzed PD and its processing. Therefore, the CMKA includes many specific procedures for operation with DBs, such as[15]:

- the generation of a SQL-query to the DBMS;
- acquisition of data from the DB in accordance to the query formed by the procedure of data acquisition from the DB;
- filtration of some data subset that is then used for the construction of a set of rules (procedure of data subset filtration); and
- conversion of data to a format that can be directly used by knowledge acquisition algorithms (procedure of data conversion).

Below is the description of the procedures that are assigned for the preparation of data selection for subsequent analysis.

Based on the generation of an SQL-query the sample for subsequent application of Data Mining algorithms is formed. The knowledge engineer selects the attributes from the DB and based on this the system generates an SQL-query. Taking into account the specific character of the Data Mining algorithms used in CMKA, the knowledge engineer carries out the procedure of extracting the dependent and independent attributes (columns) in the analyzed sample. Then the processing of the unknown values of attributes occurs.

Notice that in the local variant of the CMKA, two basic algorithms for constructing the decision trees of ID3 [16] and C4.5 [17] that allow one to construct the sets of conditionaction rules in terms of the analyses of developed decision trees are used. However, the concepts of the CART algorithm [18] are preferred in going to the distributed variant of the CMKA, since this allows one to construct binary decision trees that are more convenient during visualization and rule post processing to reduce the general number of derived rules.

The procedure of data transformation converts them into a format that can be directly used by knowledge acquisition algorithms. Once the sample for the analysis has been completed, the procedures of knowledge acquisition from a DB are immediately applied, in so doing, it provides the determination of relationships in the form of if/then rules and basing on algorithm which is beyond this work.

The final procedures are the following: assessment of the model precision in terms of the textual data; estimation of the algorithm and its parameters that provide the best results in knowledge acquisition; and the conversion of obtained rules into the required format. The required format is determined by exact application where described method is used.

In going to the distributed knowledge acquisition, the emphasis is on the synchronization of the processes of knowledge acquisition from different sources by means of special typical design procedure (TDP) incorporated in POM and the technology of IES prototype construction [1]. The applied TDP uses the technological DB of an intelligent planner of the AT-TECHNOLOGY workbench and specific software for the integration of knowledge sources serving as a basis for the integration of KF fragments the obtained from different sources. The typical design procedure "Knowledge Acquisition from DB" includes the following stages: the acquisition of KF fragments in the form of if/then rules by using the CMKA (expert interviewing and knowledge acquisition from DB) and carrying out the verification of obtained KF fragments; the integration of sets of rules due to the algorithms of comparing some KF fragments, which is based on the calculation of the adjacency coefficient [19] for each pair of rules; and verification of the united KF.

Note that the integration of rule sets is the most labor-intensive problem [20]. The automated comparison of rule sets obtained from different knowledge sources precedes this procedure. Extended decision tables (EDTs) [20] are used as the analyzed structure for the effective and rapid comparison of sets of rules in the POM. Each cell of such a table contains the data of the input and parameters of the input statement to the concrete rule, which is characterized by a headline.

Below is the detail description of the typical design procedure "Knowledge acquisition from DB" implemented in the intelligent program environment of AT-TECHNOLOGY workbench.

4   Implementation of the Typical Design Procedure "Knowledge Acquisition from Database"

Problems of development process support in developing intelligent and technological integrated expert systems (IES) with power functionality and scalable architecture are getting more and more significant and topical. For the first time these problems were reviewed in IES [1] development problem-oriented methodology and in AT-TECHNOLOGY workbench, which supports this methodology and represents knowledge engineer workstation.

The experience collected in development of multiple applied IES [1,13], tutoring IES development and usage in particular [21,22] has shown that the most of IES development problems are related to high complexity of projecting and implementation stages, and the problem domain has significant influence on organization and specificity of these lifecycle stages. The human factor also remains significant enough, because it leads to increasing of labor and development time spent. Also in the most cases the IES development technology specificity does not allow to use traditional programming methods.

Therefore a significant place in the problem-oriented methodology has been assigned to methods and instruments of intelligent program support of development processes. To all of them a common term "intelligent program environment" is applied (common methodology provisions are described in monograph [1] and another papers, for example [21]).

Today intelligent technology of integrated IES prototype development includes: development plan generation and execution with help of intelligent planner; knowledge engineer dynamical assistance based on knowledge about TDP and reusable components base intelligent program environment components; IES prototype architecture model generation; IES prototype analyzing based on knowledge about methods and models for typical problems solving; recommendation and explanation messages delivering to knowledge engineer. Intelligent planner "knows" how many and which TDPs and reusable components are registered in the workbench, and what are they designed for. Based on this knowledge, the development plan is generated.

Let us describe TDP "Knowledge Acquisition from DB" in details. Common TDP model is defined as:

$$TDP = \langle C, L, T \rangle, \tag{4}$$

where C is a set of conditions which allow TDP releasing; L execution scenario, described in internal action language; T is a set of parameters, initialized by intelligent planner when the TDP is included in IES development plan. And now, let us consider components concrete definition for TDP "Knowledge Acquisition from DB":

Component. Conditions for the TDP are defined in following way:

- a "storage" element in extended data flow diagram (EDFD) hierarchy, which represents architecture model of developing IES prototype;
- a lifecycle stage is system requirements analyzing;
- there must be at least one "unformalized operation" element in EDFD hierarchy;
- in the EDFD hierarchy a "storage" element must be connected with a "unformalized operation" element.

Component L. This TDP can be executed in two ways:

1. Initial knowledge field generation with distributed knowledge acquisition from DB algorithm without expert interviewing.
2. Knowledge field generation with distributed knowledge acquisition from DB after expert interviewing. In this variant it is necessary to execute expert interviewing task.

Component T. Context parameter P17 is set to 0 with comment that TDP "Knowledge Acquisition from DB" will be used. In the first step of TDP "Knowledge Acquisition from DB" execution, knowledge engineer selects a set of registered databases, and then forms a set of data storages with help of special program tools. These storages are analyzed with a distributed knowledge acquisition from DB algorithm [14,15]. The next step is the knowledge acquisition from DB algorithm configuring and generating with it a set of knowledge fields from each registered DB. In the third step, all knowledge fields of different types are merged. The main stag-es in this step are [15]: loading, objects merging, extended solution table and rules similarity table forming. In the stage of knowledge field fragments merging an expert sets control zones and values of float attributes coinciding. Also merging of objects, attributes types merging, and rules merging are performed. Next, a sample of rules from TDP "Knowledge Acquisition from DB" are presented.

A rule for initiating an execution of data storage forming tools:

```
<PLANRULE ID="14" Caption="Storage creation" Condition="LCStage=1
AND StorageCount(LinkToDB)>0" Parent="3" ArgType="Project"
Executor="Ware House" Action="run_warehouse" ActionType="0"
Type="1" />
```

A rule for running tools for distributed knowledge acquisition from DB:

```
<PLANRULE ID="17" Caption="Distributed knowledge acquisition from
database" Condition="LCStage=1 AND StorageCount(LinkToDB)>0 AND
AllElementCount(TDesES)>0" Parent="3" ArgType="Project"
Executor="Data Mining" Action="run_mining" ActionType="0" Type="1"/>
```

A rule for starting the tool for merging if/then rules:

```
<PLANRULE ID="18" Caption="Merge knowledge field fragmens"
Condition="LCStage=1 AND AllElementCount(TDesES)>0" Parent="3"
ArgType= "ProjectValue" Executor="Rules_src" Action="run_rules"
ActionType="0" Type="1" />
```

Samples of more complex TDPs connected with tutoring IES development are described in [22]. The difficulties of the tutoring IES development technology are caused by supporting two different work modes DesignTime, oriented to work with teachers (course/discipline ontology creating processes, different typed training im-pacts creating, etc.) and Runtime, for working with students (current student model building processes, including psychological model, etc.).

5 Conclusion

The experimental routine research of the distributed variant of the CMKA (including the collection of algorithms and procedures of knowledge processing obtained during expert interviews, as well as during the analysis of protocols of interviewing and knowledge acquisition from the DB) on several real and test DBs showed a high efficiency of the proposed approach to the solution of problems of KB incompleteness, for KBs support, and the automated updating of KBs upon the emergence of new DBs or changes of outdated ones.

In conclusion, it is necessary to point out, that today we are performing experimental research connected with intelligent support for IES prototype construction. During this experiment many weak points were already fixed, in particular connected with low performance, not sufficient technologic knowledge base content, new typical design procedures development, etc. As a result, time cost for a typical IES development prototype with AT-TECHNOLOGY workbench was reduced.

References

1. Rybina, G.V.: Theory and Technology of Construction of Integrated Expert Systems. Nauchtekhlitizdat, Moscow (2008) (in Russian)
2. Lyugger, D.F.: Artificial Intellect: Strategies and Methods for Solving Complex Problems. Williams, Moscow (2003) (in Russian)
3. Osipov, G.S.: Artificial intelligence methods. Fizmatlit Publishing House, Moscow (2011) (in Russian)

4. Chastikov, A.P., Gavrilova, T.A., Belov, D.L.: Expert System Development. The CLIPS Environment. BHV Publishing, St. Petersburg (2003) (in Russian)
5. Rybina, G.V.: Fundamentals of Intellectual System Construction. Finansy i Statistika, Moscow (2010) (in Russian)
6. Podlipskii, O.K.: Construction of Knowledge Bases by Expert Group. Komp. Issled. Modelir. 2(1) (2010) (in Russian)
7. Kobrinskii, B.A.: Extraction of Expert Knowledge: Group Varian. Novosti Iskusstv. Intell. 3 (2004) (in Russian)
8. Mendonça, D., Kelton, K., Rush, R., Wallace, W.: Acquiring and Assessing Knowledge from Multiple Experts Using Graphical Representations. Knowledge Based Systems Techniques and Applications 1, 293–326 (2000)
9. Dieng, R., Giboin, A., Tourtier, P., Corby, O.: Knowledge Acquisition for Explainable, MultiExpert, Knowledge Based Design Systems. In: European Knowledge Acquisition Workshop (1992)
10. Feldman, D., Hirsh, M.: Mining Associations in Text in the Presence of Background Knowledge. In: 2nd Internation Conference on Knowledge Discovery, pp. 343–346 (1996)
11. Finn, V.K.: About Intelligent Analysis of Data. Artificial Intelligence News 3 (2004)
12. Khoroshevskii, V.F.: Treatment of Natural-Lingual Texts: from Language Understanding Models to Knowledge Extraction Technologies. Artificial Intelligence News 6 (2002)
13. Rybina, G.V.: Problem-oriented methodology and practical applications for Integrated Expert System construction (a review of applications in static and dynamic problems). Instruments and Systems: Monitoring, Control, and Diagnostics 12 (2011)
14. Rybina, G.V.: Combined knowledge acquisition method for knowledge base construction for integrated expert systems. Instruments and Systems: Monitoring, Control, and Diagnostics 8 (2011)
15. Rybina, G.V., Deineko, A.O.: Distributed knowledge acquisition for automated integrated expert system construction. Artificial Intelligence and Decision Making 4 (2010)
16. Quinlan, J.R.: Induction of Decision Trees. Machine Learn. Journal 1, 81–106 (1986)
17. Sreerama, K., Kasif, S., Salzberg, S.: A System for Induction of Oblique Decision Trees. J. Artif. Intell. Res (JAIR) 2, 1–32 (1994)
18. Breiman, L., Fiedman, J., Olshen, R., Stone, C.J.: Classification and Regression Trees. Wadsworth Int. Group, Belmont (1984)
19. Zagoruiko, N.G.: Applied Methods for Data and Knowledge Analysis. Inst. Matem., Novosibirsk (1999) (in Russian)
20. Rybina, G.V., Deineko, A.O.: About one approach for merging IF/THEN rules acquired from different knowledge sources. Artificial Intelligence and Decision Making 4 (2011)
21. Rybina, G.V.: Intelligent tutoring systems based on integrated expert systems: Development and usage experience. Information Measuring and Control 10 (2011)
22. Rybina, G.V., Blohin, Y.M., Ivashenko, M.G.: Some aspects of the intelligent technology for tutoring construction of integrated expert systems. Instruments and Systems: Monitoring, Control and Diagnostics 4 (2013)

A Feature Selection Approach for Anchor Evaluation in Ontology Mapping

Frederik C. Schadd and Nico Roos

Maastricht University, The Netherlands
{frederik.schadd,roos}@maastrichtuniversity.nl

Abstract. Computing alignments between ontologies is a crucial task for the facilitation of information exchange between knowledge systems. An alignment is a mapping consisting of a set of correspondences, where each correspondence denotes two ontology concepts denoting the same information. In this domain, it can occur that a partial alignment is generated by a domain expert, which can then be exploited by specialized techniques. In order for these techniques to function as intended, it must be ensured that the given correspondences, also known as anchors, are indeed correct. We propose an approach to this problem by reformulating it as a feature selection task, where each feature represents an anchor. The feature space is populated with a set of reliably generated correspondences, which are compared with the anchors using a measure of alignment. We apply feature selection techniques to quantify how well the anchors align with this set of correspondences. The resulting scores are used as anchor reliability measures and combined with the anchor similarities.

We evaluate the approach by generating a set of partial alignments for the used dataset and weighting the concept similarities with anchor evaluation measure of our approach. Three different similarity metrics are used, a syntactic, structural and semantic metric, in order to demonstrate the effectiveness of our approach.

1 Introduction

The availability of semantically structured data via the semantic web [3] allows for a varied set of approaches exploiting this data, ranging from data-warehousing and web site creation and management [19,27], to querying one or multiple knowledge sources [16,6]. The semantic structure of this data is determined by an ontology written by a domain expert using expressive languages such as RDFS [4] or OWL [20]. A common issue in this field is that two ontologies describing the same information can be heterogeneous with regard to its terminology, structure, scope or granularity [8]. If the situation arises that one needs to transfer information between knowledge systems using heterogeneous ontologies, then one needs transform the data in such a way that it is in compliance with the new ontology. For every concept in the first ontology a corresponding concept in the second must be identified which is used to store the same information. The task of identifying the correspondences between ontologies is known as ontology mapping.

Creating a mapping between ontologies is a laborious task which would require a domain expert to inspect both ontologies and determine mappings, if it were done by hand.

P. Klinov and D. Mouromtsev (Eds.): KESW 2014, CCIS 468, pp. 160–174, 2014.

Doing so becomes prohibitively difficult and time consuming when faced with increasingly large ontologies, such that automatic approaches are necessary for large scale problems [13,32]. This also becomes a problem with the rise of the Semantic Web [3], which envisions autonomous agents automatically querying multiple knowledge sources for information.

Approaches which autonomously map ontologies have been an active field of research in the past decade [2,5,7,12,17,23]. These systems use a varied selection of similarity metrics to determine the similarity of ontology concepts and use these values to derive a complete mapping, also known as alignment, between the input ontologies. Typically, multiple similarity measures are used to ensure the robustness of the system in the case that certain meta-information is missing in the ontologies. These similarity measures utilize different types of meta-information of the ontology concepts with the intuition that corresponding concepts will have aspect of this information in common, e.g. similar names, properties or neighbouring concepts.

A special case of a mapping problem is where a partial mapping is already available from a domain expert. Specialized approaches can then utilize this mapping to derive further correspondences in order to produce a complete mapping [2,24,28,30]. However, these techniques rely on the correctness of the correspondences in the partial mapping, known as anchors, in order to deliver additional high quality correspondences. While, evaluating these correspondences using similarity metrics can be used for this task, they require a substantially high similarity threshold to ensure a high likelihood of correctness. This results in a large quantity of correspondences being filtered out, which also negatively affects the specialized techniques.

In this paper, we present an approach for the task of evaluating the correspondences originating from a partial alignment. This approach does not compare the concepts of these correspondences directly, allowing true correspondences whose concepts do not share much meta-information to be classified more correctly. The approach utilizes feature-selection techniques stemming from the fields of data mining and machine learning. We create a feature space with each feature representing an anchor, which is populated by generating a set of reliably correct and incorrect correspondences. The values of this feature space are computed using a measure of dissonance, which should yield predictable results only if the given anchor is correct. This predictability is then exploited using different feature selection methods. We evaluate this approach on a real-world dataset [14] by randomly generating partial alignments containing both correct and incorrect anchors and evaluating how well our approach can complement similarity-based techniques.

The remainder of this paper is structured as follows. The mapping problem is formally introduced in section 2 and detail our approach in section 3. We present the empirical evaluation in section 4. Finally, section 5 concludes the paper and suggests future research.

2   Mapping with Partial Alignments

Formally, ontology mapping is defined as the process of identifying concepts pairs, also referred to as correspondences between two ontologies which denote the similar information [9]. We define a correspondence between two ontologies O_1 and O_2 as a 5-tuple $< id, e_1, e_2, r, s >$, where id denotes a unique identifier, e_1 and e_2 denote a reference to a concept originating from O_1 and O_2 respectively, r denotes the semantic relation that is asserted between e_1 and e_2 and s denotes a confidence value lying in the interval $[0, 1]$. The classic process of ontology mapping thus receives as input two ontologies O_1 and O_2, and produces a set of correspondences $A = \{c_1, c_2, \ldots, c_n\}$, referred to as an alignment.

A special case of this process occurs when a partial alignment PA is available as additional input for the mapping process. This is an alignment that has been produced by a pre-processing approach or assembled by hand by a domain expert. However, this alignment considered to be incomplete, such that it becomes necessary to compute addition correspondences in order to generate a complete mapping between O_1 and O_2. To achieve this, the correspondences in PA can be utilized by special techniques in order to determine the remaining correspondences [24,28]. The resulting alignment A thus be considered as the merger of all correspondences given in PA, since these can be assumed to be correct, and all correspondences that have been computed.

2.1 Anchor Filtering

While the correspondences originating from a partial alignment, referred to as anchors, can be assumed to be correct, this is not always the case. In case of a generated partial alignment, there is no guarantee that the used approach has a precision of 100% for every mapping task. If the partial alignment is made by a domain expert, it can always occur that the expert makes a mistake. The presence of incorrect anchors can degrade the quality of the computed correspondences, with the degradation of quality being correlated to the quantity of incorrect anchors. In order to ensure that a mapping approach that utilizes partial alignments performs as designed, it becomes necessary to perform a pre-processing step that ensures that the provided anchors are of sufficient quality.

The procedure of pre-processing partial alignments can be described by two key steps: *anchor evaluation* and the application of a *filtering policy*. Given two ontologies O_1 and O_2, and a partial alignment PA consisting of n anchors $\{c_1, c_2, \ldots c_n\}$, the *anchor evaluation* step produces a set of n scores $S = \{s_1, s_2, \ldots, s_n\}$, with each score s_x indicating the quality of its anchor c_x. The *filtering* step uses these scores to discard any anchor which does not satisfy a given policy, creating a new partial alignment PA', such that $PA' \subseteq PA$. The entire process is illustrated in Figure 1.

Typically, the *evaluation* and *filtering* steps are achieved through the application of already existing approaches from the field of ontology mapping. The *filtering* step can be performed by simply applying a threshold to the score set S, with the threshold value set by a domain expert or learned using a training set. To evaluate the anchors, one can utilize any available concept similarity metric [31]. However, such metrics are unfortunately susceptible to concept heterogeneities, where a concept pair for which a human would immediately conclude that it denotes the same information would result in a low similarity values. Such heterogeneities can be mitigated through the combination of multiple similarity metrics, though the aggregation of several similarity values has its disadvantages. For example, given two concept pairs which respectively receive the similarity values $\{0, 1\}$ and $\{0.5, 0.5\}$ as determined by two metrics, one would be

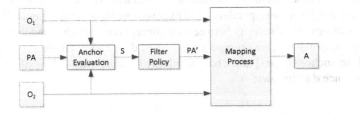

Fig. 1. Illustration of the anchor filtering process when mapping with partial alignments

more inclined to accept the first pair than the second, since it can occur that the feature on which a similarity metric relies might be absent while at the same time the maximum score of a given metric is only rarely a false positive. Computing the aggregate of two similarities would thus obscure this information. The approach presented in this paper attempts to tackle this problem by proposing a new way in which a similarity metric can be used to evaluate anchors.

3   Proposed Approach

A similarity metric can produce a small set of reliable correspondences, given a sufficiently high similarity threshold. Furthermore, one can also reliably generate a set of incorrect correspondences, given a sufficiently low threshold. One can utilize correct and incorrect correspondences for the analysis of the anchors given in the input partial alignment. To achieve this, one needs a method for evaluating anchors against this set of reliable correspondences, which allows for the distinguishment of correct and incorrect anchors.

When comparing an anchor with a given correct correspondence, one would desire a measure which assigns this comparison a certain value, regardless of the proximity between the anchor and correspondence in the taxonomy. This aspect becomes especially important when dealing with poorly designed ontologies which may lack a thoroughly structure taxonomy. For example, comparing an anchor denoting the concept *vehicle* with two correct correspondences denoting the concepts *car* and *physical object* respectively, one would desire the same outcome despite *physical object* being less related to *vehicle* than *car*. The same would also be desired when comparing a correct anchor with incorrect correspondences, albeit with the output being different than the comparison with correct correspondences. One can interpret such a measure as expressing how well an anchor aligns with a correspondences, as opposed to measuring the semantic similarity between the anchor concepts. A correct anchor would thus be expected to be better aligned with regard to a reliably classified correspondence as opposed to an incorrect anchor. To minimize the effect of outliers and utilize all available reliably classified correspondences, one should measure the degree of alignment of an anchor and all given correspondences, and measure how well this measure correlates with the expected result. A way to measure how well an anchor aligns with a given correspondence would be to compute the concept similarities between the concepts in the anchor and the concepts of the given correspondence and express how these similarities differ. To measure this difference in similarity between the concepts of an anchor and the concepts of a given correspondence, we propose a measure of dissonance. Given a correspondence $\{c_1, c_2\}$, an anchor $\{a_1, a_2\}$ and a base similarity measure $sim(a, b) \in [0, 1]$, we define the dissonance d as follows:

$$d(\{c_1, c_2\}, \{a_1, a_2\}) = |sim(c_1, a_2) - sim(c_2, a_1)| \tag{1}$$

Using the measure of dissonance, the core of the approach consists of comparing the given anchor to a set of reliably generated correspondences, correct and incorrect, and quantifying to what extend the anchor aligns with the given correspondences. Based on this quantification, the set of anchors can then be filtered. For this research, we will investigate three different metrics when used as base similarity sim.

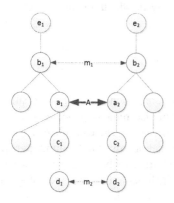
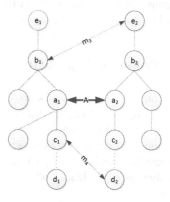

(a) Correct anchor A contrasted against two correct matches m_1 and m_2.

(b) Correct anchor A contrasted against two incorrect matches m_3 and m_4.

Fig. 2. Example scenarios of an anchor A being compared to either correct matches, illustrating the expected semantic difference between anchors and given correspondences

To illustrate the principle behind the approach, consider the examples illustrated in Figures 2 and 3. Each example illustrates two ontologies, an anchor A and two correspondences linking two other concept pairs. Figure 2a depicts a correct anchor and two correct correspondences $m_1 = [b_1, b_2]$ and $m_2 = [d_1, d_2]$. m_1 is semantically more related to A than to m_2, thus it can be expected that when calculating $sim(a_1, b_2)$ and $sim(a_2, b_1)$ results in higher values than when computing $sim(a_1, d_2)$ and $sim(a_2, d_1)$. It is reasonable to presume that $sim(a_1, b_2)$ and $sim(a_2, b_1)$ will result in equally high, and $sim(a_1, d_2)$ and $sim(a_2, d_1)$ will result in equally low values, meaning that computing the dissonance $d(m_1, A)$ and $d(m_2, A)$ will result in equally low values, indicating a high degree of alignment.

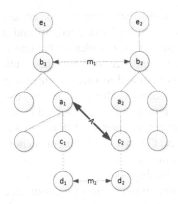

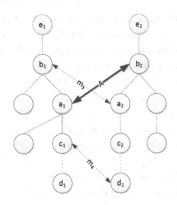

(a) An incorrect anchor A contrasted against two correct matches m_1 and m_2.

(b) An incorrect anchor A contrasted against two incorrect matches m_3 and m_4.

Fig. 3. Four example scenarios of an anchor A being compared to incorrect matches, illustrating the irregularity in the expected semantic difference between anchors and given correspondences

Comparing a correct anchor to dissimilar correspondences is expected to not exhibit this behaviour. Figure 2b illustrates a correct anchor A, consisting of the concepts a_1 and a_2, and two incorrect matches m_3 and m_4, which link the concepts b_1 with e_2 and c_1 with d_2 respectively. In this situation, a similarity calculation between a_2 and b_1 is likely to result in a higher value than the similarity between a_1 and e_2. Similarly, the concept similarity between the concepts of A and m_3 are also likely to differ, despite m_4 being semantically more apart from A than m_3.

When given an incorrect anchor, the similarity difference between the concepts of A and the concepts of either correct or incorrect matches are less likely to be predictable, as illustrated in Figure 3a and 3b. Figure 3a depicts an incorrect anchor A being compared to two correct correspondences. Here, both correspondences contain one concept, b_1 and d_2 respectively, which are semantically closer to A than their other concept. Thus, computing a similarity measure between the concepts of a correct correspondence and the concepts of an incorrect anchor will likely produce unequal results, regardless of the semantic distance of the correspondence to the anchor. However, to which degree these similarity will differ is not predictable, since this depends on how semantically related the concepts of the incorrect anchor are. If one were to compare an incorrect anchor to an incorrect correspondences, then the expected difference in concept similarities is not predictable at all, as illustrated in Figure 3b. The comparison of A with m_3 likely to produce a low difference in similarity when comparing a_1 with a_2 and b_1 with b_2. On the other hand, the similarity difference between an anchor can be very large, as illustrated with m_4.

3.1 Filtering Using Feature Selection

Having identified a measurement which leads to predictable behaviour for correct anchors and less predictable behaviour for incorrect anchors, one now needs to find a method for quantifying this predictability. As previously stated, in order for the dissonance to behave in a predictable way one must use correspondences of which their truth value is known with a high degree of certainty. The correct and incorrect comparison correspondences need to be generated reliably, such that labelling them as true and false respectively results in only few incorrect labels. Assuming that these generated correspondences have indeed their corresponding labels, one can interpret the different dissonance measures as separate samples over a feature space. Given a set of n input anchors $A = \{a_1, a_2, \ldots, a_n\}$ and the set of generated correspondences $C = \{c_1, c_2, \ldots, c_m\}$ with their respective labels $Y = \{y_1, y_2, \ldots, y_m\}$, containing both reliably correct and incorrect correspondences, each correspondence c_x would thus consist of n dissonance measurements $d_{x,i} (i = 1, \ldots n)$ and its label y_x. If an anchor a_x is correct, then evaluating the dissonances over C would lead to discernible differences for correct and incorrect correspondences, making the variable representing a_x in the feature space a good predictor of the labels Y.

To determine how well each dimension can serve as a predictor, one can utilize established feature selection techniques [15], which have become part of a set of important pre-processing techniques facilitating the use of machine learning and data-mining techniques on high-dimensional datasets. These techniques quantify how much a feature can contribute to the classification of a given labelled dataset. Their scores are then used in order to dismiss features which do not hold information that is relevant for classifying the data, allowing for the reduction of the feature space and the quicker training and execution of classifiers.

For this research, we will use the computed feature scores as evaluation metric for their corresponding anchors. Based on these values, a filtering policy can then dismiss anchors which are unlikely to be correct. Feature selection methods can utilize different underlying principles, for instance using correlation measures or information theory approaches. In order to not bias our approach to a single method, we will evaluate six different feature evaluation measures.

Pearson Correlation Coefficient. A fundamental method in the field of mathematical analysis, the *Pearson Correlation Coefficient* [22] measures the linear correlation between two variables. Having the sample set X and Y of two variables, the *Pearson Correlation Coefficient* is defined as:

$$r = \frac{\sum_{i=1}^{n}(X_i - \bar{X})(Y_i - \bar{Y})}{\sqrt{\sum_{i=1}^{n}(X_i - \bar{X})^2}\sqrt{\sum_{i=1}^{n}(Y_i - \bar{Y})^2}} \tag{2}$$

Spearman Rank Correlation. The *Spearman Rank Correlation* [22] is a method which utilizes the method of computing the *Pearson Correlation Coefficient*. However, the sample sets X and Y are transformed into the ranking sets x and y. The correlation between x and y is then computed as:

$$p = \frac{\sum_{i=1}^{n}(x_i - \bar{x})(y_i - \bar{y})}{\sqrt{\sum_{i=1}^{n}(x_i - \bar{x})^2}\sqrt{\sum_{i=1}^{n}(y_i - \bar{y})^2}} \tag{3}$$

Gain Ratio. Information theoretical approaches have also been employed as measures of feature quality. Information gain techniques compute how much impurity is left in each split after a given attribute has been employed as the root node of a classification tree [26]. To measure this impurity, the measure of entropy is commonly employed. The entropy of a variable X is defined as:

$$H(X) = -\sum_{x_i} p(x_i) log_2 p(x_i)$$ (4)

The entropy after observing another variable is defined as:

$$H(X|Y) = -\sum_{y_j} p(y_j) \sum_{x_i} p(x_i|y_j) log_2 p(x_i|y_j)$$ (5)

The information gain of X is defined as the additional amount of information left after partitioning for all values of Y:

$$IG(X|Y) = H(X) - H(X|Y)$$ (6)

The *Gain Ratio* is defined as the normalized information gain:

$$GainRatio(X|Y) = IG(X|Y)/H(X)$$ (7)

Symmetrical Uncertainty. The *Symmetrical Uncertainty* [11] is a measure that is similar to the *Gain Ratio*. It however employs a different normalization principle to counteract the bias towards larger attribute sets. Using equations 4 and 6, the *Symmetrical Uncertainty* $SU(X)$ can be computed as follows:

$$SU(X) = 2 \left[\frac{IG(X|Y)}{H(X) + H(Y)} \right]$$ (8)

Thornton's Separability Index. Instead of using a correlation measure, *Thornton's Separability Index*[33] expresses separability between the classes in a dataset. Specifically, it is defined as the fraction of data-points whose nearest neighbour shares the same classification label. It is computed as follows:

$$TSI = \frac{\sum_{i=1}^{n}(f(x_i) + f(x'_i) + 1) \mod 2}{n}$$ (9)

where f is a binary value function returning 0 or 1, depending on which class label is associated with value x_i. x'_i is defined as the nearest neighbour of x_i.

Fisher's Linear Discriminant. *Fisher's Linear Discriminant* [10] evaluates the discriminatory quality of a set of features by calculating the difference of means of the features and normalizing this distance by a measure of the within-class scatter. The dataset is transformed into a linear space using the projection w which optimizes the output of the value function. The discriminant of two features can be computed as follows:

$$J(w) = \frac{|\mu_{y_1} - \mu_{y_2}|}{s_{y_1}^2 + s_{y_2}^2}$$ (10)

where μ_y and s_y^2 denote the means and variance of class y.

Using these feature evaluation methods one can evaluate the given anchors of a partial alignments with regards to their discriminatory qualities over the dissonance feature space. Based on the evaluation values, a filtering policy can then decide which anchors to discard before continuing the mapping process. The computation of these measures has been facilitated using the Java-ML framework [1].

4   Evaluation

To evaluate the proposed technique of filtering anchors, we utilized the *conference* dataset originating from the 2013 Ontology Alignment Evaluation Initiative [14]. This dataset contains matching tasks, including reference alignments, of real-world ontologies describing the domain of scientific conferences. While this dataset does not contain predefined partial alignments as additional input, it is possible to simply generate partial alignments from the supplied reference alignments. For this domain, it is preferable that the partial alignment also contains incorrect anchors such that the capability of filtering these incorrect anchors can be adequately tested. For each mapping task, *PA* is generated randomly such that it exhibits a *precision* and *recall* of 0.5 with respect to the reference alignment. Since we assume that a similarity metric can produce limited set reliable correspondences given a high threshold, as mentioned in Section 3, we limit the set of correct correspondences in the partial alignment to correspondences which do no exhibit a high pairwise similarity. The experiments thus provide an insight to what extent we can reliably evaluate anchors for situations where a basic similarity-based evaluation produces unreliable results.

Each task is repeated 100 times and the results aggregated in order to minimize random fluctuations. For each task, the given approach evaluates the given anchors, such that from the resulting scores a ordered ranking is created. While in a real-world application a given filtering approach would discard a series anchors based on a given policy, for instance by applying a threshold, for an experimental set-up it is more appropriate to perform a precision vs. recall analysis. Such an analysis allows for a comparison of performances without having to limit oneself to a set filtering policies.

To evaluate the dissonance between an anchor and a comparison correspondence, as stated in Section 3, a base similarity metric *sim* is required. We investigate three different categories of base similarity metrics:

Syntactic. A comparison between concept names and labels using a specific algorithm. The Jaro [18] similarity was applied for this purpose.
Structural. A comparison between concepts which also includes information of related concepts in its computation. As an example of a structural similarity, a profile similarity [25] has been evaluated. A profile similarity gathers syntactical information, e.g. concept names, labels and comments, from a given concept and its related concepts into a collection, which is referred to as profile. The similarity of two profiles determines the similarity of the corresponding concepts.
Semantic. A similarity of this type aims to identify the meanings of concept senses within a lexical resource. The senses of the lexical resource are related with each other using semantic relations, e.g. *'is-a-kind-of'* relations, forming a taxonomy

of senses. Concept similarities are determined by identifying the correct concept senses and determining the distance of these senses within the lexical taxonomy. This distance is then transformed into a similarity metric. For this evaluation a semantic similarity using WordNet as a lexical resource has been evaluated [29].

The final score of each anchor is determined by computing the pairwise similarity of the anchor concepts, also computed using sim, and multiplying this similarity with the anchor consistency score as determined using the proposed approach, using one of the tested feature evaluation methods. We will compare the rankings of our approach with a *baseline*, which is obtained by computing the pairwise similarities of the anchor concepts using the base similarity sim, while omitting the evaluation of the anchors using our approach. The comparison with the *baseline* allows us to establish how much our approach contributes to the evaluation of the given anchors.

The presented approach requires a method of generating the set of correspondences C which serve as individuals of the feature space. In order to apply feature selection techniques on a dataset, the class labels y of each individual must be known, and ideally also correct. Since a single similarity metric can produce a reliable set or correct correspondences, albeit limited in size, one can use this set as the part of C which represent true correspondences. In order to generate reliably incorrect correspondences, one can simply select two concepts at random while ensure that their pairwise similarity is below a threshold. For the experiments, the quantity of incorrect correspondences is set to be equal to the quantity of reliably correct correspondences. To generate C the *Jaro* similarity with thresholds 0.75 and 0.3 was utilized to ensure that the correspondences had a sufficiently high or low similarity.

4.1 Syntactic Similarity

In the first performed experiment the *Jaro* similarity was evaluated when applied as sim in order to evaluate a syntactical similarity. The generated anchors are evaluated and ranked according to their evaluation scores. We evaluate these rankings by computing their aggregated interpolated precision vs. recall values, displayed in Figure 4.

From the results depicted in Figure 4 several observations can be made. The most striking observation to be made is that all six tested feature evaluation methods produced a better ranking than the un-weighted baseline. At low recall levels this resulted in an increased precision of up to .057. At the higher recall levels we observe an increase in precision of up to .035.

With regard to the individual feature evaluation metrics a few trends are observable. First of all, we can see that the information theoretical approaches, meaning the *Gain-Ratio* and the *Symmetrical Uncertainty* improve the precision fairly consistently across all recall levels. On average, these measure improve the precision by approximately 0.3. The *Spearman rank correlation* and *Fisher's discriminant* only display a marginal improvement for lower recall levels, however show a more significant improvement for higher recall levels. The most significant improvements for the lower recall levels are observed when applying *Thornton's separability index* and *Pearson's correlation coefficient*.

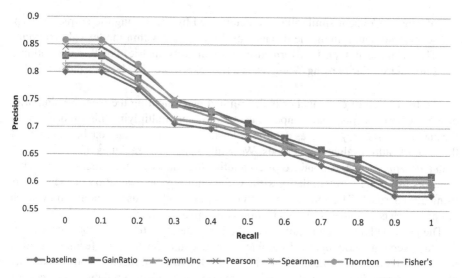

Fig. 4. Precision vs. recall of the rankings created using a syntactic similarity weighted by the evaluated feature selection methods. The un-weighted variant of the syntactic similarity is used as baseline.

4.2 Structural Similarity

For the second evaluation of our approach, we replaced the *Jaro* similarity with a *profile* similarity for *sim*. The *profile* similarity [25] compiles meta-information, primarily the name, comments and annotations, of a given concept and concepts that are linked to the given concept using relations such as *'is-a'* and *'domain-of'*. A profile similarity can be classified as a structural similarity due the utilization of information originating from related concepts. The gathered meta-information is represented as a weighted document-vector, also referred to as a profile. The similarity between two concepts is determined by computing the cosine similarity of their corresponding document vectors. The results of evaluating our approach using a profile similarity as *sim* can be seen in Figure 5.

From Figure 5 we can observe a more mixed result compared to the previous evaluation. The information-theoretical methods, namely *Gain Ratio* and *Symmetrical Uncertainty* outperform the baseline at lower recall levels, maintaining a near-perfect precision of 0.99 for one additional recall level and outperforming the baseline by a margin of roughly .022 at a recall of 0.3. However, for higher recall levels this margin drops until both measures perform roughly on par with the baseline at the highest recall levels. *Thornton's Separability Index* outperforms the baseline only at lower recall levels, while *Pearson's correlation coefficient* performs lower than the baseline. The most promising measures in this experiment were *Fisher's linear discriminant* and the *Spearman rank correlation*, which performed higher than the baseline for all recall levels. Contrary to the baseline, both measures produce a near perfect ranking of 0.99 at a recall of 0.2. The *Spearman rank correlation* produces rankings which have an

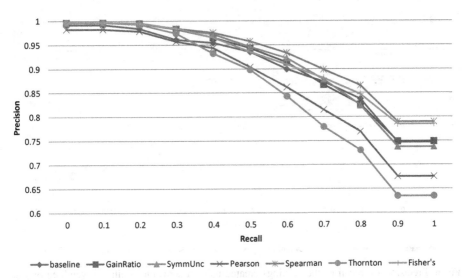

Fig. 5. Precision vs. recall of the rankings created using a structural similarity weighted by the evaluated feature selection methods. The un-weighted variant of the structural similarity is used as baseline.

increased precision of roughly .025 for most recall levels, while for the highest recall levels this difference is widened to roughly .045.

4.3 Semantic Similarity

In the third performed evaluation, we evaluated our approach when utilizing a semantic similarity as sim. A semantic similarity derives a similarity between two concepts by identifying their intended senses within a corpus and computing the semantic or taxonomic distance between the senses. The resulting distance value is then transformed into a similarity measure. For a semantic similarity to functions it is necessary that the given corpus also models the domains of the two input ontologies. To ensure this, WordNet [21] has been utilized as corpus, which aims at modelling the entire English language. The result of utilizing a semantic similarity as sim can be seen in Figure 6.

From Figure 6 several key observations can be made. First of all, the baseline displays a distinctively constant precision of .82 up to a recall level of .5. For the lower recall levels, our approach outperforms the baseline by a significant margin using any of the tested feature evaluation methods. Most measures produced an interpolated precision and recall of approximately .9, indicating an improvement of .08. When increasing the recall levels, the performance of these measures slowly approaches the performance of the baseline, while still staying above it. The exception is *Pearson's correlation coefficient*, which performs lower than the baseline at higher recall levels.

The clearly best performing measure is *Thornton's separability index*, which produced a precision higher than both the baseline and the other measures for all recall levels. At recall levels of .3 and higher Thornton's separability index improved upon

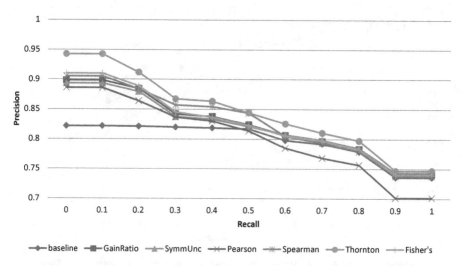

Fig. 6. Precision vs. recall of the rankings created using a semantic similarity weighted by the evaluated feature selection methods. The un-weighted variant of the semantic similarity is used as baseline.

the baseline by up to .047. At recall levels of .0 and .1 Thornton's separability index produced rankings with a precision of approximately .94, an improvement of .12 compared to the baseline. At a recall level of .2 it still produced rankings with a commendable precision of .91, which is .09 higher than the baseline.

Improvements of this magnitude are particularly important for the utilization of partial alignments, since they allow a significantly larger amount of anchors to be utilized while maintaining a degree of certainty that the anchors are correct. An approach which utilizes partial alignments relies on the quantity and quality of the anchors, but is likely biased towards the quality of the anchors. Thus in order to perform well, such an approach is likely to enforce stringent criteria on the given anchors instead of risking wrong anchors to be included in its computation. In the case of using a semantic similarity to achieve this, our approach would lead to a significantly higher amount of correct anchors being retained.

5   Conclusion and Future Research

In this paper we presented an approach of filtering correspondences of partial alignments, known as anchors, using feature selection techniques. By defining a measure of dissonance, with which one can compare anchors to correct or incorrect correspondences, and observing that this measure only renders predictable results if the anchors represent correct correspondences, we can formulate the task of evaluating anchors as a feature selection problem. Since this approach does not utilize the direct comparison of the anchor concepts, its resulting scores should display better results for anchors whose concept similarities do not allow for a reliable positive classification.

A variety of feature evaluation methods are empirically evaluated. A syntactical, structural and semantic similarity are evaluated as base similarity of our approach and compared to a baseline rankings obtained from computing the pairwise similarity of the anchors. We observe improvements for all tested base similarity measures, with the most significant improvements observed when utilizing the syntactic and semantic similarity. For the syntactic similarity all tested feature evaluation methods outperformed the baseline with regard to precision for all recall levels by approximately .057. For the semantic similarity we observed a particularly significant increase in precision up to .12 for lower recall levels, and a considerate increase for the remaining recall levels up to .047.

Overall, we conclude that our proposed approach displayed a promising start as a novel approach for evaluating anchors when mapping with partial alignments.

References

1. Abeel, T., Van de Peer, Y., Saeys, Y.: Java-ml: A machine learning library. Journal of Machine Learning Research 10, 931–934 (2009)
2. Aumueller, D., Do, H.H., Massmann, S., Rahm, E.: Schema and ontology matching with coma++. In: Proceedings of the 2005 ACM SIGMOD International Conference on Management of Data, pp. 906–908. ACM (2005)
3. Berners-Lee, T., Hendler, J., Lassila, O.: The semantic web. Scientific American 284(5), 34–43 (2001)
4. Brickley, D., Guha, R.V.: RDF Vocabulary Description Language 1.0: RDF Schema (February 2004), http://www.w3.org/TR/rdf-schema
5. Cheatham, M.: Mapsss results for oaei 2011. In: Proceedings of the ISWC 2011 Workshop on Ontology Matching, pp. 184–190 (2011)
6. Cruz, I., Xiao, H.: Ontology driven data integration in heterogeneous networks. Complex Systems in Knowledge-based Environments: Theory, Models and Applications, 75–98 (2009)
7. David, J., Guillet, F., Briand, H.: Matching directories and owl ontologies with aroma. In: Proc. of the 15th ACM International Conference on Information and Knowledge Management, pp. 830–831 (2006)
8. Euzenat, J.: Towards a principled approach to semantic interoperability. In: Proceedings of the IJCAI 2001 Workshop on Ontologies and Information Sharing, pp. 19–25 (2001)
9. Euzenat, J., Shvaiko, P.: Ontology Matching, vol. 18. Springer, Berlin (2007)
10. Fisher, R.A.: The use of multiple measurements in taxinomic problems. Annals of Eugenics 7(2), 179–188 (1936)
11. Flannery, B.P., Press, W.H., Teukolsky, S.A., Vetterling, W.: Numerical recipes in c. Press Syndicate of the University of Cambridge, New York (1992)
12. Giunchiglia, F., Autayeu, A., Pane, J.: S-match: An open source framework for matching lightweight ontologies. Semantic Web 3(3), 307–317 (2012)
13. Giunchiglia, F., Yatskevich, M., Avesani, P., Shvaiko, P.: A large dataset for the evaluation of ontology matching. The Knowledge Engineering Review Journal 24, 137–157 (2009)
14. Grau, B.C., Dragisic, Z., Eckert, K., Euzenat, J., Ferrara, A., Granada, R., Ivanova, V., Jiménez-Ruiz, E., Kempf, A.O., Lambrix, P., et al.: Results of the ontology alignment evaluation initiative 2013. In: Proc. 8th ISWC Workshop on Ontology Matching (OM), pp. 61–100 (2013)
15. Guyon, I., Elisseeff, A.: An introduction to variable and feature selection. Journal of Machine Learning Research 3, 1157–1182 (2003)

16. He, B., Chang, K.C.C.: Automatic complex schema matching across web query interfaces: A correlation mining approach. ACM Transactions on Database Systems (TODS) 31(1), 346–395 (2006)
17. Hu, W., Qu, Y.: Falcon-ao: A practical ontology matching system. Web Semantics: Science, Services and Agents on the World Wide Web 6(3), 237–239 (2008)
18. Jaro, M.: Advances in record-linkage methodology as applied to matching the 1985 census of tampa, florida. Journal of the American Statistical Association 84(406), 414–420 (1989)
19. Kim, W., Seo, J.: Classifying schematic and data heterogeneity in multidatabase systems. Computer 24(12), 12–18 (1991)
20. McGuinness, D., van Harmelen, F.: OWL web ontology language overview. W3C recommendation, W3C (February 2004)
21. Miller, G.A.: Wordnet: A lexical database for english. Communications of the ACM 38, 39–41 (1995)
22. Myers, J.L., Well, A.D., Lorch Jr., R.F.: Research design and statistical analysis. Routledge (2010)
23. Ngo, D., Bellahsene, Z., Coletta, R.: Yam++-a combination of graph matching and machine learning approach to ontology alignment task. Journal of Web Semantic (2012)
24. Noy, N.F., Musen, M.A.: Anchor-prompt: Using non-local context for semantic matching. In: Proceedings of the ICJAI Workshop on Ontologies and Information Sharing, pp. 63–70 (2001)
25. Qu, Y., Hu, W., Cheng, G.: Constructing virtual documents for ontology matching. In: Proceedings of the 15th International Conference on World Wide Web, WWW 2006, pp. 23–31. ACM, New York (2006)
26. Quinlan, J.R.: Induction of decision trees. Machine Learning 1(1), 81–106 (1986)
27. Rahm, E., Bernstein, P.A.: A survey of approaches to automatic schema matching. The VLDB Journal 10(4), 334–350 (2001)
28. Schadd, F.C., Roos, N.: Anchor-profiles for ontology mapping with partial alignments. In: Proceedings of the 12th Scandinavian AI Conference (SCAI 2013), pp. 235–244 (2013)
29. Schadd, F., Roos, N.: Coupling of wordnet entries for ontology mapping using virtual documents. In: Proceedings of The Seventh International Workshop on Ontology Matching (OM 2012) Collocated with the 11th International Semantic Web Conference (ISWC 2012), pp. 25–36 (2012)
30. Seddiqui, M.H., Aono, M.: An efficient and scalable algorithm for segmented alignment of ontologies of arbitrary size. Journal of Web Semantics 7(4), 344–356 (2009)
31. Shvaiko, P., Euzenat, J.: A survey of schema-based matching approaches. In: Spaccapietra, S. (ed.) Journal on Data Semantics IV. LNCS, vol. 3730, pp. 146–171. Springer, Heidelberg (2005)
32. Shvaiko, P., Euzenat, J.: Ten challenges for ontology matching. In: Meersman, R., Tari, Z. (eds.) OTM 2008, Part II. LNCS, vol. 5332, pp. 1164–1182. Springer, Heidelberg (2008)
33. Thornton, C.: Separability is a learners best friend. In: 4th Neural Computation and Psychology Workshop, London, April 9-11, pp. 40–46. Springer (1998)

Linked-Data Integration for Workflow-Based Computational Experiments

Pavel A. Smirnov and Sergey V. Kovalchuk

e-Science Research Institute
ITMO University
Saint-Petersburg, Russia
smirnp@niuitmo.ru

Abstract. Accumulated volumes of semantically annotated data which are distributed over the Internet deliver a valuable source of material for computational-intensive scientific experiments according to E-Science paradigm. However, the diversity of Linked Open Data sources and ontological structures within these structures raise a problem of search, extraction and import of relevant data from third-party endpoints. In this paper we present a solution, which helps users to create workflow-based applications with LOD-data without manual typing SPARQL queries. The solution is a functional extension for Virtual Simulation Objects toolbox [1]. Its concept and technology propose knowledge-based composite application design process. We describe LOD-data import process, which is implemented with "generic pattern" specification. A faceted browsing tool with basic filtration mechanisms was used in the experiments and a use-case from meteorology domain was also presented.

Keywords: Scientific experiment, workflow composite application, data integration.

1 Motivation

With the appearance of semantic web technologies a lot of plain-text information has been automatically formalized into semantic-enabled structures [2]. Diversity of inter-linked ontologies in LOD Cloud[1] demonstrates that the formalized content belongs to a variety of domains: education, science, geospatial, media, social networks, etc. Some of the information may be a valuable source of data for E-Science tasks. The main problems for the scientists, who are not familiar with semantic-web technologies, occur at the phases of data search, filtration and integration into their applications. For specialists with semantic-web technologies' background, it's not a problem, but the most of eScience researchers are not familiar with technologies such as RDF, OWL and SPARQL. So, the problem makes it impossible for them to use LOD-data for their domains-specific tasks solution.

Motivation for this work is to give researchers the ability to easily browse and capture required facts from linked data sources in order to use them in simulation modeling analyses. The contribution of this paper is a linked data import process

---

[1] http://lod-cloud.net/

P. Klinov and D. Mouromtsev (Eds.): KESW 2014, CCIS 468, pp. 175–183, 2014.

based on Virtual Simulation Objects (VSO) concept and technology. The difference of import process is in a phase of "generic pattern" abstraction, which brings flexibility into design and management of newly-created Virtual Objects based on imported data.

The remainder of the paper is organized as follows. Section 2 describes the background and key VSO terms and features. Section 3 specifies the proposed data import process. Sections 4 and 5 are devoted to implementation details and a real scientific use-case demonstration regarding meteorology domain. Section 6 includes discussion, related works and future plans.

2   Background

Scientific workflows are targeted to make scientists more productive due to automation of their data driven and computational-intensive analyses [3]. In comparison to business-process workflows, where quality of service is the most valuable criterion [4], scientific workflows bring some novel scientific results and should be sharable and easy reproducible to be verified by other scientists.

According to model driven architecture [5] three levels of workflow composition are outlined: a concrete workflow – platform-dependent computational model with invocation of particular software services on particular nodes in the network; abstract workflow – contains platform-independent computational model with abstract services' invocation; conceptual workflow (or meta-workflow) – application model, which combines several platform-independent computational models.

In our previous paper [1] a Virtual Simulation Objects concept and technology have been introduced. It describes that user designs his application at top level of abstraction (meta-level). In this case all underlying levels (abstract and concrete) are generated automatically. The most valuable component of implemented VSO-toolbox is a knowledge base (KB) with catalog of VSO-images – virtual objects patterns with predefined structures, set of properties and default values. To provide the ability to use several exemplars of one VSO-image within working environment (i.e. single VSO-project), an instantiation mechanism was implemented. VSO-instances usually differ from their images by particular values of input parameters, which are obtained as a result of automatic or manual composition. Instantiation mechanism allows us to save VSO-projects into KB without any impact on original images. If VSO-images for composition do not exist, they should be preliminary designed via VSO-editor application. In order to simplify VSO-images design, the following user-support functionality has been implemented: integration with platform's package base and provenance captured data [6].

For the better description of the problem of semantic data integration into workflow-based applications, let us introduce some abstract use-case without binding it to any particular domain. Suppose that in any third-party ontology, user has found a set of ontological concepts, which he wants to analyze by a sequence of software packages (i.e. workflow-based application). For example, processing such a diversity of concepts performs a quantitative analysis and allows us to verify (or improve) any simulation model implemented in one of the packages. Traditionally, process of data harvesting from LOD-source goes in the following way. User should find out a query interface, manually or he should select the needed concepts via faceted browser and save the results into XML or CSV file. Next, to process the downloaded concepts in pipeline mode, the user is required to create a certain parser, generate workflow or an application (for example, a console) which invokes the consequence of target packages with the values of the particular concepts. Even to do these trivial things, the user should basically understand semantic web technologies and be ready to apply some programming skills. To avoid these actions, we propose a data import process with parsing results "on the fly" and save parsed concepts into knowledge-base as new VSO-images, described above. An additional phase is called "generic image abstraction" and it is performed during data import. It improves classification and future management of the imported concepts.

3   Data Import with Generic Image Abstraction

Process of data capturing of heterogeneously structured LOD-sources requires an algorithm declaring how this data should be gathered and structured. The elaborated algorithm uses VSO-images as basic entities. They will be stored in knowledge base and present the imported data. The algorithm is presented at Fig. 1 and the key elements are described below.

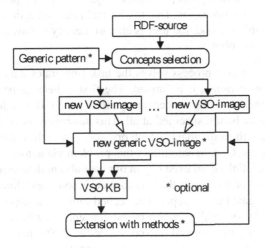

Fig. 1. Import process via generic-pattern specification

Formally the import process using VSO-images consists of the following stages:

1. *RDF source.* User should manually specify RDF-object's URI or upload an RDF-file. Search of the required dataset is out of the scope of the task.
2. *Required concepts' selection.* After the user has specified an RDF-source, he should manually select the particular properties and values, which are necessary to be imported. Properties selection depends highly on user's goals and is aimed to filter unnecessary relations to be processed further (such "abstract", "sameAs", "hasPicture", etc.).

3. *Generic pattern's specification (optional)*. Generic pattern is homogenously structured specification, which may be applied for all the imported concepts. The generic pattern also impacts on the previous phase. Applied as "a mask" it allows us to check if the selected concepts satisfy the specified requirements. Inheriting the structure of generic pattern by all the imported concepts may be easily extended with new properties and executable methods in a pipeline mode.
4. *Submission to KB* is the final stage during import process. The stage is performed in automatic mode. According to selected data and generic pattern (if it was specified) a set of VSO-images will be generated and submitted into knowledge base. The result of this stage is a set of newly created VSO-images, which may be dragged-and-dropped into workspace (VSO-environment application). VSO-images participate in virtual environment design process with further workflow code generation as proposed in [1].
5. *Extension of images by computational methods (optional)*. Newly created VSO-images (which either inherit some genetic image or not) may be extended by existing executable methods or some additional properties. Extension means encapsulation of the structure of methods (scenarios, implementations, executable packages order and parameters) into particular VSO-image structure. This phase is optional and these methods may be also invoked out of the created images, but physical encapsulation into particular virtual object's structure provides a piece of expert's knowledge formalization. Due to physical interconnection between virtual object and executable method, the user is able to identify the available methods to be performed over the object.

Though the proposed import process solves the task (integrates data from LOD into workflow-based computations), it is limited. The first is heterogeneity of concepts' structures. Some of the importing concepts may either have different formats, or these required properties may be not specified at all. This heterogeneity of data is a natural problem of semantic web technologies which originates from the collaborative contribution of the ontologies. Certain solution of this problem via automatic analysis content through "sameAs" links does exist [2]. In our case absent data specification either may be done manually or it requires the user to specify some additional parsing logic, which was not investigated in the paper. The second limit is the depth of hierarchy of importing concepts. Theoretically, import of the concepts may have any hierarchical structures to be correctly transformed into corresponding VSO-image. But in practice it is almost unreal to provide a pipeline import of complex hierarchical concepts due to high heterogeneity of their inner concepts. Examples of both limitations are presented in section 5.

4   Implementation

To provide the user with a mechanism for concepts' selection, a faceted browser was implemented and integrated into existing VSO-editor application as custom Silverlight control. RDF-data browsing is organized as horizontal sequence of the lists (see Fig.2), where the level of depth depends on a current focused item. The top level of

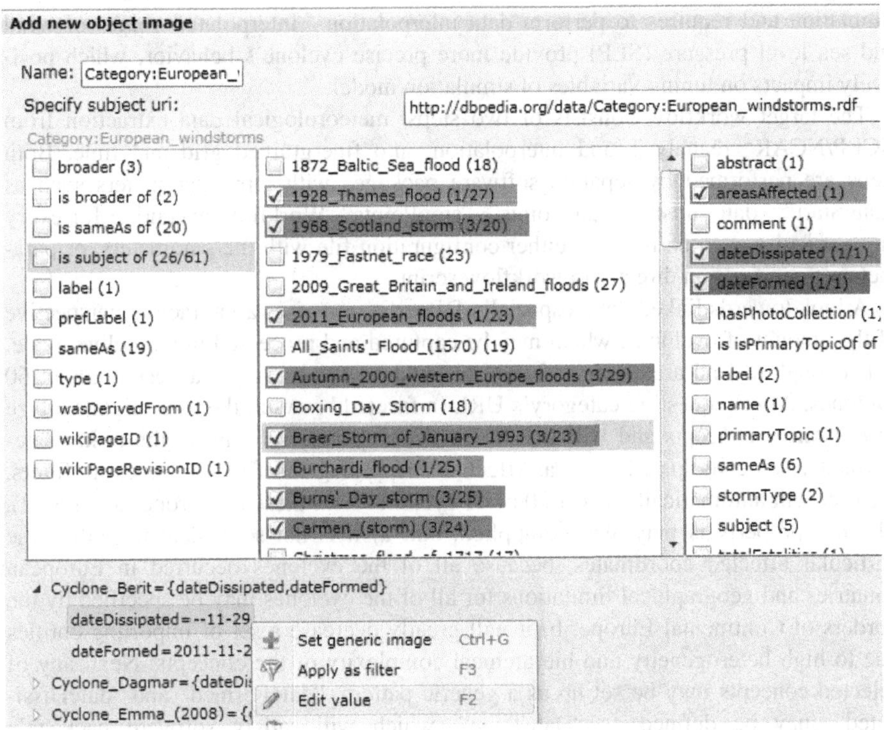

Fig. 2. LOD-browser control with filters

the tree is an item, which has been initially requested via user-specified URI. Lower levels contain dynamically requested properties or values of the current focused item. Levels are loading asynchronously and appending at the right side of the interface.

To facilitate the validation of selected records, a hierarchical tree-view list was placed under the browser control (see Fig.2). The tree is organized according to the inner structures of the importing concepts. User's navigation over its items provides automatic selection of corresponding concepts in the faceted browser above.

To make data selection more convenient, an automatic filtration mechanism is offered to the user. Having chosen any property at any level of depth, the user may apply it as a condition to filter similar concepts with that property. The property will be marked by a random color and on the same level other relevant concepts will be marked the same way. For example, 26 out of 61 concepts from category "European storms" contain the property "dateDissipated" (marked with blue at Fig.2).

5   Use Case

To prove the feasibility of the proposed import process, an ordinary use case from meteorology domain has been chosen. The task is devoted to the cyclone's behavior simulation and requires to perform data interpolation. Interpolated values of wind and sea level pressure (SLP) provide more precise cyclone's behavior, which positively impacts on tuning variables of simulation model.

The target workflow consists of two steps: meteorological data extraction from NCEP/NCAR[2] reanalysis and interpolation onto fine-grained grid and time. Both steps are performed by separate software packages with input parameters such as "dateStart", "dateFinish", "startPoints", "stopPoints". Workflow execution for every any particular cyclone requires either configuration file with the parameters, or parameters' specification directly in workflow script.

A look towards linked data, especially DBpedia, promises an attractive perspective of the amount of cyclones, which may be captured and processed in a pipeline mode. It is enough to find a category "European windstorms" to get an access to about 60 cyclones. After requesting category's URL in faceted browser, the user might analyze any of target concepts and will find at least 3 properties relevant to the task: "date-Formed", "dateDissipated", "areasAffected". Applying the first two ones as filters, the user will automatically select 20 of 61 cyclones with these two properties (Fig. 2). The last property is may also be applied, but: a) it is not so critical to outline the particular affected coordinates, because all of the cyclones occurred in European countries and geographical limitations for all of the cyclones may be specified by the borders of Continental Europe; b) it will greatly decrease a set of importing entities due to high heterogeneity and hierarchical complexity of the concepts. Next, any of selected concepts may be set up as a generic pattern. "dateFormed" and "dateDissipated" may be defined as "DateTime", which will satisfy software package's requirement. Application of generic pattern as a mask for filtration of matching concepts has shown that only dates of 5 cyclones out of 20 can be correctly parsed as DateTime (due to the accuracy of specified values).

After the selection stage has been finished, the selected cyclones will be created as new VSO-images and will inherit the generic-one called "Cyclone". According to the original workflow described above, the generic image should be manually extended with two VSO-models, which perform an invocation of data extraction and functionality of interpolation (see Fig.3a). These models may be developed preliminary during the original workflow implementation. Extension is performed as drag-and-drop operation in the VSO-editor application. Due to objects' inheritance, all the imported cyclone's images will be extended in the same way.

The result of data import according to the proposed algorithm is a set of new VSO-images submitted into knowledge base. It is available for virtual system construction via by VSO-environment application (see Fig.3b). User may add any amount of imported cyclone images into environment and simulate all of them in one click. Workflow script will be generated automatically and may be executed in parallel mode due to distributed and scalable architecture of execution middleware. In our case, this is a CLAVIRE platform [7].

---

[2] http://www.esrl.noaa.gov/psd/data/gridded/data.ncep.reanalysis.html

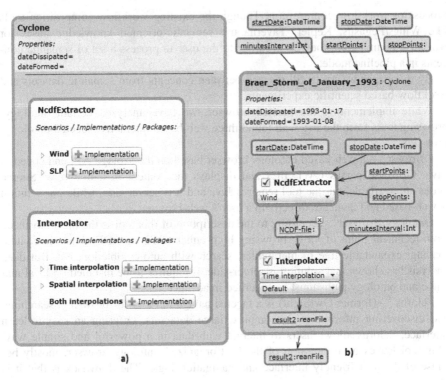

Fig. 3. a) Generic VSO-image extended with two models b) A Braer-Storm VSO-instance during workflow composition

6   Discussion and Conclusion

This paper proposes an idea of workflow-based analysis of semantic concepts and demonstrates our effort to implement it. Analyzing the literature devoted to the linked data integration, we have found that the papers devoted to construction of federated ontologies [8,9,10], missed   links' discovery [11,12], evaluation of the level of similarity between entities from different ontologies [8][13], data visualization [14] and so on. Even a guide with a rather clear caption "How to integrate LINKED data into your application" [15] offers to perform operations like "Vocabularies normalization" and "Identifiers resolving" in order to integrate several ontologies into a federated one. Only after that it offers to access it via SPARQL-endpoint. The problem is that all of these operations are unknown to researchers from the majority of domains except semantic web. There is a lack of user-friendly ontology-accessing tools to provide an access to Open Data without requirements for additional skills like SPARQL syntax. Another analysis of workflow composition tools with semantic web technologies was presented in our previous paper [16]. It has shown that there is no clear solution to integrate semantic-enabled data from third-party LOD-sources into design process of workflow composition. Though the existing workflow-composition tools like Wings/Pegasus, Kepler, Taverna use semantic-oriented knowledge bases for workflows annotation, they do not offer to the user to process a set of semantic concepts in a pipeline mode.

By this paper we try to fill the gap between concepts from semantic datasets and workflow-based scientific experiments.

While implementing the faceted browser, we have analyzed certain ontology-browsing tools from the list[3] and found three web-based interactive faceted ontology-browsers:

OBrowse[4] – a web-based ontology browser based on the Protégé-API and coded in Java. OBrowse parses OWL files and displays the content in a tree-view. Source codes are available, but the tool requires Java and it is server-side, while our solution is web-based and launches directly in a user's web-browser.

Ontology Browser[5] according to the description of this tool is the most advanced from technical point of view: browsing both either OWL or RDF, dynamic content loading, expandable tree of hierarchies, search with auto-completion, etc. But deep analysis has shown that solution is server-side. It requires to be installed on local machine and ontology paths must be specified in advance.

Pelorus [6]– (former OwlSight) is a faceted navigation tool for browsing, searching, and discovering information in complex, large data sets. Offering an easy-to-learn interface, Pelorus allows users to interact with data in a powerful and simple way. This tool leaves an impression of the best-organized ontology browser, mostly because of the user-friendly interface and navigation logic. The drawback is that it is proprietary.

Our faceted browser is client-side, and all the requests and processing are performed by user's machine, which do not require any server-side installations. The browser is also connected to a tree-view control above and responds to interactive actions received from the tree-view.

In the future, we plan to implement new features to solve the discovered problems like disjunction filtering, autocomplete functionality and so on. Perhaps, to solve the problem of data heterogeneity we will use a library, which generates C#-classes directly from RDF and dynamically compiles the logic as executable application. It should be automatically instantiated into CLAVIRE and be able to be invoked during concepts' selection phase. Probably, an approach will make the user to execute dynamically transformations with importing data in order to increase a number of homogenous concepts satisfying the specified generic pattern.

Acknowledgement. This paper is partially supported by Russian Scientific Foundation, grant #14-11-00823.

---

[3] http://wiki.opensemanticframework.org/index.php/Ontology_Tools
[4] http://sourceforge.net/projects/obrowse/
[5] https://code.google.com/p/ontology-browser/
[6] http://pelorus.clarkparsia.com/

References

1. Smirnov, P.A., Kovalchuk, S.V., Boukhanovsky, A.V.: Knowledge-Based Support for Complex Systems Exploration in Distributed Problem Solving Environments. In: Klinov, P., Mouromtsev, D. (eds.) KESW 2013. Communications in Computer and Information Science, vol. 394, pp. 147–161. Springer, Heidelberg (2013)
2. Lehmann, J., et al.: DBpedia-a large-scale, Multilingual Knowledge Base Extracted from Wikipedia. In: Semantic Web Journal (2013) (Under review)
3. McPhillips, T.: Scientific Workflow Design for Mere Mortals. Future Generation Computer Systems 5(25), 541–551 (2009)
4. Shen, J., et al.: Aligning Ontology-based Development with Service Oriented Systems. Future Generation Computer Systems 32, 263–273 (2014)
5. Cerezo, N., Montagnat, J., Blay-Fornarino, M.: Computer-Assisted Scientific Workflow Design. Journal of Grid Computing 3(11), 585–612 (2013)
6. Smirnov, P.A., Kovalchuk, S.V.: Provenance-Based Workflow Composition with Virtual Simulation Objects Technology. To appear in: Proceeding of the 11th International Conference on Fuzzy Systems and Knowledge Discovery (FSKD), Xiamen, China (August 2014)
7. V Knyazkov, K., et al.: CLAVIRE: e-Science Infrastructure for Data-driven Computing. Journal of Computational Science 3(6), 504–510 (2012)
8. Zhao, L., Ichise, R.: Instance-Based Ontological Knowledge Acquisition. In: Cimiano, P., Corcho, O., Presutti, V., Hollink, L., Rudolph, S. (eds.) ESWC 2013. LNCS, vol. 7882, pp. 155–169. Springer, Heidelberg (2013)
9. Chen, Z., et al.: Semantic Integration and Knowledge Discovery for Environmental Research. Journal of Database Management 18(1), 43–67 (2007)
10. Tarasova, T., Argenti, M., Marx, M.: Semantically-Enabled Environmental Data Discovery and Integration: Demonstration Using the Iceland Volcano Use Case. In: Klinov, P., Mouromtsev, D. (eds.) KESW 2013. CCIS, vol. 394, pp. 289–297. Springer, Heidelberg (2013)
11. Ngomo, A.C.N., Auer, S.: LIMES - A Time-Efficient Approach for Large-Scale Link Discovery on the Web of Data. In: Proceedings of the Twenty-Second International Joint Conference on Artificial Intelligence, vol. 3, pp. 2312–2317 (2011)
12. Isele, R., Jentzsch, A., Bizer, C.: Silk Server - Adding Missing Links while Consuming Linked Data. In: 1st International Workshop on Consuming Linked Data (COLD 2010), Shanghai (2010)
13. Rodríguez, M.A., Egenhofer, M.J.: Determining Semantic Similarity Among Entity Classes from Different Ontologies. IEEE Transactions on Knowledge and Data Engineering 2(15), 442–456 (2003)
14. Klímek, J., Helmich, J., Nečaský, M.: Application of the Linked Data Visualization Model on Real World Data from the Czech LOD Cloud. To appear in the Proceedings of the WWW 2014 Workshop on Linked Data on the Web (LDOW 2014), Seoul, Korea (April 2014)
15. Schultz, A., et al.: How to Integrate LINKED Data into your Application, http://mes-semantics.com/wp-content/uploads/2012/09/Becker-etal-LDIF-SemTechSanFrancisco.pdf
16. Smirnov, P.A., Kovalchuk, S.V., Dukhanov, A.V.: Domain Ontologies Integration for Virtual Modelling and Simulation Environments. Procedia Computer Science 29, 2507–2514 (2014)

Ontology for Resource Self-organisation in Cyber-Physical-Social Systems

Nikolay Teslya[1,2], Alexander Smirnov[1,2], Tatiana Levashova[1], and Nikolay Shilov[1]

[1] St. Petersburg Institute for Informatics and Automation of the Russian Academy of Sciences
39, 14th line, St. Petersburg, Russian Federation, 199178
[2] ITMO University, 49, Kronverkskiy av., St. Petersburg, Russian Federation, 197101
{teslya,smir,tatiana.levashova,nick}@iias.spb.su

Abstract. Cyber-Physical-Social Systems (CPSSs) are expected to be context-aware. Sharable contexts lie at the heart of the context-aware systems. Ontologies provide means to create sharable ontology-based context models. Such ontologies are referred to as context ontologies. Context is an ontology-based model specified for actual settings. The present research inherits the idea of context ontologies usage for modelling context in CPSSs. In this work, an upper level context ontology for CPSSs is proposed. This ontology is applied in the domain of self-organising resource network. A case study from the area of proactive recommendation systems demonstrates the proposed approach.

Keywords: Cyber-physical-social systems, upper context ontology, resource self-organization.

1   Introduction

Cyber-Physical-Social Systems (CPSSs) is a relatively new research field. It takes ideas from, but goes significantly beyond, the current progress in cyber-physical systems, socio-technical systems and cyber-social systems to support computing for human experience [1]. CPSSs tightly integrate physical, cyber, and social worlds based on interactions between these worlds in real time. Such systems rely on communication, computation and control infrastructures commonly consisting of several levels for the three worlds with various resources as sensors, actuators, computational resources, services, humans, etc.

Semantics is the basis to ensure that several resources arrive at the same meaning regarding the situation and data/information/knowledge being communicated. Ontologies provide for a shared and common understanding of some domain that can be communicated across the multiple CPSS' resources. They facilitate knowledge sharing and reuse in open and dynamic distributed systems and allow entities not designed to work together to interoperate [2].

CPSSs belong to the class of variable systems with dynamic structures. Their resources are too numerous, mobile with a changeable composition. Planned resource interactions in such systems are just impossible. Resource self-organisation is the most efficient way to organise interactions and communications between the resources making up CPSSs.

P. Klinov and D. Mouromtsev (Eds.): KESW 2014, CCIS 468, pp. 184–195, 2014.

The paper contributes to the areas of development of ontologies for CPSSs and of CPSS' resource self-organisation. It proposes an upper-level ontology for CPSSs. This ontology is used for multi-level self-organisation of CPSS' resources. A case study from the area of proactive recommendation systems demonstrates the proposed approach.

The paper is structured as follows. Section 2 discusses the upper-level ontology for CPSSs. Section 3 introduces the approach for multi-level self-organisation of CPSS' resources and presents the domain-specific view on the upper ontology from the self-organization perspective. A case study from the area of proactive recommendation systems is described in Section 4.

2   Upper Ontology

CPSSs are expected to be context-aware. Sharable contexts lie at the heart of the context-aware systems. Ontologies provide means to create sharable ontology-based context models. Such ontologies are referred to as context ontologies. The context ontologies consist of the upper ontology for general concepts, and domain specific ontologies representing knowledge of different application domains [3, 4, 5]. The upper ontology is shared by these domains. As a rule, the upper ontology represents concepts that are common for all context-aware applications (*Context Entity, Time, Location, Person, Agent, Activity, Device*, etc.) and provide flexible extensibility to add specific concepts in different application domains (i.e., *Cell Phone* can be a sub-category of the category *Device*) [6, 7, 8]. Context is described as an ontology-based model specified for actual settings. Multiple sources of data/information/knowledge provide information about the actual settings. This information is integrated within the ontology-based model. The context model is a result of the integration.

The present research inherits the idea of context ontologies usage for modelling context in CPSSs. Although a number of ontologies have been created by now, e.g., in the area of socio-technical systems [9, 10, 11], the purpose of the present research is to propose an ontology convenient to use for self-organization.

According to [12], any information describing an entity's context falls into one of five categories for context information: individuality, activity, location, time, and relations (Fig. 1). The individuality category contains properties and attributes describing the entity itself. The category activity covers all tasks this entity may be involved in. The context categories location and time provide the spatio-temporal coordinates of the respective entity. Finally, the relations category represents information about any possible relation the entity may establish with another entity.

CPSS consists of cyber space, physical space, and mental space [13]. These spaces are represented by sets of *resources*. In the upper ontology (Fig. 2) proposed for CPSSs, the resources are thought of as the entities whose contexts are to be described. The physical space consists of various interacting information and computational *physical devices*. These devices united on the communication basis organize the cyber space. The mental space is represented by *humans* with their knowledge, mental capabilities, and sociocultural elements. Information from cyberspace *interacts* with physical space (*physical device*) and mental space (*human*).

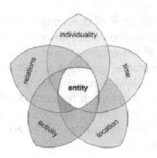

Fig. 1. Five fundamental categories for context information [12]

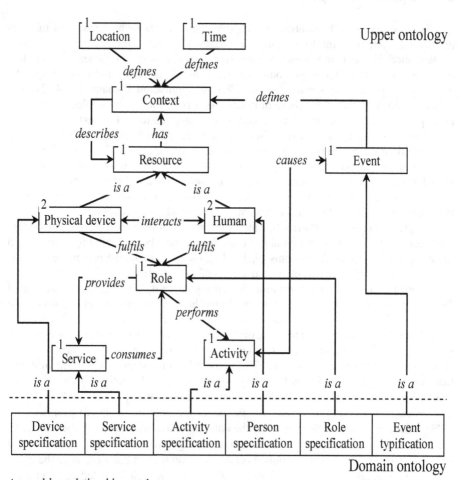

is a and *has* relationships are 1:∞
arities of other relationships are undefined

Fig. 2. Upper ontology for cyber-physical-social systems (CPSSs)

Resource's *context* is defined by *location, time, resource* individuality, and *event*. Resources perform some *activity* according to the *roles* they fulfil in the current context and depending on the type of *event*. On the other hand, the type of *activity* that a *resource* performs *causes* a type of *event*. For example, the *event* of a phone call defines the human *activity* as answer the phone. But, when a person raises the hand at the lecture time, this *activity causes* an *event* as, for instance, lecture interruption. This explains bidirectionality of '*causes*' relationship between *event* and *activity*.

The resources have some functionality in result of which they provide *services*. The services *provided* by one resource are *consumed* by other resources.

In Fig. 2, upper indices in boxes representing the ontology concepts indicate the taxonomical level of these concepts. All the concepts of the upper ontology are intended to be specialised in the application domains. An example of usage of the proposed ontology for self-organization of a service network in a CPSS is presented below.

3   Resource Self-organization

In order for distributed systems like CPSSs to operate efficiently, they have to be provided with self-organisation mechanisms. In a CPSS such mechanisms concern self-organisation of CPSS' resources. The goal of the resource self-organisation is support of humans in their decisions, activities, solution of the tasks, etc. At that, humans are the participants of the self-organisation process, as well.

3.1   Multi-level Self-organization

Social world as a distinguishing feature of CPSSs suggested using ideas from team organisations. The analysis of literature related to organizational behaviour & team management has showed that the most efficient teams are self-organizing teams working in the organizational context (Fig. 3). For example, social self-organisation has been researched by Hofkirchner [14], Fuchs [15], etc. However, in this case there is a significant risk for the group to choose a wrong strategy preventing from achieving desired goals. For this purpose, self-organising groups / systems need to have a certain guiding control from an upper level. This consideration produces the idea of multi-level self-organization.

The process of self-organisation of a network assumes creating and maintaining a logical network structure on top of a dynamically changing physical network topology. This logical network structure is used as a scalable infrastructure by various functional entities like address management, routing, service registry, media delivery, etc. The autonomous and dynamic structuring of components, context information and resources is the essential work of self-organisation [17]. The network is self-organised in the sense that it autonomously monitors available context in the network, provides the required context and any other necessary network service support to the requested services, and self-adapts when context changes.

To guide self-organising groups / systems, the guiding control via policy transfer from an upper level is used in the proposed approach [18]. This control enables a more efficient self-organisation based on the "top-to-bottom" configuration principle, which assumes conceptual configuration followed by parametric configuration. In this regard, each level can be considered as a scenario-based decision arena following certain complex knowledge patterns related to adaptable business models.

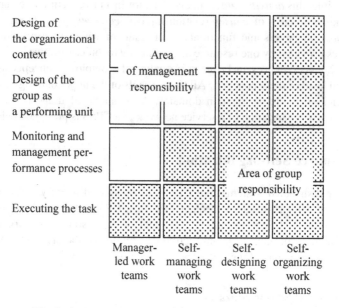

Fig. 3. Authority of work group types (adapted from [16])

The approach is based on the following principles: self-management and responsibility, decentralization, as well as integration of chain policy transfer (a formal chain of policies running from top to bottom) with network organisation (without any social hierarchy of command and control within a level), initiative from an upper level and co-operation within one level. The idea can be interpreted as producing "guided order from noise". In accordance with [19] such system falls into the class of purposeful systems.

Intra-level self-organisation is considered as a threefold process of (i) cognition (where subjective context-dependent knowledge is produced), (ii) communication (where system-specific objectification or subjectification of knowledge takes place), and (iii) synergetical co-operation (where objectified, emergent knowledge is produced). The Individually acquired context-dependent (subjective) knowledge is put to use efficiently by entering a social co-ordination and co-operation process. The objective knowledge is stored in structures and enables time-space distanciation of social relationships.

In order to achieve the dynamics and self-organisation of the CPSS, its components (resources) have to be creative, knowledgeable, active, and social. The resources that are parts of a system permanently change their joint environment what results in a synergetic collaboration and leads to achieving a certain level of collective intelligence. This is also supported by the fact that individual resource behaviour is partially determined by the social environment the resources are contributing to (called "norms"). For this purpose a protocol has been developed based on the BarterCast approach [20] that originates from the following ideas: (i) each service builds a network representing all interactions it knows about; (ii) the reputation of a service depends on the reputation of other services in the path between this service and the service connecting to it.

The overall scheme of the approach is shown in Fig. 4. In the approach, agents represent various CPSS' resources. Since the structures and self-organisation models of all the levels are identical, the developed framework is fully scalable. This makes it possible to perform conceptual development of the agents, i.e. to define kinds of agents needed, their characteristics, etc. Then, at the implementation stage, the particular behaviour and functionality of the agents may vary in different application domains.

The interoperability between the agents at the technological level is provided via usage of common standards and protocols, the interoperability at the level of semantics is ensured via usage of a common ontology.

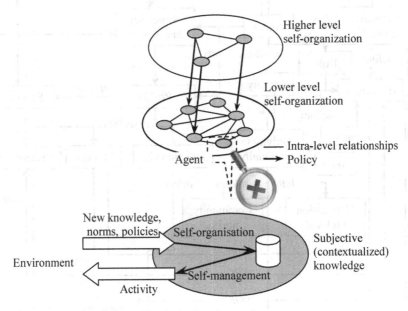

Fig. 4. Approach overview

3.2 Ontology for Self-organization of Resource Agents

Fig. 5 represents the developed ontology for self-organisation of agents in a CPSS. It is a middle-level ontology based on the upper ontology above. The concepts of the upper ontology are greyed. The concepts defined in the middle-level ontology are expected to be specified in particular application domains. The main concepts are described below.

Agent is used to represent CPSS' resources of both types: physical devices and humans. The agent is an acting unit of the multilevel self-organisation process. The agent has *structural knowledge*, *parametric knowledge*, and *profile*. The agent is characterized by such properties as self-organisation, self-management, autonomy, and proactiveness and performs some *activities in the community*.

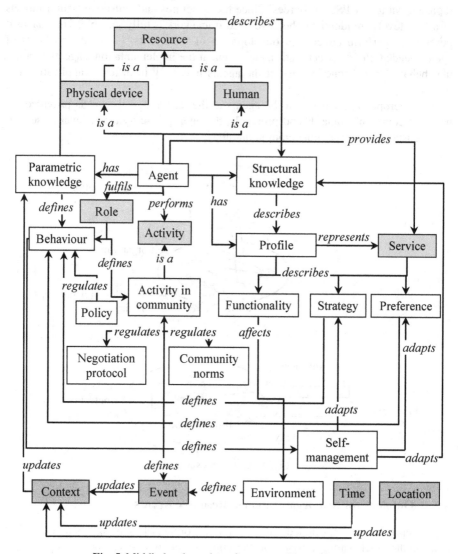

Fig. 5. Middle-level ontology for agent self-organisation

Structural Knowledge is a conceptual description of problems to be solved by the *agent*; the agent's internal *ontology* represents this kind of knowledge. The internal ontology harmonises with the common ontology. The structural knowledge describes the structure of the agent's *parametric knowledge* and the structure and the terminology of the agent's *context* and *profile*. Depending on the situation the structural knowledge can be modified (adapted) by the *self-management* capability.

Parametric knowledge is the knowledge about the actual situation. This knowledge is the structural knowledge filled with the information characterising this situation.

The agent's *context* is any information that can be used to characterize the situation of the agent. The context is purposed to represent only relevant information and knowledge from the large amount of those. Relevance of information and knowledge is evaluated on a basis how they are related to a modelling of an ad hoc problem. The context is represented by means of the agent's internal *ontology*. It is updated depending on the current *event, location*, and *time*. Information from the agent's *environment* and results of its *activity in the community* define *events* and vice-versa.

The context updates the agent's *parametric knowledge*, which in turn defines the agent's *behaviour* according to the agent's *role*. The presented approach exploits the idea of self-organisation to autonomously adapt *behaviours* of multiple agents to the situation in order to provide their *services* according to this context and to propose context-aware decisions.

The agent's *profile* is represented by means of the agent's internal *ontology* and in a way understandable by other agents of the CPSS. It represents the *services* this agent provides. The set of *services* defines the agent's *functionality*. *Functionality* is a set of cyber-physical-social functions the agent can perform. Via the *functionality* the agent can modify its *environment*. The agent's functionality can be modified in certain extent via the *self-management* capability.

As well, the agent's *profile* describes *preferences* and *strategies* of this agent. *Preference* is an agent's attitude towards a set of own and/or environmental states and/or against other states. The *preferences* affect the agent's *behaviour*. The agent can modify its *preferences* through *self-management*. *Strategy* is a pre-defined plan of actions rules of action selection to change the agent's own state and the state of the *environment* from the current to the preferred ones. The strategy defines the agent's *behaviour*. The agent can modify its strategy through *self-management*.

Environment is the surroundings of the CPSS the agent is a part of, which may interact with the CPSS. The environment produces events, which in turn affect the agent's *context*. The agent can affect the environment if it has appropriate *functionality* (e.g., a manipulator can change the location of a corresponding part).

Self-Management is an agent's capability achieved through its *behaviour* to modify (reconfigure) its internal *ontology, functionality, strategy*, and *preferences* in response to changes in the environment.

Behaviour is the agent's capability to perform certain actions (*activity in community* and/or *self-management*) in order to change the own state and the state of the *environment* from the current to the preferred ones. The *behaviour* is defined by the agent's *preferences* and *strategies*, as well as by the *policies* defined on a higher level of the self-organisation.

Policy is a set of principles and/or rules coming from a higher level of self-organisation to guide *behaviour* and achieve rational outcomes on a lower level of self-organisation.

Activity in community is a capability of the agent to communicate with other agents and negotiate with them through the agent's *behaviour*. It is regulated by the *negotiation protocol* and *community norms*.

Negotiation protocol is a set of basic rules so that when agents follow them, the system behaves as it supposed to. It defines the *activity in community* of the agents.

Community Norm is a law that governs the agent's *activity in community*. Unlike the negotiation protocol the community norms have certain degree of necessity ("it would be nice to follow a certain norm").

4   Case Study

The approach demonstration is based on the following scenario [21]: *You need to re-fuel the car (based on the automatic gas level identification) and have some rest and a dinner in a decent restaurant (based on the automatic fatigue level identification depending on how long you have been driving). Instead of finding a cheapest gas station, the system finds a gas station located near a restaurant, which has good feedback from its customers or belongs to the brand preferred by you.*

This solution consists of two actions (visiting a restaurant and refuelling the car) and involves three negotiating agents: restaurant advisor, gas station advisor [22] and planner (this agent, responsible for time keeping, is involved in almost any scenario in order to avoid solutions which would suggest driving too far away). Each of the three agents are assigned certain functions calculating degree of usefulness of their suggestions for the driver (e.g., visiting a café with average customer ratings has a lowest utility, visiting a nice restaurant with high customer ratings is estimated has a higher utility, and visiting the favourite driver's restaurant has the highest utility). The utility scale of the planner agent might depend on usual distances driven by the driver, his/her preferences and current schedule. The total utility of the solution depends on the contributions of each participating agent. The appropriate mathematical models are yet to be developed.

In order for such a mechanism to operate efficiently, it requires a continuous adjustment of the agent's utilities. This can be done through collecting information and knowledge from different sources. A taxonomy of sources can be found in [23, p. 369]. This taxonomy is matched against the middle-level ontology (Fig. 5). Among the sources, referred in the taxonomy, the following ones can be mentioned:

1. User feedback (the driver can increase or reduce the utility of a certain agent). This is a reliable information source; however, in real life it is very unlikely, that the driver will provide such feedback.

2. Initial driver profile (the driver can fill out the initial preferences in his/her profile). This is also a reliable information source but such information will be outdated after some time.

3. Analysis of driver decisions (the system can analyse if the driver followed the proposed solution, or which solution is preferred if several alternative solutions are presented to the driver). This is a less reliable information source, but such information

will never be outdated and development of learning algorithms can significantly improve such feedback.

4. Analysis of decisions of drivers with similar interests/habits. This source originates from the method of collaborative filtering used in group recommendation systems.

The resulting low-level ontology is not presented here because of its largeness.

The interaction between agents is presented in Fig. 6. It is based on usage of AppLink [24] for interaction with the vehicle. In addition to the information already stored in the agents (associated databases, user settings, revealed preferences, etc.), they acquire the following information from other agents, namely:

- Gas station advisor obtains current car location, gas level, and predefined driver preferences.
- Restaurant advisor obtains current car location and predefined driver preferences.
- Planner obtains driver's schedule from his/her smartphone and predefined driver preferences to estimate current time restrictions.

After that, the agents negotiate in order to generate one or several alternative solutions based on the driver requirements. During this negotiation, they can query available navigation system to estimate the driving time between different locations. Finally, the generated solutions are transferred to the AppLink screen so that the driver could choose the most appropriate one, and to the in-car navigation system.

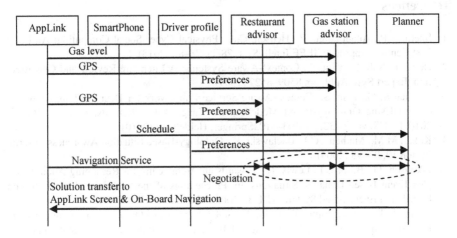

Fig. 6. Agent interaction example

5   Conclusion

The present research deals with a new research field of CPSSs. In the research, a CPSS is considered consisting of sets of resources representing cyber, physical, and mental spaces. The paper presents the upper ontology for CPSSs and its application for self-organization of CPSS' resources.

The main concepts of the upper ontology show their share ability in the application area. The concept "resource" distinguishing two types of resources (physical devices and humans) indicated that there is no necessity in this division. In the application domain the two resource types were merged into one concept. That is, humans are full members of the CPSSs. Sometimes they fulfil role of resources in providing information, knowledge, services, etc. Another time they are users of the CPSSs in consuming information, knowledge, services, etc.

The ideas behind the research were verified in the area of proactive recommendation systems. So far, small number of resources participated in the negotiation to self-organise. Further, the number of resources is planned to be enlarged to become closer to real-worlds systems.

Acknowledgements. The present research was partly supported by the Project 213 (the research program "Information, control, and intelligent technologies & systems" of the Russian Academy of Sciences (RAS)), grant 074-U01 (the Government of the Russian Federation), and grant KA322 «Development of cross-border e-tourism framework for the programme region (Smart e-Tourism)» (Karelia ENPI programme, which is co-funded by the European Union, the Russian Federation and the Republic of Finland).

References

1. Sheth, A.P., Anantharam, P., Henson, C.A.: Physical-Cyber-Social Computing: An Early 21st Century Approach. IEEE Intell. Syst. 28(1), 78–82 (2013)
2. Hong, J., Suh, E., Kim, S.: Context-Aware Systems: A Literature Review and Classification. Expert Syst. Appl. 36, 8509–8522 (2009)
3. Cagalaban, G., Kim, S.: Context-Aware Service Framework for Decision-Support Applications Using Ontology-Based Modeling. In: Kang, B.-H., Richards, D. (eds.) PKAW 2010. LNCS, vol. 6232, pp. 103–110. Springer, Heidelberg (2010)
4. Kokar, M.M., Matheus, C.J., Baclawski, K.: Ontology-Based Situation Awareness. Inform. Fusion 10, 83–98 (2009)
5. Jakobson, G., Buford, J., Lewis, L.: Towards an Architecture for Reasoning About Complex Event-Based Dynamic Situations. In: Proceedings of the International Workshop on Distributed Event-based Systems (DEBS 2004), Edinburgh, UK (2004)
6. Chen, H., Perich, F., Finin, T., Joshi, A.: SOUPA: Standard Ontology for Ubiquitous and Pervasive Application. In: Proceedings of International Conference on Mobile and Ubiquitous Systems: Networking and Services, Boston, August 22-25, pp. 258–267 (2004)
7. Wang, X.H., Gu, T., Zhang, D.Q., Pung H.K.: Ontology Based Context Modeling and Reasoning Using OWL. In: Proceedings of the 2nd IEEE Conference on Pervasive Computing and Communications, Workshop on Context Modeling and Reasoning. IEEE CS Press, pp. 18–22 (2004)
8. Heckmann, D., Schwartz, T., Brandherm, B., Schmitz, M., von Wilamowitz-Moellendorff, M.: GUMO – the general user model ontology. In: Ardissono, L., Brna, P., Mitrović, A. (eds.) UM 2005. LNCS (LNAI), vol. 3538, pp. 428–432. Springer, Heidelberg (2005)

9. Massacci, F., Mylopoulos, J., Zannone, N.: An Ontology for Secure Socio-Technical Systems. In: Rittgen, P. (ed.) Handbook of Ontologies for Business Interaction, pp. 188–206. Information Science Reference, Hershey (2008)

10. Porello, D., Setti, F., Ferrario, R., Cristani, M.: Multiagent Socio-Technical Systems. An Ontological Approach. In: Balke, T., Dignum, F., van Riemsdijk, M.B., Chopra, A.K. (eds.) COIN 2013. LNCS (LNAI), vol. 8386, pp. 42–62. Springer, Heidelberg (2013)

11. van Dam, K.H., Nikolic, I., Lukszo, Z. (eds.): Agent-Based Modelling of Socio-Technical Systems. Agent-Based Social Systems, vol. 9. Springer, Netherlands (2013)

12. Zimmermann, A., Lorenz, A., Oppermann, R.: An Operational Definition of Context. In: Kokinov, B., Richardson, D.C., Roth-Berghofer, T.R., Vieu, L. (eds.) CONTEXT 2007. LNCS (LNAI), vol. 4635, pp. 558–571. Springer, Heidelberg (2007)

13. Liu, Z., Yang, D.-S., Wen, D., Zhang, W.-M., Mao, W.: Cyber-Physical-Social Systems for Command and Control. IEEE Intell. Syst., 92–96 (July/August 2011)

14. Hofkirchner, W.: Emergence and the Logic of Explanation. In: An Argument for the Unity of Science. Acta Polytechnica Scandinavica. Mathematics, Computing and Management in Engineering Series, vol. 91, pp. 23–30 (1998)

15. F.C.: Globalization and Self-Organization in the Knowledge-Based Society. TripleC http://triplec.uti.at 1(2), 105–169 (2003)

16. Hackman, J.R.: The Design of Work Teams. In: Lorch, J.W. (ed.) Handbook of Organizational Behavior. Prentice Hall, Upper Saddle River (1987)

17. Ambient Networks Phase 2. Integrated Design for Context, Network and Policy Management, Deliverable D10.-D1 (2006), http://www.ambient-networks.org/Files/deliverables/D10-D.1_PU.pdf (retrieved from May 16, 2014)

18. Smirnov, A., Sandkuhl, K., Shilov, N.: Multilevel Self-Organisation of Cyber-Physical Networks: Synergic Approach. Int. J. Integrated Supply Management 8(1/2/3), 90–106 (2013)

19. Jantsch, E.: Design for Evolution. George Braziller, New York (1975)

20. Meulpolder, M., Pouwelse, J.A., Epema, D.H.J., Sips, H.J.: BarterCast: A practical approach to prevent lazy freeriding in P2P networks. In: IEEE International Symposium on Parallel & Distributed Processing (2009), doi:10.1109/IPDPS.2009.5160954

21. Smirnov, A., Shilov, N., Makklya, A., Gusikhin, O.: Context-Based Service Fusion for Personalized On-Board Information Support. In: 18th International Forum on Advanced Microsystems for Automotive Applications (AMAA 2014) "Smart Systems for Safe, Clean, and Automated Vehicles", Berlin, Germany, June 23-24 (accepted for publication in 2014)

22. Klampfl, E., Gusikhin, O., Theisen, K., Liu, Y., Giuli, T.J.: Intelligent Refueling Advisory System. In: Proceedings of 2nd Workshop on Intelligent Vehicle Control Systems, Madeira, Portugal, pp. 60–72 (2008)

23. Burke, R., Ramezani, M.: Matching Recommendation Technologies and Domains. In: Ricci, F., Rokach, L., Shapira, B., Kantor, P.B. (eds.) Recommender Systems Handbook. Springer (2011)

24. SYNC AppLink Overview, http://support.ford.com/sync-technology/applink-overview-sync (accessed May 16, 2014)

Words Worth Attention: Predicting Words of the Week on the Russian Wiktionary

Dmitry Ustalov[1,2,3]

[1] Krasovsky Institute of Mathematics and Mechanics, Ekaterinburg, Russia
[2] Ural Federal University, Ekaterinburg, Russia
[3] NLPub, Ekaterinburg, Russia
dau@imm.uran.ru

Abstract. Such collaborative lexicography projects as Wiktionary are becoming strong competitors for traditional semantic resources just as Wikipedia has already become for expert-built knowledge bases. Keeping the data obtained from the general public crowd in good quality is a very challenging problem because of the fuzzy nature of the crowdsourcing phenomena. The presented study focuses on predicting the *word of the week* articles on the Russian Wiktionary by treating this problem as a binary classification task. The best proposed model is based on the Naïve Bayes classifier and has weighted average precision, recall, and F_1-measure values of 87% by evaluating on the provided dataset.

Keywords: Russian Wiktionary, semantic resources, word of the week, quality assessment.

1 Introduction

A significant problem of the Semantic Web is the lack of the data which can be used in the applications as queries have become useless. One way of approaching this problem is to convert existent resources into such Semantic Web formats as RDF and OWL. But what if these resources are produced by the crowd, presented in unstructured form and need to be pre-processed even before conversion?

A thesaurus is a crucial component of many natural language processing and knowledge engineering applications. Although it is well known how to transform a regular thesaurus into the SKOS format [2], this thesaurus must be of a good quality. For instance, Wiktionary—a crowdsourced thesaurus—is considered today as a rival for expert-built lexicons [10] and there is an approach of transforming the Russian one[1] into a relational database [8]. It is necessary to maintain the Wiktionary quality to make it possible to be used in the real Semantic Web applications. Indeed, assessing the quality of the Russian Wiktionary is a challenging yet important topic because of the fuzzy nature of the crowdsourcing phenomena.

---

[1] http://ru.wiktionary.org/

P. Klinov and D. Mouromtsev (Eds.): KESW 2014, CCIS 468, pp. 196–207, 2014.

This paper is organized as follows. Section 2 focuses on related work on Wikipedia and its quality assessment studies. Section 3 briefly describes the Russian Wiktionary and its individual qualities. Section 4 presents the quality assessment model for the Russian Wiktionary to be applied in the classification task. Section 5 describes the created dataset to be used during the evaluation task. Section 6 is concerned on evaluating the proposed model on several popular classification algorithms. Section 7 discusses and interprets the obtained results. Section 8 concludes with final remarks and directions for the future work.

2 Related Work

The English Wikipedia quality is being thoroughly studied because of it being the largest and the most developed Wikipedia containing more than 4 500 000 articles. Many works propose sophisticated quality assessment approaches based either on regression or classification tasks with various tricky features including readability measures, article structure properties, linguistic observations, collaborative evidences, etc.

An early study of Wikipedia and its quality was performed by Wilkinson & Huberman [13], who found a statistically significant correlation between page edits, talkpage conversations and the quality of these pages. Another study of Wikipedia's quality and its dependency on author's authority was conducted by Hu et al. [6], who proposed a PROBREVIEW model which represents contributors and their reviewing behaviour. Also a NAÏVE model based on article word count was proposed and demonstrated similar performance on large sets of articles.

One of the most cited papers in this field is the study conducted by Kittur & Kraut [7] in which the influence of number and concentration of editors to article quality was found. The more editors are concentrated on the article, the higher quality can be achieved.

A quantitative study of Wikipedia articles and workflow was performed by Stvilia et al. [12] in which several issues of Wikipedia articles were discussed and the descriptive statistics of the information quality problems found in featured articles were demonstrated.

One approach seems to be slightly amusing to think of, yet proves to be very effective to identify high quality articles in Wikipedia. This is a binary classification by word count proposed by Blumenstock [3]. The mentioned approach treats all pages having less than 2 000 words as non-featured and more than 2 000 words as featured.

A major study of Wikipedia quality conducted by Dalip et al. [5] proposes a lot of informative features which can be used in a support vector machine-based regression method. Some of these features including readability measures can be applied for the English language only.

De la Calzada et al. [4] conducted another study on Wikipedia article quality with strong focus on separating articles into "stabilized" and "controversial" categories; this author presents special-purpose models for both categories.

A study by Arazy & Nov [1] continues the study by Kitter & Kraut and gives special attention to an editor's Wikipedia-wide global activity and his article-specific local activity, and found that global inequality has more significant impact on article quality.

One very interesting study is dedicated to the Thai Wikipedia [11]. The paper in question has become one of the significant reasons for conducting the present research due to the proposed framework. The Thai Wikipedia has less than 100 000 articles[2] written by more than 200 000 users (only 1 000 of those are active). As it will be shown in the next section, the Russian Wiktionary is quite similar to the Thai Wikipedia in terms of its size.

Despite of many studies of Wikipedia being available, it is problematic to apply their approaches to Wiktionary—especially the Russian Wiktionary—since it is less developed, has sufficiently strict article structure, and the Russian language behaves differently from English on such natural language processing tasks as readability estimation.

3   The Russian Wiktionary

The Russian Wiktionary is the 8th largest Wiktionary composed of more than 520 000 articles—one article represents a word—written by more than 120 000 users (only 164 users are active participants) since 2004.

Every article in the Russian Wiktionary is written in the Russian language and is laid out using a convenient word page template with predefined structure. Despite the Russian Wiktionary being not a true Linked Data resource, its content is (semi-)structured and allows one to easily parse it into a machine-readable thesaurus [8] that can be transformed into SKOS [2] or other formats.

Communities behind many popular Wiki resources often maintain lists of featured articles, good articles, high quality articles and the like. These articles are selected collectively by the majority vote of Wiki's administrators and moderators, and such an article should conform to a set of formal quality standards.

Unfortunately, the English Wiktionary along with the Russian Wiktionary are not engaged in such an activity as article promotion. For instance, the Russian Wiktionary has only one featured article on the word *water*. The reason for this is that in Wikipedia a featured article status may be assigned to thank its author for a hard yet productive work. In the Russian Wiktionary does not have such resources and available work force. Generally, Wiktionaries including the Russian one use a slightly different concept called *word of the day* and in addition to it the latter uses a concept called *word of the week*.

The first one, *word of the day* is a special label for an article that makes the labeled article appear on the main page of the Wiktionary on the specified day. It does not necessary mean that the article is good or of a high quality—these articles are often incomplete—but it is designed to concentrate the community efforts on the specified word instead.

The second one, *word of the week* is a currently inactive project, aimed at annotating various prominent articles of higher-than-average quality in order to provide other community members with examples. This study is concerned with

---

using these *words of the week* to assess the quality of the Russian Wiktionary pages. The *word of the week* project was being run from 2007 to 2012.

4 The Model

This study treats the quality assessment problem as a binary classification task. Specifically, an article is to be classified into one of two classes: one class represents *featured* article and another one represents ¬*featured* article. This notation will be used in this paper to denote these class labels.

4.1 Features

The model will be initially composed of thirteen simple features arranged into three groups (CONTENT, LINGUISTIC and REVISION features) and of a class label (*featured* or ¬*featured*). Some features are derived from the related studies in which those have been found useful.

CONTENT features are the features that implicitly or explicitly represent some parts of an article's content. There are five of those.

CharacterCount $\in \mathbb{Z}$ is a number of all characters in an article including wiki markup and spaces [5].
WordCount $\in \mathbb{Z}$ is a number of words in the text [3,5].
InterwikiLinks $\in \mathbb{Z}$ is a number of interwiki links to other Wiktionary pages [5,11].
Links $\in \mathbb{Z}$ is a number of links to external websites [5,11].
Pictures $\in \mathbb{Z}$ is a number of pictures embedded into an article [5,11].

LINGUISTIC features represent Wiktionary-specific article aspects that reflect various properties of a particular word. There are six of those.

Frequency $\in \mathbb{R}$ is a relative word frequency obtained from the Russian National Corpus [9]. In case of morphological homonymy and when a word has several possible part-of-speech tags, their frequencies are summed up for a given word.
Definitions $\in \mathbb{Z}$ is a number of Wiktionary definitions of a word. The intuition behind this and the following four features is like this: the more linguistic data a word has been provided with, the better the article is.
Synonyms $\in \mathbb{Z}$ is a number of provided quasi-synonyms of a word.
Antonyms $\in \mathbb{Z}$ is a number of provided antonyms of a word.
Hypernyms $\in \mathbb{Z}$ is a number of provided hypernyms of a word.
Hyponyms $\in \mathbb{Z}$ is a number of provided hyponyms of a word.

REVISION features represent editor activity on the article since many studies confirm that revision-based features have a strong correlation with article quality. There are only two of those.

Revisions $\in \mathbb{Z}$ is a number of an article revisions [6,7,5].
Protection $\in \{true, false\}$ is a status of edit protection of an article representing whether an article is blocked from anonymous edits or not.

Densities of all the continuous features' distributions are skewed at Fig. 1.

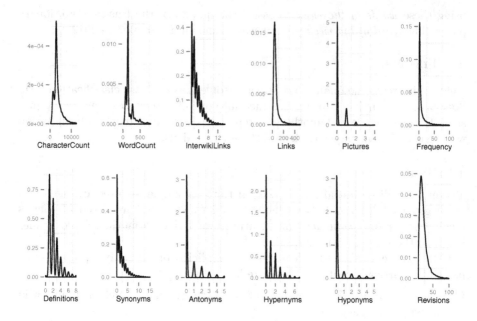

Fig. 1. Densities for all the proposed continuous features

4.2 Discretization

Such features as *CharacterCount, Frequency, Revisions*, etc are represented by continuous values. Before applying classification algorithms it is crucial to discretize these features and transform them from the ratio and interval scales into the nominal or ordinal scales. This has been done manually by considering the features' densities and splitting them into discrete groups according to Fig. 1. The splits are presented in the set-builder notation (Table 1).

5 The Dataset

In order to create a dataset for this study a set of words provided with the Russian National Corpus frequencies [9] and the Wiktionary *words of the week* have been chosen to be included into the dataset, which contained 20 385 different words. The correspondent Russian Wiktionary pages have been obtained with such metadata as revision information, interwiki & external links information, etc. For each page only the Russian section has been considered. Then, each word was mapped into a set of features. After that a dataset containing 20 385 feature vectors was saved into a comma-separated values file.

Since the class distribution in the dataset is highly imbalanced (294 *featured* and 20 091 ¬*featured* words) the resulting dataset was additionally split into ten smaller datasets. Each of those includes the same set of 294 *featured* and a

Table 1. Discretization of the continuous features

Group	Feature	Levels		
CONTENT	CharacterCount	$low \in [0, 2000]$,	$medium \in]2000, 7000]$,	$high \in]7000, +\infty[$
	WordCount	$low \in [0, 200]$,	$medium \in]200, 400]$,	$high \in]400, +\infty[$
	InterwikiLinks	$low \in [0, 5]$,	$medium \in]5, 10]$,	$high \in]10, +\infty[$
	Links	$low \in [0, 100]$,	$medium \in]100, 200]$,	$high \in]200, +\infty[$
	Pictures	$zero \in [0, 1[$,	$one \in [1, 2[$,	$many \in [2, +\infty[$
LINGUISTIC	Frequency	$low \in [0, 50]$,	$medium \in]50, 400]$,	$high \in]400, +\infty[$
	Definitions	$low \in [0, 5]$,	$medium \in]5, 10]$,	$high \in]10, +\infty[$
	Synonyms	$low \in [0, 5]$,	$medium \in]5, 10]$,	$high \in]10, +\infty[$
	Antonyms	$zero \in [0, 1[$,	$many \in]1, +\infty[$	
	Hypernyms	$zero \in [0, 1[$,	$low \in]1, 5]$,	$high \in]5, +\infty[$
	Hyponyms	$zero \in [0, 1[$,	$low \in]1, 10]$,	$high \in]10, +\infty[$
REVISION	Revisions	$low \in [0, 50]$,	$medium \in]50, 100]$,	$high \in]100, +\infty[$

random sample of ¬*featured* articles, the number of which is four times greater than that of the *featured* ones. Thus, each of these smaller datasets is composed of *featured* articles by 20% and of ¬*featured* by 80%.

6 Evaluation

The model will be evaluated by using 10-fold cross-validation on all of the ten datasets with ten repetitions, the obtained results are properly combined and the best evaluated model is expected to maximize the weighted average F_1-measure which is computed as

$$\mathrm{wF_1} = \frac{\sum_{c \in C} \mathrm{F_1}(c) \cdot |c|}{\sum_{c \in C} |c|},$$

where C is a set of class labels and $F_1(c)$ denotes a computed F_1-measure for the particular class label c. It may be useful to note that such values as weighted average precision and recall are computed similarly w.r.t. the correspondent terms. During the evaluation assigning the ¬*featured* label to a *featured* article is treated as a type I error.

The following classification algorithms were involved in the evaluation process: "zero rule", "one-attribute-rule", Naïve Bayes, logistic regression, support vector machine, C4.5, random forest. All of these algorithms are implemented in and evaluated using the Weka 3.6.11 machine learning software[3] running on a 64-bit GNU/Linux system with Oracle® Java® 7u51 and 16 GB of RAM.

6.1 Classifiers

ZeroR. The "zero rule" algorithm selects the majority class in the dataset and uses that to make all the predictions. Since the provided dataset is composed of *featured* words by 20% and of ¬*featured* words by 80%, the classifier will always assign ¬*featured* class to any given word in this study.

---

[3] http://www.cs.waikato.ac.nz/ml/weka/

OneR. The idea of the "one-attribute-rule" association rules algorithm is to find the only attribute to use that makes the fewest prediction errors. In this study, the *OneR* algorithm has selected *Revisions* as such an attribute (Table 4).

NaïveB. The Naïve Bayes algorithm is an application of the Bayes' theorem that performs very well on document categorization tasks. In this study, the classifier uses a maximum *a posteriori* probability estimate. Since all the features are nominal and are already discretized, no additional feature processing is required.

LogReg. Logistic regression is a binary classifier which then measures the relationship between a categorical dependent variable and one or more independent features. Early experiments on logistic regression with the same but undiscretized continuous features showed that discretized nominal features perform better on this dataset.

SVM. The sequential minimal optimization algorithm for training a support vector classifier with radial basis function kernel and $c = 1$ was also evaluated in this study.

C4.5. C4.5 is a decision tree algorithm that builds decision trees from a set of training data using the concept of information entropy. The pruned *J48* implementation of the algorithm has been used in this study.

RForest. Random forest is an ensemble learning method that constructs a forest of random trees and assigns classes by majority vote of these trees. In this study the algorithm was executed with ten trees.

6.2   Performance on the *Featured* Class

Table 2 presents the evaluation results obtained using 10-fold cross-validation and the confusion matrix for the *featured* class treated as a positive class.

The **SVM** classifier has statistically significantly outperformed all other classifiers on precision except **OneR** and **LogReg** as according to the corrected paired two-tailed *t-test* with the significance level of .05. **OneR** and **LogReg** classifiers have approximately the same precision as the **SVM** classifier.

The **NaïveB** classifier has outperformed all other classifiers on recall as according to the corrected paired two-tailed *t-test* with the significance level of .05. Other classifiers have approximately the same recall except the **ZeroR** classifier which treated any article as ¬*featured* and therefore has recognized no *featured* articles.

NaïveB has also statistically significantly outperformed all other classifiers on F_1-measure as according to the corrected paired two-tailed *t-test* with the significance level of .05. However, its precision is statistically significantly worse than **OneR**, **LogReg** and **SVM** as according to the corrected paired two-tailed *t-test* with the significance level of .05. The **C4.5** and **RForest** classifiers have approximately the same precision as the **NaïveB** classifier.

Table 2. True positive and negative, false positive and negative rates, precision, recall and F_1-measure for the *featured* class treated as a positive class (numbers in parentheses represent standard deviations of the correspondent values)

	ZeroR	OneR	NaïveB	LogReg	SVM	C4.5	RForest
TPR	.00(.00)	.45(.10)	.67(.09)	.54(.09)	.47(.09)	.52(.09)	.55(.09)
TNR	1.0(.00)	.96(.02)	.92(.03)	.95(.02)	.97(.02)	.94(.02)	.92(.03)
FPR	.00(.00)	.04(.02)	.08(.03)	.05(.02)	.03(.02)	.06(.02)	.08(.03)
FNR	1.0(.00)	.55(.10)	.33(.09)	.46(.09)	.53(.09)	.48(.09)	.45(.09)
precision	.00(.00)	.74(.10)	.67(.08)	.73(.09)	.78(.09)	.70(.09)	.64(.08)
recall	.00(.00)	.45(.10)	.67(.09)	.54(.09)	.47(.09)	.52(.09)	.55(.09)
F_1-measure	.00(.00)	.55(.09)	.66(.07)	.62(.08)	.58(.09)	.59(.07)	.57(.08)

6.3   Overall Performance

Overall performance of the evaluated algorithms is shown in Table 3. Weighted average values show how well a classifier performs both in identifying *featured* instances and also in identifying ¬*featured* examples.

The **NaïveB** classifier has outperformed **ZeroR**, **OneR** and **RForest** on weighted average precision as according to the corrected paired two-tailed *t-test* with the significance level of .05. However, **LogReg**, **SVM** and **C4.5** classifiers have approximately the same weighted average precision as **NaïveB**.

SVM has performed better than **ZeroR**, **OneR** and **RForest** on weighted average recall as according to the corrected paired two-tailed *t-test* with the significance level of .05. However, **NaïveB**, **LogReg** and **C4.5** have approximately the same weighted average recall as the **SVM** classifier.

Finally, **NaïveB**, **LogReg**, **SVM** and **C4.5** have approximately the same weighted average F_1-measure as according to the corrected paired two-tailed *t-test* with the significance level of .05. The rest of classifiers have performed statistically significantly worse.

Table 3. Accuracy, area under the ROC curve, weighted average precision, recall and F_1-measure (numbers in parentheses represent standard deviations of the correspondent values)

	ZeroR	OneR	NaïveB	LogReg	SVM	C4.5	RForest
accuracy	.80(.00)	.86(.02)	.87(.03)	.87(.02)	.87(.02)	.86(.02)	.84(.03)
AUC	.50(.00)	.70(.05)	.90(.03)	.90(.03)	.72(.05)	.78(.05)	.84(.04)
precision	.64(.01)	.85(.03)	.87(.03)	.86(.03)	.86(.03)	.85(.03)	.84(.03)
recall	.80(.00)	.86(.02)	.87(.03)	.87(.02)	.87(.02)	.86(.02)	.85(.03)
F_1-measure	.71(.00)	.84(.03)	.87(.03)	.86(.03)	.85(.03)	.85(.03)	.84(.03)

7   Discussion

According to the obtained results it seems that **NaïveB** tends to assign the *featured* label to given examples and the rest of classifiers tend to classify examples into the ¬*featured* class instead. This can also be confirmed by considering the values of true positive and false positive rates in Table 2. Since it is necessary to maximize the weighted average F_1-measure when preserving high positive rate, it is assumed that the Naïve Bayes classifier provides the best output.

7.1 Quality of the Training Set

The main problem of the dataset is the training set quality because there is the lack of *featured* training examples. Classifiers may perform better if more features can be induced from the data and magnitudes of the training and the test sets will be the same. The *word of the week* was shut down in 2012 and additional human expert-produced annotations might be very useful.

7.2 Does Size Matter?

Table 4. Features ranked by information gain and "one-attribute-rule" on a complete dataset with discretized features using 10-fold cross-validation (numbers in parentheses represent standard deviations of the correspondent values)

Group	Feature	InfoGain	OneR
CONTENT	CharacterCount	.117(.005)	83.401(.267)
	WordCount	.122(.004)	80.514(.477)
	InterwikiLinks	.143(.006)	81.837(.733)
	Links	.117(.005)	81.769(.248)
	Pictures	.082(.004)	82.109(.297)
LINGUISTIC	Frequency	.072(.003)	81.565(.157)
	Definitions	.065(.005)	80.748(.391)
	Synonyms	.057(.004)	80.952(.159)
	Antonyms	.021(.002)	80.000(.037)
	Hypernyms	.064(.004)	81.429(.209)
	Hyponyms	.060(.005)	80.616(.121)
REVISION	Revisions	.146(.006)	85.850(.248)
	Protection	.009(.001)	80.000(.037)

Table 5. F_1-measure values for the *featured* class when only one feature is used (numbers in parentheses represent standard deviations of the correspondent values)

	ZeroR	OneR	NaïveB	LogReg	C4.5	RForest
CharacterCount	.00(.00)	.51(.09)	.42(.10)	.41(.10)	.53(.11)	.47(.08)
WordCount	.00(.00)	.39(.09)	.32(.10)	.26(.10)	.49(.10)	.39(.08)
Revisions	.00(.00)	.56(.08)	.51(.09)	.52(.09)	.55(.10)	.51(.09)

According to high rank of the **CharacterCount** (computing using the information gain measure) and **Revision** (computed by both **OneR** and information gain measures) features in Table 4, another study has been conducted using each of those continuous values as the only feature to classify the examples. The **WordCount** feature was also evaluated in a similar manner in order to compare the results with the similar study [3]. The results are provided in Table 5. The **SVM** method was not used due to inacceptable execution time on these models.

On the one hand, it seems that the Russian Wiktionary articles have similar sizes and the sole use of such length-based features as **CharacterCount** or **WordCount** can not produce good result. On the other hand, the sole use of the **Revisions** feature results into the same outcome. It seems to be a better decision to toss a coin with 50% probability instead of using these three models.

7.3 "It Was on the Front Page Before It Was Featured"

In order to ensure that the possibility of article attributes of the featured articles represent the state of these articles before having been featured (i.e. before the article has been exhibited on the front page of the Wiktionary) is excluded, another evaluation has been performed using *words of the day* combined with *words of the week* in the same way as it was conducted above. All these *words of the day* as well as the *words of the week* appeared at least once on the front page. In this case the dataset consisted of 1 866 *featured* words and 18 518 ¬*featured* words.

As a result, **LogReg** has the highest precision of .63(.04) and **NaïveB** has shown both the highest recall and F_1-measure of .44(.04) and of .48(.03) correspondingly. This means that *words of the day* behave noticably worse than *words of the week* presented in Table 3 and predicting the "featuredness" of an article based on attributes that already exclude the effect of being featured is a kind of circular argument.

8 Conclusion

The best proposed model is based on the Naïve Bayes classifier and has weighted average precision, recall, and F_1-measure values of 87% by evaluating on the provided dataset. Future work may be concerned with the following directions:

1. extending the number of REVISION features because such features may significantly improve the model [13,6,7,1],
2. providing the less skewed dataset may increase the performance of the present model,
3. performing the full-scale test in the field may be useful in revealing the real qualities of the model,
4. investigating the patterns of two or three features may result in much simpler model despite of slightly decreased performance,
5. evaluating on simpler and more interpretable algorithms (e.g. hierarchical regression) than such algorithms as **SVM**, **RForest** and other ones. This will allow the investigator to "learn" from the data as well.

The presented dataset and the supplementary scripts are available[4] under Creative Commons Attribution-ShareAlike 3.0 and MIT licenses, respectively. These scripts are implemented in the Ruby programming language without external dependencies.

Acknowledgements. This work is supported by the Russian Foundation for the Humanities, project 13-04-12020 "New Open Electronic Thesaurus for Russian". The author would like to thank Andrew Krizhanovsky for fruitful discussions and valuable suggestions. The author is also grateful to the anonymous referees who offered very useful comments on the present paper.

References

1. Arazy, O., Nov, O.: Determinants of Wikipedia Quality: The Roles of Global and Local Contribution Inequality. In: Proceedings of the 2010 ACM Conference on Computer Supported Cooperative Work, pp. 233–236. ACM (2010)
2. van Assem, M., Malaisé, V., Miles, A., Schreiber, G.: A Method to Convert Thesauri to SKOS. In: Sure, Y., Domingue, J. (eds.) ESWC 2006. LNCS, vol. 4011, pp. 95–109. Springer, Heidelberg (2006)
3. Blumenstock, J.E.: Size Matters: Word Count as a Measure of Quality on Wikipedia. In: Proceedings of the 17th International Conference on World Wide Web, pp. 1095–1096. ACM (2008)
4. De la Calzada, G., Dekhtyar, A.: On Measuring the Quality of Wikipedia Articles. In: Proceedings of the 4th Workshop on Information Credibility, pp. 11–18. ACM (2010)
5. Dalip, D.H., Gonçalves, A.M., Cristo, M., Calado, P.: Automatic Quality Assessment of Content Created Collaboratively by Web Communities: A Case Study of Wikipedia. In: Proceedings of the 9th ACM/IEEE-CS Joint Conference on Digital Libraries, pp. 295–304. ACM (2009)
6. Hu, M., Lim, E.P., Sun, A., Lauw, H.W., Vuong, B.Q.: Measuring Article Quality in Wikipedia: Models and Evaluation. In: Proceedings of the Sixteenth ACM Conference on Conference on Information and Knowledge Management, pp. 243–252. ACM (2007)
7. Kittur, A., Kraut, R.E.: Harnessing the Wisdom of Crowds in Wikipedia: Quality Through Coordination. In: Proceedings of the 2008 ACM Conference on Computer Supported Cooperative Work, pp. 37–46. ACM (2008)
8. Krizhanovsky, A., Smirnov, A.: An approach to automated construction of a general-purpose lexical ontology based on Wiktionary. Journal of Computer and Systems Sciences International 52(2), 215–225 (2013)
9. Lyashevskaya, O., Sharov, S.: The frequency dictionary of modern Russian language. Azbukovnik, Moscow (2009)
10. Meyer, C.M., Gurevych, I.: Wiktionary: A new rival for expert-built lexicons? Exploring the possibilities of collaborative lexicography. Electronic Lexicography, 259–291 (2012)

---

[4] http://ustalov.imm.uran.ru/pub/ruwiktionary-skewed.tar.gz

11. Saengthongpattana, K., Soonthornphisaj, N.: Assessing the Quality of Thai Wikipedia Articles Using Concept and Statistical Features. In: Rocha, Á., Correia, A.M., Tan, F., Stroetmann, K. (eds.) New Perspectives in Information Systems and Technologies, Volume 1. AISC, vol. 275, pp. 513–523. Springer, Heidelberg (2014)
12. Stvilia, B., Twidale, M.B., Smith, L.C., Gasser, L.: Information Quality Work Organization in Wikipedia. Journal of the American Society for Information Science and Technology 59(6), 983–1001 (2008)
13. Wilkinson, D.M., Huberman, B.A.: Cooperation and Quality in Wikipedia. In: Proceedings of the 2007 International Symposium on Wikis, pp. 157–164. ACM (2007)

Deriving of Thematic Facts from Unstructured Texts and Background Knowledge

Nataliya Yelagina and Michail Panteleyev

Saint-Petersburg State Electrotechnical University "LETI", Russia
{natyelagin,mpanteleyev}@gmail.com

Abstract. When developing information-analytical systems (IAS) for various purposes it is often necessary to gather *thematic facts* which are of interest to experts in the field. The paper presents an approach that allows one to increase the completeness of fact extraction by using basic domain knowledge. The main idea of the approach is deriving new facts on the basis of facts explicitly stated in the text and basic knowledge contained in the corresponding ontologies. An architecture and algorithms of the system are discussed. The approach is illustrated by an example of extracting relevant facts using inference rules.

1   Introduction

The Internet and corporate databases store huge amount of unstructured documents. Therefore the problem of automated extraction of relevant information from these documents is attracting the attention of many researchers in the field of Text Mining and Information Extraction. In these areas a lot of approaches and techniques have been proposed many of which are specifically tailored to particular problems that they are meant to address [1].

When developing IAS for decision making support the experts are interested in getting facts characterizing various aspects of the analyzed objects. However, relevant facts are not always mentioned in the analyzed texts explicitly. These facts in some cases can be inferred from the facts contained in the texts and some basic knowledge. This paper presents the approach to solving this task. The paper is organized as follows. Section 2 provides an overview of related work. Section 3 explains the proposed approach and basic models. Section 4 presents the algorithms of the FactE system implementing the approach. In Section 5 implementation details of FactE system prototype are presented. In Section 6 some preliminary experimental results is discussed. Finally, the conclusion discusses the possible directions for improving the system.

2   Related Work

Fact extraction from unstructured text is currently the subject of many works. Some of them have the objective to solve the general task of information extraction while others aim at extracting facts of a more complex structure. Several approaches to fact extraction are known; the ontology-based one is considered in

P. Klinov and D. Mouromtsev (Eds.): KESW 2014, CCIS 468, pp. 208–218, 2014.

this paper. The fundamental work [2] reveals the state-of-the-art of this subfield of information extraction and presents the corresponding systems.

Paper [3] considers the task of extracting facts as RDF-triples by identifying specific instances of the ontology in sentences of the text, and composing RDF-triples, replenishing the ontology. The approach to the problem is based on extracting each of the triple elements by searching the corresponding parse tree. The paper presents the Onto-Text system implementing the approach.

The SOBA system [4] is able to automatically create a knowledge base while analyzing texts. The system allows to process documents from heterogeneous sources – text, tables, and image captions. SOBA includes a webcrawler which allows to find new sources on the subject, linguistic annotation module and mapping module that allows to project the information found in the sources on the ontology elements. Text processing is guided by extraction rules.

Most existing ontology-based information extraction (OBIE) systems allow to identify knowledge, explicitly mentioned in text, by using ontological knowledge while analyzing the documents. In addition to the broad descriptive features ontologies also have the advanced features of inferring knowledge. Some systems actively use reasoning as a partial replacement to the traditional techniques of extracting information. BOEMIE [5], for instance, is a generic content analysis system processing texts, video, audio inputs, etc. Inference in BOEMIE is based on automatically acquired rules that operate information extracted from the source. This system only uses knowledge, explicitly mentioned in the text.

Use and expansion of the accumulated knowledge ontology is implemented in SOFIE system [6]. This system is capable of reasoning upon accumulated knowledge, as well as the knowledge acquired while processing text, to test hypotheses and define semantics of words and phrases more precisely. The hypotheses that were confirmed extend SOFIE's ontology, and the system receives new extraction templates (linguistic rules), which further can be used for information extraction.

This paper presents a system that implements an ontological approach to extracting facts from text. Unlike existing systems, which target mainly extraction of the desired category of facts mentioned explicitly in the text of the analyzed document, this system allows obtaining new facts not stated in the text explicitly. The proposed approach improves the completeness of fact extraction due to: (1) use of ontologies to extract facts from the text and (2) deriving the facts not mentioned in the texts. The inference of implicit facts is based on the facts acquired in text analysis and the basic knowledge of the ontology.

3   The Approach and Basic Models

Under a *thematic fact* (TF) we understand an assertion characterizing some entity S (the subject of the fact) in a certain aspect. The aspect, in which the subject of the fact is characterized, defines the base relation R connecting S to another entity O (the object of the fact). Thus, a thematic fact can be formally represented using the language of binary relations:

$$TF = R(S, O) \ .$$

The relation R specifies the corresponding *fact category* (FC).

The proposed approach is implemented in the context of developing an IAS designed for evaluation of innovative technologies. For that reason new technologies are considered as subjects of the facts. However, the proposed approach is universal and can be used in other areas.

Particular aspects characterizing technology (generally, the fact subject) determine the appropriate categories of facts to be extracted from unstructured texts. Such categories include, for instance, companies that develop the technology, the readiness degree of the technology, companies that are potential consumers of the technology etc. The list of fact categories is known in advance and is used in the system design.

Two main issues impede the fact extraction process:

1. Skipping some relevant facts contained in texts due to the variety and complexity of their possible formulations. Facts can be not retrieved due to:
   - *Lexical* diversity of TF's structural elements: subjects, objects and relations. An example of the base relation synonymy: "Enterprise E is *developing* technology T" and "Enterprise E is *working on creation* of technology T".
   - *Syntactic* diversity of TF's expression. The order of TF's structural elements in a sentence is not strictly fixed, for instance: "Enterprise E is developing technology T" and "Technology T is being developed by enterprise E".
2. The absence of explicit mentions of relevant facts in texts, despite the fact that such facts can be logically inferred from those already found in texts using some general knowledge.

The proposed approach addresses these problems and provides an increase of the fact extraction completeness, which is interesting for the system's user (an expert). Specific aspects of the approach are discussed in detail below.

3.1 Using Ontologies for Thematic Fact Extraction

Facts of various categories are extracted from texts with the use of corresponding *extraction template* (ET). To improve the completeness of TF extraction, elements of templates that correspond to different FCs are associated with elements of a *lexical ontology*. This allows to fully use the possible lexical expression forms of TF subject, object and relation, as well as clearly define their semantic identity. For each given FC a set of ETs was developed. These templates determine generically the category-specific subject, object and relation as elements in lexical ontology. For example, the ET for a FC about the companies-consumers of a given technology can be generally defined as follows:

$$element\_specifying\_Interest(element\_specifying\_Technology,$$
$$element\_specifying\_Enterprise) \quad (1)$$

The problem of syntactic diversity of a TF is solved by ontological description of the ET structure by listing its elements without strictly fixing their order.

The OBIE approach enables one to use a lexical ontology for managing the fact extraction process. To organize this, all developed ETs are specified in the ontology using the corresponding *template relations*. Template relations are binary relations linking the entity, representing the FC template, with entities, representing each of the template elements. There exist three relations of this kind for each ET:

$$is\_Template\_Subject(FC\_template, ET\_subject),$$
$$is\_Template\_Object(FC\_template, ET\_object),$$
$$is\_Template\_Relation(FC\_template, ET\_relation).$$

Thus the lexical ontology defines:

1. Entities corresponding to the elements of ETs for each FC;
2. Hierarchical relations and relations of lexical synonymy;
3. Template relations for every ET defined in the IAS.

The entities of high level abstraction in the lexical ontology include the following: Fact_Category (FC), Fact_Subject (FS), Fact_Relation (FR) and Fact_Object (FO). When developing ET the concrete subclasses of these high-level classes are defined. These subclasses then specify corresponding template relations among each other. The elements of ETs are represented by *descriptive instances* of ontological classes matching the defined relation, its subject and object. A descriptive instance (DI) is an instance of an ontological class which implements its object properties. DIs allow to formalize ontological knowledge. They specify a set of characteristic object relations, their domains and ranges at the class level, and allow to implement these relationships for specific instances. For every DI a set of *lexical instances*, belonging to the same class, can be defined. A lexical instance (LI) is an instance of an ontology class, which expresses the lexical word form of the class. All the LIs specified for a DI are semantically identical, i.e. they are lexical synonyms.

Let us consider an example demonstrating the concepts of DI and LI. There exists a generic class named "Fact_Category", which has a relation "has_Relation" with the range of class "Fact_Relation". We will consider the FC of enterprises, which are consuming some technology; the corresponding ET is specified as (1). Based on (1), a subclass named "Enterprises_Consumers" is created for the "Fact_Category" class, and for the "Fact_Relation" class a subclass named "Interest" is created. It is not possible to connect the new classes with the "has-Relation" relation directly, and for each of them corresponding DIs are created, which are linked by this relation. Then, for the "Enterprises_Consumers" and "Interest" classes lexical filling is to be specified, i.e. LIs are to be created. To connect a set of LIs to an ET, there exists a "hasLexicalForm" relation, which connects every LI to the corresponding DI of its class. For instance, the "Interest" class may contain LIs named "interested", "plans to buy", etc.

Having one or more LIs for all structural components of the template (in a random order) in the structural element of a document is the basis for the extraction of this element as a thematic fact.

Fig. 1 shows a fragment of the lexical ontology that describes knowledge about enterprises-consumers of the required technology. Considering the introduced definitions, the ET for this category is specified as follows:

$$DI\_of\_Interest\_Class(DI\_of\_Technology\_Class,$$
$$DI\_of\_EnterprisesConsumers\_Class)$$

On Fig. 1 the elements of the ontology are shown in the following way: high-level classes and basic subclasses participating in fact extraction process – in thick borders; their instances – in dotted-line borders; the subclass relation ("isSubclassOf") – (*); the type relation ("isA") – dotted-line arrows; the lexical form relation ("hasLexicalForm") – (**). Number "1" specifies the template's relation "hasObject", number "2" – the template's relation "hasRelation", number "3" – the template's relation "hasSubject".

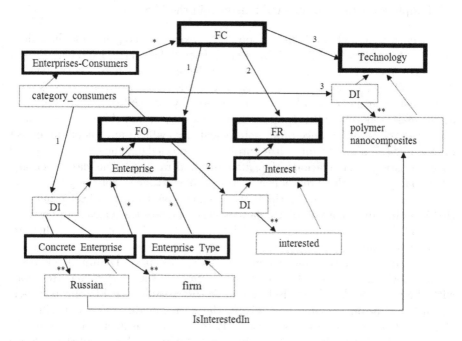

Fig. 1. A fragment of the lexical ontology describing knowledge about enterprises-consumers of the required technology

The lexical ontology expands during the text analysis process by the *extracted TF* (EF). Each EF is normalized and added to the ontology as a statement (a triple) represented by an *object property* specified for the considered FC. This object property links the lexical forms of the TF subject and relation, which were found in texts. For instance, for the considered FC the lexical ontology may expand by a triple "IsInterestedIn (polymer nanocomposites, Russian Helicopters)". This new relation is shown in Fig. 1.

3.2 Deriving Facts Based on the Basic Knowledge and Facts Extracted in the Document Analysis Process

The discussion of the approach to deriving of relevant facts not contained explicitly in texts (derived facts, DF) we begin with an example. Let us assume that an expert is interested in facts about the companies being potential consumers of some technology T. We also assume that for certain classes of products, there exists a basic knowledge (i.e. knowledge specific to a given area) of two types stored in the ontological knowledge base:

- Knowledge about the structure of the products as a hierarchy of items that make up the given class of products: subsystems, components, elements; sub-properties of "hasPart" property (e.g. "hasSubsystem", "hasComponent") and its inverse property "partOf" are used;
- Knowledge about the materials used in the manufacturing of certain subsystems (components). Here the "usedMaterial" property is used (and its inverse property "isUsedIn").

Let us suppose that in the process of text analysis a fact was found stating that the analyzed technology T is perspective for the production of material M. In addition, another fact has been extracted stating a certain company is planning to produce a certain type of product P. Using the basic knowledge that this type of products contain components which use material M in their manufacturing it can be concluded that the enterprise is a potential consumer of technology T. Here is a possible inference rule for this kind of facts:

$$hasSubsystem(?Product, ?Subsystem) \land$$
$$hasComponent(?Subsystem, ?Component) \land$$
$$isUsedIn(?Material, ?Component) \land$$
$$isUsedFor(?Technology, ?Material) \land$$
$$planToProduce(?Enterprise, ?Product)$$
$$\Longrightarrow$$
$$isPotentialConsumer(?Technology, ?Enterprise) \qquad (2)$$

The model of deriving of implicit facts can be formally written as follows:

$$(BK, EF) \underset{IR}{\models} DF$$

where BK – $Background\ Domain\ Knowledge$; EF – $Extracted\ Facts$; IR – $Inference\ Rules$; DF – $Derived\ Facts$.

The algorithms of system's prototype operation that implements this approach to facts extraction are presented in the next section.

4   Algorithms

This section presents two algorithms which implement the approach discussed above: i) extracting TF that are explicitly stated in documents and ii) deriving of facts using basic knowledge and facts, extracted from texts.

Let us introduce the required abbreviations: *LexOntology* — lexical ontology; *query* — user query; $\{FC\}$ — the array of thematic fact's categories; $\{IFC\}$ — the array of inferred facts categories; *FS* — fact subject; *FO* — fact object; *FR* — fact relation; *DC* — document corpora that is being processed; *Doc* — a document; Doc_{pt} — a document in plain text; *DI* — descriptive instance; $\{fact\_category\_tag\}$ — the array of fact categories tags; $\{IR\}$ — inference rules; $\{extracted\_fact\}$ — the array of extracted facts; $\{inferred\_fact\}$ — the array of logically inferred facts; *BackgroundKnowledge* — basic domain knowledge. The process of extracting facts from documents is presented in Algorithm 1.

On step 1 the *descriptive instance* (DI), corresponding to the FS is extracted from the lexical ontology. On step 2 the subject of the current query is added to the ontology using the *hasLexicalForm* relation of the extracted DI. In cycle 3 all of the documents of the corpora being analyzed are converted to plain-text (4), divided into sentences (5), and the sentenced that are considered to be potential facts (according to the user query) are detected (6). Step 7 introduces a cycle on all the potential facts; this cycle contains another cycle on fact categories (8).

Step 9 extracts the DI for the ontological class representing the current FC. On step 10 following the *hasObject* relation the DI of the class representing the FO for the FC is extracted. On step 11 the DI of the class representing the relation of the FC is extracted using the *hasRelation* relation.

On steps 12-13 all the lexical forms for FO and FR DIs are extracted from the lexical ontology by the *hasLexicalForm* relation. Step 14 forms an extraction template from the lexical forms, and the extraction template is matched against the potential fact in step 15. If a match was found, step 17 extracts an instance from the lexical ontology which is corresponding to the lexical form of the FO. Step 18 extracts a relation which is specific for the current FC. Finally, on step 19 the extracted TF is added to the lexical ontology. The sentence under consideration is tagged with the FC tag (20) and is added to the extracted facts array on step 21.

For each of the inferred fact categories a cycle 1 is organized: on step 2 an inference rule specific for the IFC is determined. On step 3, using the metadata stated for all the predicates in the inference rule, the array of facts to be extracted is formed. On step 3, using the metadata stated for all the predicated in the extraction rule, the basic knowledge to be used to derive new facts is formed. Steps 7-8 address the Algorithm 1, which allows to extract the required facts from the initial document corpora. The extraction template is already specified for this stage: the object and the relation of the pattern are determined by their lexical forms. If the required fact has been extracted, a new fact is derived using the basic knowledge (step 10). On step 12 the derived fact is added to the array of derived facts.

Algorithm 1. Extracting thematic facts from texts

---

    input $LexOntology, query, \{FC\}, \{fact\_category\_tag\}, DC$
    output $\{extracted\_fact\}, LexOntology$
  1: $FSDI \leftarrow getDescInstance(LexOntology)$
  2: $User\_Query\_Instance$
       $\leftarrow updateLexOnto(hasLexicalForm(FSDI, query), LexOntology)$
  3: **for all** $Doc \in DC$ **do**
  4:     $Doc_{pt} \leftarrow toPlainText(Doc)$
  5:     $\{Sentence\} \leftarrow splitText(Doc_{pt})$
  6:     $\{PossibleFactSentence\} \leftarrow getPossibleFacts(FS(query), \{Sentence\})$
  7:     **for all** $PossibleFact \in \{PossibleFact\}$ **do**
  8:         **for all** $fc \in \{FC\}$ **do**
  9:           $FCDI \leftarrow getDIForFactCategory(LexOntology, fc)$
10:           $FODI \leftarrow getDIForFactObject(LexOntology, hasObject(FCDI))$
11:           $FRDI \leftarrow getDIForFactRelation(LexOntology, hasRelation(FCDI))$
12:           $\{FO\_lexical\_form\} \leftarrow getLexicalForms(LexOntology,$
             $hasLexicalForm(FODI))$
13:           $\{FR\_lexical\_form\} \leftarrow getLexicalForms(LexOntology,$
             $hasLexicalForm(FRDI))$
14:           $lexicalPattern \leftarrow formLexicalPattern(\{FO\_lexical\_form\},$
             $\{FR\_lexical\_form\})$
15:           $[is\_Match, MatchedSubjectLexicalForm]$
             $\leftarrow conductPatternMatching(PossibleFact, lexicalPattern)$
16:           **if** is_Match **then**
17:              $FOLexicalFormInstance \leftarrow getInstance(LexOntology,$
               $MatchedSubjectLexicalForm)$
18:              $Relation \leftarrow getOntologicalRelationForFC(LexOntology, fc)$
19:              $LexOntology \leftarrow updateOntology(LexOntology,$
               $FOLexicalFormInstance, User\_Query\_Instance, Relation)$
20:              $Fact \leftarrow tagFact(tag, PossibleFact)$
21:              $\{extracted\_fact\} \leftarrow addFact(\{extracted\_fact\}, Fact)$
22:           **end if**
23:         **end for**
24:     **end for**
25: **end for**

---

5   Implementation

The proposed approach to facts extraction has been implemented in the FactE framework. FactE is a subsystem of Information-analytical system which takes the user query containing the name of the innovative technology, as well as a corpus of texts to be processed, as an input. The list of fact categories and inference rules for deriving of new facts are believed to be given in advance.

The FactE architecture has been developed on the basis of the above presented algorithms. As seen from Fig. 2, FactE has two functional modules:

Algorithm 2. Deriving of facts using basic knowledge and texts

---

    input $\{IFC\}$, $\{IR\}$, BackgroundKnowledge
    output $\{inferred\_fact\}$
1: **for all** $ifc \in \{IFC\}$ **do**
2:    $IR \leftarrow getInferenceRuleForCategory(ifc, \{IR\})$
3:    $\{Required\_Fact\} \leftarrow getRequiredFacts(IR)$
4:    $\{Required\_Fact\} \leftarrow getRequiredFacts(IR)$
5:    $\{Background\_Knowledge\} \leftarrow getBackgroundKnowledge(IR,$
        $BackgroundKnowledge)$
6:    **for all** $required\_fact \in \{Required\_Fact\}$ **do**
7:        **for all** $Doc \in \{DC\}$ **do**
8:            Apply **Algorithm 1**, steps [2, 4-5, 6-8, 14-15] with input:
                $FC = ifc$, $FO = required\_Fact.Object$,
                $FR = required\_Fact.Relation$
9:            **if** is_Match **then**
10:               $Inferred\_Fact \leftarrow applyRule(PossibleFact,$
                    $\{Background\_Knowledge\})$
11:            **end if**
12:            $\{Inferred\_Fact\} \leftarrow addInferredFact(\{Inferred\_Fact\},$
                $Inferred\_Fact)$
13:        **end for**
14:    **end for**
15: **end for**

- linguistic processor, designed for fact extraction using filled extraction templates, which are provided by the lexical ontology and
- fact derivation module, which is intended to organize the logical inference of new facts.

The functioning of the mentioned modules is controlled by the system ontology which describes and stores both lexical knowledge (managing the process of extraction of implicitly mentioned facts) and basic knowledge (used for new facts inference).

The following third-party software was used for solving particular problems when implementing the FactE framework: Apache HttpClient [7], Apache Tika [8], GATE [9], Apache Open NLP SentenceSplitter [10], Apache Lucene [11], Apache Jena Core [12], Apache Jena SDB [13].

6 Preliminary Experimental Results

The system's prototype is now at the early development stage. Particularly, the amount of data in domain ontologies containing basic knowledge is small, and the set of the experimental results obtained is limited at this point. Below a real result obtained while testing the prototype is described. The testing was held on the basis on Internet sources in Russian language.

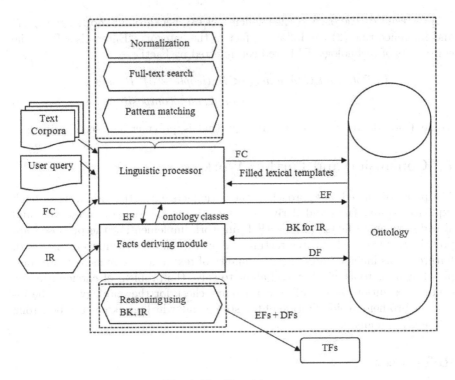

Fig. 2. FactE architecture

The query contained the technology of producing polymer composites. The fact category was "potential consumers of the technology". In the analysed text corpora the document [14] was included amongst others. This document contains the sentence "The joint company "Helicopters of Russia" intends to create a perspective multipurpose commercial helicopter". The algorithm of fact extraction reveals the following fact:

$$Plans\_To\_Produce(\ll Helicopters\ of\ Russia \gg, helicopter) \qquad (3)$$

The background knowledge of FactE includes the following statements:

$$Includes(helicopter, ballscrew) \qquad (4)$$

$$Contains(ballscrew, blades) \qquad (5)$$

$$Used\_for\_Production(CPRF, blades) \qquad (6)$$

$$May\_Be\_Used\_For\_Manufacturing\_Material($$
$$polymernanocomposites, CPRF) \qquad (7)$$

As a result on the basis of the explicit fact (3), background knowledge (4)–(7) and inference rule (2) the following fact of the category "Enterprises-Potential consumers of technology T" have been inferred by FactE:

$$Is\_Potential\_Consumer(\ll Helicopters \ of \ Russia \gg,$$
$$polymernanocomposites) \ . \tag{8}$$

where T stands for the given technology (that is, polymer nano-composites).

7 Conclusion and Further Work

The paper discussed an approach to thematic facts extraction, allowing to fetch explicitly stated facts and derive new facts using the domain knowledge and already extracted facts. The FactE framework implementing the proposed approach was presented, its architecture and operational algorithm were discussed. Future works include improving the quality of text analysis by using more complex linguistic tools which would allow to solve the problem of coreference and context resolution. Above all, a consistency check for the ontology is to be introduced to help avoid addition of the statements which are known to be wrong in the given domain.

References

1. Feldman, R., Sanger, J.: The Text Mining Textbook: Advanced Approaches in Analyzing Unstructured Data. Cambridge Univ. Press (2007)
2. Wimalasuriya, D., Dou, D.: Ontology-based information extraction: An introduction and a survey of current approaches. J. of Inf. Science 36(3), 306–323 (2010)
3. Anantharangachar, R., Ramani, S., Rajagopalan, S.: Ontology Guided Information Extraction from Unstructured Text. Int. J. of Web & Sem. Tech. 4(1), 19–36 (2013)
4. Buitelaar, P., Cimiano, P., Frank, A., Hartung, M., Racioppa, S.: Ontology-based Information Extraction and Integration from Heterogeneous Data Sources. Int. J. of Human Computer Studies 66, 759–788 (2008)
5. Petasis, G., Möller, R., Karkaletsis, V.: BOEMIE: Reasoning-based Information Extraction. In: Proceedings of the 1st Workshop on Natural Language Processing and Automated Reasoning, pp. 60–75 (2013)
6. Suchanek, F.M., Sozio, M., Weikum, G.: SOFIE: A self-organizing framework for information extraction. In: Proceedings of the 18th International Conference on World Wide Web, Madrid, Spain, pp. 631–640 (2009)
7. Apache Http Client, http://hc.apache.org
8. Apache Tika, http://tika.apache.org/
9. GATE: General Architecture for Text Engineering, https://gate.ac.uk/
10. Apache Open NLP, https://opennlp.apache.org/
11. Apache Lucene, http://lucene.apache.org
12. Apache Jena Core, https://jena.apache.org/documentation/rdf/
13. Apache Jena SDB, http://jena.apache.org/documentation/sdb/
14. A PROMISING HIGH-SPEED HELICOPTER (PSV) V-37, http://bastion-karpenko.ru/v-37_psv/

A Collaborative Development of Ontology-Based Knowledge Bases

Oleg Dyachenko and Yury Zagorulko

Novosibirsk, A.P. Ershov Institute of Siberian Branch of Informatics Systems
of Russian Academy of Sciences
dyachenko.oleg@gmail.com, zagor@iis.nsk.su

Abstract. The paper describes the model of collective development of knowledge bases (KB), based on ontologies, and knowledge base editor that implements this model. In addition, the paper discusses the requirements for knowledge base editors that support collaborative KB building. The model proposed uses asynchronous editing mode as default and knowledge base version control system. The model supports integration of notifications and discussions into the development process, as well as the presence of the flexible roles and permissions management system to support groups of developers and experts with various levels of ontological competence and areas of expertise. The implementation of this model in KB editor integrated into the thematic intelligent scientific Internet resource (ISIR) is described. Collaborative KB building is supported by version control subsystem that constantly monitors the consistency of the knowledge base, and by the notification subsystem intended to make development transparent for users and to integrate the discussions to the development process.

Keywords: Collective Knowledge Bases, Collaborative Knowledge Base Building, Ontology Management.

1 Introduction

Currently, there is a rapid growth in demand in different knowledge bases (KB), and the knowledge base themselves become so large in size and covered domains of knowledge. That makes their support by one expert or a small group of experts inefficient or even impossible. Development of knowledge bases becomes more a collective task, therefore it requires the means supporting their building and maintenance. At the same time, only a small number of existing editors support collaborative development of knowledge bases. Thus, as a rule, in these editors, such support is incomplete, i.e. does not cover all the needs of collaborative development. Therefore, none of the existing editors can be taken as default editor for all cases of collective KB development. Moreover, the scientific community has not yet formulated a fairly complete list of requirements to be met by such development tools regardless of the context and their application.

P. Klinov and D. Mouromtsev (Eds.): KESW 2014, CCIS 468, pp. 219–228, 2014.
© Springer International Publishing Switzerland 2014

2 Requirements for KB Editors Supporting Collaborative KB Building

In this paper by knowledge bases we understand the knowledge bases based on ontologies. We adhere to the classic definition given by T. Gruber – "ontology is an explicit specification of a conceptualization" [1] where a conceptualization is understood as a simplified representation of the world that models the subject domain in the form of a set of concepts, objects and other entities available, and relationships between them.

One of the main problems related to the collaborative construction of KBs, is managing the interaction and communication between users, because even within the same area of knowledge the same concept can be interpreted in different ways. In this situation, ontologies play an important role, serving as an agreement of a group of people on some domain of knowledge. It is worth noting, that this interpretation of the ontologies focuses on the consent of its content in the sense that a group of people agrees about shared usage of the same concepts, relations, attributes, and axioms provided by ontology.

Knowledge base building is necessarily an iterative and a dynamic process. It is unlikely that the ontology will be immediately built in a perfect way and will be used throughout the entire period of its existence unchanged. Typically, developing a knowledge base starts from the initial "sketch", that is subsequently revised, refined and filled with details. At the same time errors may occur, so error detection and management, competitive management and modification of data are important problems of KB building.

In addition, there are the following problems [2,3] related to the collaborative building of ontologies: data access control, recognition of intellectual property rights on generated knowledge and attribution.

The knowledge bases based on ontologies predominantly are edited with specialized tools – ontology editors. Therefore, they should provide a full support of the KB building during the course of their development. In particular, such tools should meet the set of requirements to ensure the needs of ontology development.

KB editors satisfying the requirements should ensure convenient and efficient construction and modification of the quality and consistent knowledge bases. These requirements were suggested and considered by different authors [3,4]. Based on them, we will give the list of requirements for the editors of knowledge bases

- **Functional Requirements.** Any ontology contains the classes, class attributes, relationships between classes, and set of instances of classes with the properties from classes. A set of elementary operations indivisible into smaller operations that can be made with these parts of the ontology can be most easily described as "add", "delete", and "edit". More difficult, complex changes, for example, design operations on ontology like deletion of the subclass, are often more meaningful. Their implementation requires the application of a cascade of changes related to maintaining the consistency of the knowledge base and coupled with the risk of loss/damage of data in the system. Providing complex changes functionality can accelerate the process of KB building and development since the developer will not have to perform the proper sequence of elementary operations on knowledge base to achieve the desired effect.

- **User's Supervision Requirements.** As for complex changes, in some cases there are various ways of making changes after their request. Therefore, mechanisms are needed to enable the user to choose the way to deploy the complex changes, instead of performing the change using the pre-determined pattern.

- **Development Transparency Requirement.** The changes in one part of the ontology may cause a cascade of changes in other parts of it. In most cases, it is hard for user to determine the extent of the changes being made. KB editor should provide the experts or developers with detailed information on changes that are going to be made before confirming. At the same time it's natural to group similar changes notifications with an option to view them in details.

- **Reversibility of Changes.** The editor should support the ability to revert the changes or their sequence on demand. In some cases, the application of an inverse operation may not be enough, it should be possible to return the editor to the state it was in before making changes so as not to provoke the user to unwanted extra undo operation.

- **Version Control.** Version control means monitoring and detailed logging of all changes and their metadata, time and author.

- **Knowledge Base Refinement.** The system should be able to determine the desired changes for the KB by analyzing the various KB characteristics and offer them to developers. For example, system should suggest user to revise the class in case it have only one subclass.

- **Usability Requirement.** The system should provide a variety of tools to quickly determine the current state of knowledge base – highlight errors, show tooltips and other additional information available.

- **Integration of Discussions to the KB Building Process.** When building ontologies and knowledge bases there can be situations when developers have different views on how, for example, to model a particular object. For resolving such problems it is natural to use tools that support discussions. These tools should retain the context of related part of KB and be integrated into the development process so as to remain accessible within the components of the KB.

- **Roles and Permissions Management.** KB editor's capabilities to manage user roles and permissions in a flexible manner are necessary for the control of developers' and experts' competence and areas of expertise especially from the moment when the size of KB and the number of users increase.

- **Support of Synchronous and Asynchronous Editing Modes.** Undoubtedly, simultaneous editing mode allows faster development, because every change made is immediately available to all users. At the same time, this mode leaves the possibility for developers to make changes without discussion or objections from other developers. In this regard, the editor must support not only synchronous but asynchronous KB building.

This list of requirements for the editors, of course, is not a complete one, but the editor that meets these requirements will undoubtedly be a useful tool for the collaborative development of high-quality ontologies and knowledge bases.

3   Related Work

In this section, we will briefly describe several approaches to develop collective knowledge bases:

- Ontolingua Server
- $(KA)^2$
- Co4
- Collaborative Protégé
- WebProtégé
- ContentCVS

Ontolingua Server [5] was one of the first systems that implemented the collective construction of ontologies. From the standpoint of the requirements described in the previous section, the collaborative work in this system was not well supported. Despite this, the undoubted merit of this system can be regarded as successful attempts of the implementation of collective development and monitoring of global consistency. Collaborative development in Ontolingua Server is supported through general sessions for users. In a single session while visiting the changed object's page users can receive notifications about changes made by other users. Control of user permissions is made similarly to the group policies of file systems.

The idea of $(KA)^2$ (Knowledge Annotation Initiative of the Knowledge Acquisition Community) [6] approach is the idea of modeling knowledge acquisition using ontologies developed by a group of experts. In the framework of $(KA)^2$ experts were developed multiple ontologies, such as ontology organizations, projects, people, publications, etc. Adding instances was delegated to community. Using ontologies $(KA)^2$ to annotate web-documents primarily by their owners to enable intelligent access to them was suggested. Special editing tools were developed to accelerate the process of annotation. That approach offers a convenient and easy way to create distributed ontologies, although it is limited in terms of functionality, time-consuming and highly dependent on the users' initiative.

Co4 approach [7] in its model of collective knowledge base building uses the analogy of reviewing a scientific journal articles. In the Co4 system each user has a knowledge base that he has the permissions to edit. To construct a coherent KB private users' knowledge bases are organized into a tree. In this tree leaves are private KB and intermediate vertices are called group KBs and contain knowledge agreed between their sons. Users do not have the rights to edit group KBs. In Co4 each user's KB remains hidden from other users as long as the owner has not send it in whole or in part to group of developers on a discussion. This change proposal is shown to other group KB's subscribers as a request for comment. Users must give one answer as an response: "accept" when they believe that the proposed knowledge must be integrated into a coherent knowledge base, "reject" or "offer its own version" otherwise. When all members of the group agree to accept the change received, it is accepted and recorded to the group KB, and then transmitted to all its subscribers.

Collaborative Protégé [8, 9] is an addition to the popular editor Protégé that implements the functionality of collaborative development. As part of this addition the following functionality was provided: integration of discussions and annotations into the development process, extensible annotation classes to describe proposals, votes, tips, comments, etc. were introduced to serve this purpose; changes management, logging of changes, votes and other changes in the system in a user-accessible form; roles and permissions management; workflow support, i.e. definition of a set of operations that is required to perform to make changes in KB. Collaborative Protégé provides a wide range of options to control data consistency and communication between users. Editing ontology on server goes in a synchronous way when any change is automatically delivered to all connected users.

WebProtégé [10] is a lightweight ontology editor and knowledge acquisition tool for the Web. It provides extensive collaboration support, including change tracking, contextualized threaded discussions, watches and notifications and a flexible access policy mechanism. WebProtégé aims at providing an ontology tool that a large spectrum of users, ranging from ontology experts to domain experts. Thus, its interface may be customized for users with different levels of expertise.

ContentCVS [11] is the plugin for Protégé. Its approach adapts concurrent versioning paradigm to allow several developers to make changes concurrently to ontology. It provides conflict detection and resolution features based on techniques that take the structure and semantics of the ontology versions into account.

4   KB Editor's Model

We have proposed a model of collaborative knowledge base building and architecture of a software system that implements it, using asynchronous editing mode as default and supporting KB version control [12]. Proposed model of collective KB development is focused on meeting the requirements for KB editors described in Section 2.

4.1   KB Version Control

According to the proposed model, each user of the system has its own private knowledge base "branched" from the public KB. The users can edit only their knowledge bases. From the transparency requirements private copies are private only in terms of the changes, they are available for all users of the system to view. When a developer is confident enough in the knowledge entered to his KB, he can send the changes to other users for discussion and voting. If the proposed change passes vote successfully it is transferred to the public knowledge base and is broadcasted to all remaining users.

As a version control model for the ontology we use the model analogous to the one proposed in [13]. The convenient formalism for change tracking and conflicts' detection that occur when trying to merge two working copies of the ontology to a single base are considered there. In the simplified version of this formalism the use of function S comparing two versions of ontology is suggested. This function returns the set of additions, deletions and modifications. It's possible to use it to track the conflicts that arise when combining versions of KB. Let $v1$, $v2$ be two private KBs and $v0$ – public one, then the conflict can be tracked using two values of $S – S(v0,v1)$ and $S(v0,v2)$ – there is a conflict if both values have different changes made to KB's object. When using this model, good part is the fact that when dealing with a large knowledge base and many users we do not need to store multiple copies of private KBs containing repeating unchanged "basic" part, and we need to store only the changes made relatively to public KB. Though the general form of the function S or algorithm to obtain its value is unknown, but it is possible to get the values $S(v0,v1)$ and $S(v0,v2)$ by logging changes during the process of making changes by users in their private KBs.

One of the sources of changes in the real information systems are automated programs, such as the collectors of ontological information, supplementing the knowledge base of scientific knowledge portals [14]. While working such programs can generate a large number of changes. These changes should be made to the KB directly, without "distracting" other developers.

4.2   User's Roles and Permissions

Developers and experts with various levels of ontological competence and areas of expertise may participate in the development of the KB, so it is important to provide a flexible permissions and roles management system. Group policies similar to those used in modern file systems are not satisfactory way to manage permissions. In our approach, we use the following model to grant users rights to view and edit KB. Identification of the competence group that has specific rights to modify, delete, create objects KB is given in a flexible manner with respect to a base relation in the ontology, for example, ISA. By selecting vertices in the tree constructed by this relation, we can define the rights of the group to edit only this vertex or the sub-tree rooted at this vertex. An user who belongs to several groups merges rights of these groups. It seems reasonable to divide the rights to design (working with classes and class attributes of ontology) and editorial (only adding and modifying of instances of classes).

4.3   Integration of Discussions to the Development Process

Undoubtedly, when editing ontology it is important to have all the information and discussion in one place. For users to be in the context of the discussion when editing KB, the discussion should be fully and easily accessible in the process of changing or viewing this part of the KB. It applies not only to the components of the knowledge base, but also to every change user makes and sends other users to vote. The meta-information such as information about the author, creation date, and the vote results is integrated into the development process.

4.4   Changes and Notifications Controllers

Two working components in the architecture of the proposed system are the changes and notifications controllers.

The changes controller manages the changes at different stages of editing private KB and application of approved edits to the public knowledge base. This component of the system performs the following tasks:

- KB version control,
- detection of user changes and their conflicts,
- management of complex changes,
- application of approved changes to the public KB and broadcasting them to the private KBs.

Notifications controller is responsible for users notifications about errors, available actions, the consequences complex change will have, ensuring transparency of manipulations with the private KBs. The messages can be either informational or active. The former, for example, include status messages, the latter – the messages that prompt the user to perform an action, for example, remove the detected errors.

5   KB Editor's Functionality and Its Implementation

Ontology editor is based on ontology description language with expressivity equivalent to OWL Lite [15].

As it was mentioned above, the model assumes existence of public KB, inaccessible to users for editing and the number of users' private KBs, where users can make changes. This section describes the common user scenarios taking place in the collective development of KB.

Any change in the public knowledge originates from changes made by the end user in his KB. At the level of changes in private KBs development goes in a mode similar to the single-user system.

When a user makes changes to its knowledge base through the editor's interface, the system determines the basic changes will be made with the knowledge base, as well as a cascade of changes caused by user action. For example, deleting a class attribute will also lead to the removal of the attribute values for all its instances. A list of these changes is shown to the user for confirmation by notification controller. After the confirmation these changes are recorded in the user's knowledge base with the unique change identifier, date, author, and other metadata.

Usually during an opened session expert makes many changes to the knowledge base, so for convenience of making edits and sending them to other users, users can "commit" a group of changes analogously to commit operation in textual version control systems [16].

The user can undo the single unfixed change as well as delete an entire group of the committed changes. In this case, these changes are removed from the list of changes.

Not only each class, attribute, instance, relationship, and any other object in the knowledge base, but each committed change has a discussion connected to it.

After the change is recorded to a private KB, the user can send it to other users on the discussion. Each of the members having the permissions to edit parts of KB changed receives a request for comment. Possible applications of the incoming changes: accept or reject them.

- If changes were rejected no changes in receiving user's KB occur.
- In case user accepts changes but does not have own changes intersecting with received, then accept the changes and record them to the list of his changes.
- If the receiving user has already made changes that overlap with received ones and contradict them – there is a conflict, in this case the user is notified about conflicting changes, with a list of actions to resolve the conflict: to cancel, to fully accept or accept preserving own changes.

Accepting of the incoming changes or rejecting them is the heart of the system's voting process. Model of accepting changes by voting may be determined in various ways depending on the number of users. The simplest of them is to accept the changes, if the majority of users supported them, or to accept the changes approved by all users.

At that moment when the change was accepted by voting, it is moved into a public knowledge base. Since each user has a set of KB changes made in comparison with public KB, the new change is removed from the list of changes of users who have already accepted it. Users who do not have the permissions to manage this change also receive it, and users who rejected it get a second request to accept or reject change. If this change is rejected again, then the user will get automatically created change, preserving the state of his knowledge base intact.

These user scenarios fully describe the process of collaborative knowledge base building in terms of changes management and version control in the system.

6   Conclusion

The paper summarizes the requirements for editors supporting collaborative KB building, as well as a brief overview of several tools for collaborative development of knowledge bases based on ontologies. The survey revealed that none of the editors considered fulfills the requirements for such tools. It should be noted that a complete list of requirements for systems of this type has not yet emerged in the scientific community, and a list of requirements for the editors of KB presented in this paper is only a part of them. Determination of the other requirements is possible only after the accumulation of experience in usage of systems for collaborative KB and ontologies in real-world applications and representative collection of the reviews about them from experts and developers.

The original model of collaborative development of knowledge bases, based on ontologies, was proposed. The model proposed uses asynchronous editing mode as default and knowledge base version control system. The model supports integration of notifications and discussions into the development process, as well as the presence of the flexible roles and permissions management system to support groups of developers and experts with various levels of ontological competence and areas of expertise. The implementation of this model in KB editor integrated into the thematic intelligent scientific Internet resource (ISIR) is described [17]. Collaborative KB building is supported by version control subsystem that constantly monitors the consistency of the knowledge base, and by the notification subsystem intended to make development transparent for users and to integrate the discussions to the development process.

References

1. Gruber, T.: Toward Principles for the Design of Ontologies Used for Knowledge Sharing. International Journal of Human-Computer Studies 43(5-6), 907–928 (1995)
2. Yu, Z.: Techniques and Methodologies for the Ontologies Development, Maintenance and Reengineering. In: Proceedings of Workshop "Ontological modeling" – Moscow: IIP RAS, pp. 135–162 (2008) (in Russian)
3. Zagorulko, Y., Borovikova, O.: Technology of Ontology Building for Knowledge Portals on Humanities. In: Wolff, K.E., Palchunov, D.E., Zagoruiko, N.G., Andelfinger, U. (eds.) KONT/KPP 2007. LNCS (LNAI), vol. 6581, pp. 203–216. Springer, Heidelberg (2011)
4. Stojanovic, L., Motik, B.: Ontology Evolution within Ontology Editors. In: Proceedings of the OntoWeb-SIG3 Workshop (2002)
5. Farquhar, A., Fikes, R., Rice, J.: The Ontolingua Server: A Tool for Collaborative Ontology Construction. International Journal of Human-Computer Studies 46(6), 707–727 (1997)
6. Benjamins, R., Fensel, D., Decker, S., Gomez-Perez, A. (KA)^2: Building Ontologies for the Internet, Mid Term Report. International Journal of Human Computer Studies 51, 687–712 (1999)
7. Euzenat, J.: Building Consensual Knowledge Bases: Context and Architecture. Towards Very Large Knowledge Bases. In: 2nd International Conference on Building and Sharing Very Large-scale Knowledge Bases (KBKS), pp. 143–155. IOS Press, Amsterdam (1995)
8. Tudorache, T., Noy, N.F., Tu, S., Musen, M.A.: Supporting Collaborative Ontology Development in Protégé. In: Sheth, A.P., Staab, S., Dean, M., Paolucci, M., Maynard, D., Finin, T., Thirunarayan, K. (eds.) ISWC 2008. LNCS, vol. 5318, pp. 17–32. Springer, Heidelberg (2008)
9. Correndo, G., Alani, H.: Survey of Tools for Collaborative Knowledge Construction and Sharing. In: Workshop on Collective Intelligence on Semantic Web (CISW 2007), November 2-5 (2007)
10. Tudorache, T., Nyulas, C., Noy, N., Musen, M.: WebProtégé: A Collaborative Ontology Editor and Knowledge Acquisition Tool for the Web. Semantic Web 4(1), 89–99 (2013)
11. Jiménez-Ruiz, E., Cuenca Grau, B., Horrocks, I., Berlanga, R.: Supporting Concurrent Ontology Development: Framework, Algorithms and Tool. Data & Knowledge Engineering Journal 70(1), 146–164 (2011)
12. Dyachenko, O., Yu, Z.: An Approach to Collaborative Building of Ontologies and Knowledge Bases. In: Proceedings of Russian Conference with Int. Participation "Knowledge – Ontologies – Theories", vol. 1, pp. 141–149 (2013) (in Russian)
13. Zaikin, I.: Ontology Versioning System. Proceedings of Russian Conference with Int. Participation "Knowledge – Ontologies – Theories" 1, 142–145 (2011) (in Russian)
14. Yu, Z., Borovikova, O.: An Approach to Constructing Knowledge Portals. Optoelectronics, Instrumentation and Data Processing 44(1), 75–82 (2008)

15. OWL Web Ontology Language Overview, http://www.w3.org/TR/owl-features/ (access date: March 15, 2014)
16. Pro Git Book, http://git-scm.com/book (access date: March 15, 2014)
17. Zagorulko, Y.A., Zagorulko, G.B., Shestakov, V.K., Kononenko, I.S.: Concept and Architecture of Thematic Intelligent Scientific Internet Resource. In: Proceedings of 15th international conference "Digital Libraries: Advanced Methods and Technologies, Digital Collections" (RCDL 2013), Yaroslavl, Russia, October 14-17, pp. 57–62 (2013)

A Tool to Convert Linked Data of E-Learning System to the SCORM Standard

Fedor Kozlov

ITMO University, St. Petersburg, Russia
kozlovfedor@gmail.com

Abstract. This paper presents a tool to convert linked data of an e-learning system to the SCORM standard. The conversion method is based on predefined templates. The tool receives content related to a specific course from semantic data stored in the ontology-based e-learning system. Using predefined templates the tool creates learning content for Learning Management Systems. This paper describes the overall system architecture and the methods of course's content conversion.

1 Introduction

1.1 The Ontology-Based E-Learning System

The ontology-based e-learning system provides key features for working with educational materials for tutors and students. The system data thoroughly reflects the structure of education process via the relations between courses, modules, lectures and terms. All data are stored in a semantic format which supports data reuse, flexible data modeling and entity relations analysis[1].

The ontology-based e-learning system is built on top of the Information Workbench platform[1]. The Information Workbench platform provides functions to interact with Linked Open Data[2]. The platform is built on top of open source modules. The user interface of the system is based on the Semantic MediaWiki module[3]. An extension of the standard Wiki view Information Workbench provides predefined templates and widgets. RDF data management is based on the OpenRDF Sesame framework. The platform has support of SPARQL queries. The system has open SPARQL-endpoint for sharing its content.

1.2 The SCORM Standard

The Sharable Content Object Reference Model(SCORM) is a set of standards for e-learning systems[4]. SCORM describes the format of learning content for Learning Management Systems. The most common versions of the SCORM Standard are:

- AICC HACP,
- SCORM 1.1,

---

[1] http://www.fluidops.com/information-workbench/

P. Klinov and D. Mouromtsev (Eds.): KESW 2014, CCIS 468, pp. 229–236, 2014.

– SCORM 1.2,
– SCORM 2004.

Learning courses built using the SCORM standard can be played in any SCORM-conformant Learning Management System[5].

The main feature of the SCORM standard is the processing of the result of the course, such as time and score. The analog of the SCORM Standart is the Tin Can API specification. The Tin Can API allows for several new capabilities that SCORM didn't, such as taking e-learning outside of the web browser and team-based e-learning. The SCORM standard has simple interface and better suited for development of the conversion tool.

1.3 Problem Description

The learning content of the ontology-based e-learning system can not be integrated into Learning Management Systems such as Moodle. This is one of the main problems of integrating systems learning content into local environment of the university.

The analog of the designed tool is the tool to export the linked data into the SCO objects in the SlideWiki system. The SlideWiki is the system to share corporate knowledge using presentations[6]. The SlideWiki SCORM Converter can generate SCORM learning courses from presentations. In the SlideWiki SCORM Converter, there are no templates for SCORM course pages. The rendering process is based on the copying of presentation slides.

The main goal of the designed tool is to export learning courses from the ontology-based e-learning system and convert it to SCORM-conformant learning content.

Exporting courses to SCORM standard will make it more affordable to use in e-learning systems.

The designed tool has to solve a range of problems, such as:

– To extract the semantic data from the ontology-based e-learning system,
– To create the learning content by predefined templates,
– To build a SCORM-conformant learning content,
– To support different interfaces for interaction with the service, such as user interface and REST API.

The designed tool must be integrated into the ontology-base e-learning system environment.

2 The Ontology Model

The ontology model of the ontology-based e-learning system is built on top of top-level ontologies such as AIISO[2], BIBO[3] and MA-ONT[4]. The AIISO ontology

---

[2] http://purl.org/vocab/aiiso/schema#
[3] http://purl.org/ontology/bibo/
[4] http://www.w3.org/ns/ma-ont#

is used to describe a collection of learning objects such as Course and Module. The BIBO ontology is used to describe the bibliographic resources related to the course. The MA-ONT ontology is used to describe media content of the lecture. The ontology model of the system describes relations between courses, modules, lectures and terms and helps to represent its properties and media content.

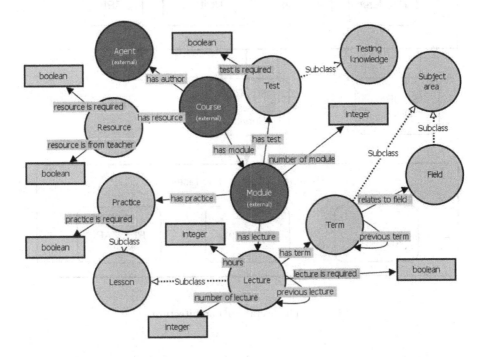

Fig. 1. The ontology model of the system

The described system functionality was designed on the material of three courses: 1) analytic geometry and linear algebra, 2) graph theory and 3) physics. Each course has modules. Each module has a number of lectures. Material of the lecture is described by a number of terms (annotations objects or a set of keyphrases from the user's point of view) and media resources.

The ontology model of the system is shown in Fig. 1.

3 Implementation

3.1 Overall Architecture

The designed tool uses functions from Information Workbench API modules. The tool also strongly integrates into the Information Workbench environment.

The core of the designed tool is the SCORM Conversion Service. This service interacts with framework modules and external libraries and provides basic interface to convert semantic learning content to SCORM format.

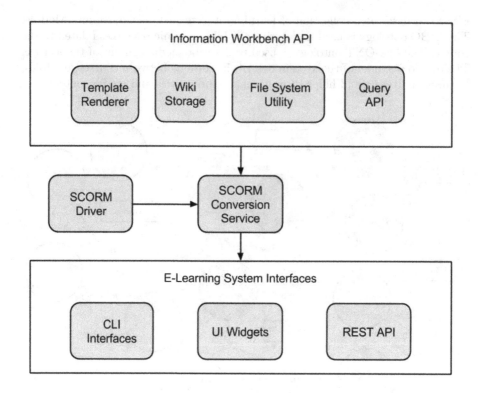

Fig. 2. The overall tool architecture

The SCORM Conversion Service is implemented in Java. A set of modules from the Information Workbench provides methods for interaction with semantic data. The SCORM Conversion Service collects semantic data through the Query API. The Wiki Storage is used to collect all necessary predefined templates. The Template Renderer binds semantic data with predefined templates and creates HTML content. The File System Utility provides functions to manipulate the files. The SCORM Conversion Service uses the SCORM Driver as external library. The SCORM Driver is a wrapper for final learning content.

All technologies used in designed tool, have been chosen based on the compatibility with technologies of the ontology-based e-learning system.

Different modules for end-users, such as UI widgets, REST API services and CLI utils, can be built on top of the SCORM Conversion Service.

The overall tool architecture is shown in Fig. 2.

3.2   Conversion Methods

In order to generate SCORM-compliant content, the relevant learning content needs to be identified and prepared. The learning content for SCORM must be represented as a standalone set of HTML pages and media resources. In this case the designed tool must be used to extract semantic data of single course and generate a learning content.

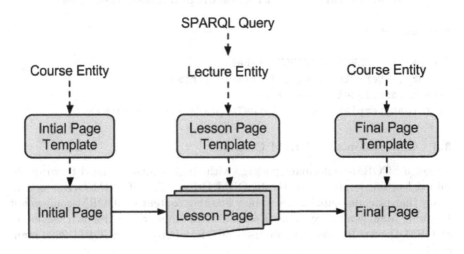

Fig. 3. The structure of learning content

HTML page generation occurs with predefined templates and the learning content comprises:

- the initial page,
- lesson pages,
- the final page.

For each type of HTML page a template must be defined. Initial and final pages are generated by a course entity. Lesson pages are generated by lecture entities. Lecture entities are obtained by predefined SPARQL query. The structure of learning content for SCORM generation is shown in Fig. 3.

Predefined templates are based on the Semantic MediaWiki syntax and stored inside the Information Workbench system. Templates support HTML tags, SPARQL queries and nested templates.

The conversion tool of the Information Workbench creates the body of the page using predefined templates. The SCORM Conversion Service performs additional processing of the content. The service extracts media resources from the content and sets additional headers, styles and controls to pages.

The following example of part of a predefined template for the lesson page is suggested.

```
= $this.rdfs:label$ =

=== About ===

'''Module''': $this.learningRu:isLectureOf$
'''Number of lecture''': $this.learningRu:numberOfLecture$

=== Terms ===

{{#sparql: SELECT DISTINCT ?label
 WHERE { ?term learningRu:isTermOf {{this}} .
 ?term rdfs:label ?label } }
 | format=template  | template=Template:ListTemplate}}
```

3.3   Generation of SCORM Content

To get a SCORM-conformant package with single course we need to wrap obtained learning content into the SCORM Driver. The SCORM Driver is a library that provides capabilities to play learning content in SCORM-conformant Learning Management Systems. Each SCORM standard has its own version of SCORM Driver. In this work we used SCORM Driver for SCORM 2004 standard.

The common steps of SCORM generation are:

- To wrap learning content into the SCORM Driver,
- To set-up manifest files,
- To add bookmarking and completion code to HTML pages,
- To add links to the next page,
- To create a ZIP archive of wrapped learning content.

In the result of the SCORM generation the designed tool receives a SCORM package for a single course.

3.4   Integration

To integrate the designed tool into an ontology-based e-learning system the following steps have been made:

- To create a new solution for Information Workbench framework,
- To create a service based on the designed tool's interface,
- To create UI widget to insert on system Wiki pages,
- To build and deploy a solution in the system environment,
- To create a ZIP archive of wrapped learning content,
- To define templates of initial, lesson and final pages for SCORM generation,
- To insert UI widget into a course page.

As a result of integration the ontology-based e-learning system has its own tunable UI component for SCORM course generation. The widget configuration interface is shown in Fig. 4.

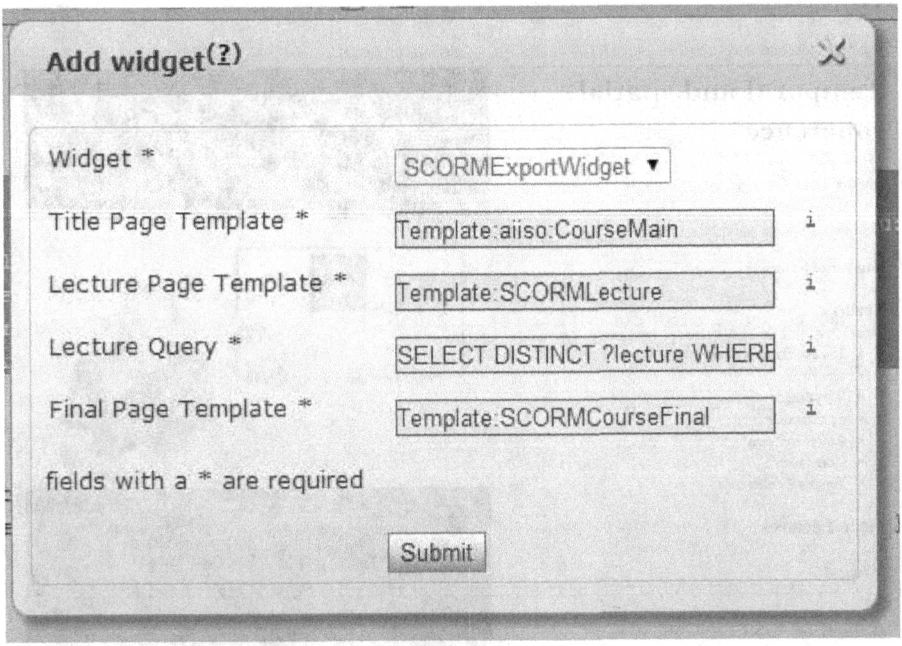

Fig. 4. The widget configuration interface

4   Conclusion

In this paper a tool to convert Linked Data of an e-learning system to a SCORM standard was described. The tool was developed and successfully integrated into the ontology-based e-learning system. A demo widget is available on any page of the course in e-learning system. The demo widget for a Physics Course can be found at http://openedu.ifmo.ru:8888/resource/Phisics:Physics.[5]

As the main output, the tool generates an archive with SCORM-conformant learning content. The archive was successfully tested out in the SCORM Cloud framework. The lesson page of the obtained SCORM package is shown in Fig. 5.

In future versions of the designed tool the following will be included:

- further support of SCORM standards,
- Tin Can API support,
- REST API service,
- CLI service,
- support of new tags and widgets in predefined templates,
- increase in the speed of page rendering,
- extended UI widgets for the tool.

---

[5] See https://github.com/ailabitmo/linked-learning-scorm-converter for the source code.

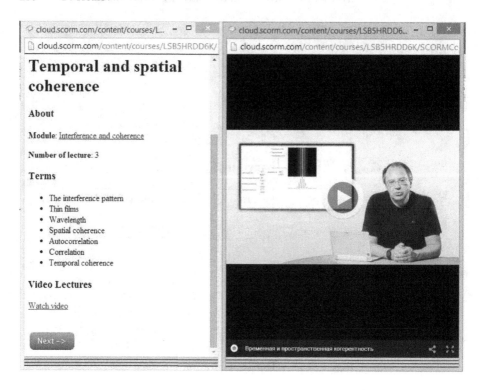

Fig. 5. The lesson page of obtained SCORM package

References

1. Mouromtsev, D., Kozlov, F., Parkhimovich, O., Zelenina, M.: Development of an Ontology-Based E-Learning System. In: Klinov, P., Mouromtsev, D. (eds.) KESW 2013. CCIS, vol. 394, pp. 273–280. Springer, Heidelberg (2013)
2. Haase, P., Schmidt, M., Schwarte, A.: The Information Workbench as a Self-Service Platform for Linked Data Applications. In: Consuming Linked Open Data Workshop (2011)
3. Krötzsch, M., Vrandečić, D., Völkel, M.: Semantic MediaWiki. In: Cruz, I., Decker, S., Allemang, D., Preist, C., Schwabe, D., Mika, P., Uschold, M., Aroyo, L.M. (eds.) ISWC 2006. LNCS, vol. 4273, pp. 935–942. Springer, Heidelberg (2006)
4. Bohl, O., Scheuhase, J., Sengler, R., Winand, U.: The sharable content object reference model (SCORM)—a critical review. Computers in Education, 950–951 (2002)
5. Qu, C., Nejdl, W.: Towards interoperability and reusability of learning resources: A SCORM–conformant courseware for computer science education. In: Proceedings of the 2nd IEEE International Conference on Advanced Learning Technologies, Kazan, Russia (2002)
6. Khalili, A., Auer, S., Tarasowa, D., Ermilov, I.: SlideWiki: Elicitation and sharing of corporate knowledge using presentations. In: ten Teije, A., Völker, J., Handschuh, S., Stuckenschmidt, H., d'Acquin, M., Nikolov, A., Aussenac-Gilles, N., Hernandez, N. (eds.) EKAW 2012. LNCS, vol. 7603, pp. 302–316. Springer, Heidelberg (2012)

OntoFast: Construct Ontology Rapidly

Abdul-Mateen Rajput[1], Marzio Pennisi[2], Santo Motta[2], and Francesco Pappalardo[3]

[1] Bonn-Aachen International Center for Information Technology [B-IT], University of Bonn, Germany
Abdul-Mateen.Rajput@uni-bonn.de
[2] Department of Mathematics and Computer Science, University of Catania, Italy
{mpennisi,motta}@dmi.unict.it
[3] Department of Drug Sciences, University of Catania, Italy
francesco.pappalardo@unict.it

Abstract. Ontology construction is a time consuming and labor intensive task. It may take many months to construct an ontology as according to standard practices each concept must have synonyms, domain specific definition, unique identifier and references. Current practices of ontology construction require manual data input to feed this data via programs such as Protégé etc. We designed a small application that speeds up the development of new ontologies. It provides an easy to use and convenient interface that allows to theoretically build an ontology within few days. The output of our program can be easily opened and then used into a standard ontology editor like Protégé. Availability: The software is freely available visiting this link: http://www.francescopappalardo.net/ontofast.zip.

Keywords: Ontology engineering, semantic web tools, ontology population.

1   Introduction

An ontology is a formal specification of a shared conceptualization [4]. Manual ontology construction is a time consuming process and it takes many months to construct an ontology from beginning. Application and objective of the ontology have to be defined and searching for the relevant concepts and metadata associated with each of the concept is a challenging task which usually takes much more time than anticipated. Due to the efforts and time consumption of constructing ontology, several approaches and applications have been developed. Some of them are automated and others are semi automated. Most of the automated ontology construction tools require technical expertise of computing and natural language processing making it difficult for people without computational background and it may take few months to couple of years to learn and master those tools. For example, as reported in a recent survey [6], learning and working with Protégé (which is not exactly an automated ontology construction tool though) is a time consuming task and it was found that six months experience was not sufficient to learn it. In addition, most of the automated tools work on a corpus to construct a hierarchical ontology. This means that the results could vary significantly on the basis of the content of the corpus. Some of these tools help to

P. Klinov and D. Mouromtsev (Eds.): KESW 2014, CCIS 468, pp. 237–241, 2014.
© Springer International Publishing Switzerland 2014

construct de-novo ontologies but cleaning the concepts which are not required and integrating associated metadata required in ontology are also cumbersome tasks. Some of the tools are presented as follows. ASIUM [3] (Acquisition of Semantic Knowledge Using Machine Learning Methods) acquires ontological knowledge from text given as an input. The system is based on conceptual and hierarchical clustering. Doddle II [10] is a system which can exploit the machine readable dictionary and text corpus to populate the domain specific ontology. KnowItAll [2] extracts facts from the web by using linguistic and statistics method and it is mainly designed for large scale information extraction. In addition, to the best of authors knowledge, there are few more programs such as MedSynDikate [5], OntoLearn [9], String-IE [8] and Text2Onto [1], but none of them provide an interface where a list of concepts can be given and associated metadata could be added in an automated way to construct an ontology.

Figure 1 shows the difference between a manual addition of a concept in an ontology and concept population via OntoFast. Adding a concept in an ontology roughly takes several minutes depending upon the size of metadata associated with it.

Steps to follow for a **single** concept addition in an ontology manually

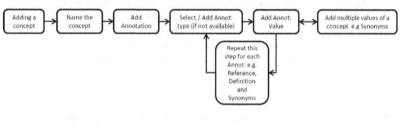

Steps to follow for **many** concepts addition in an ontology via OntoFast

Fig. 1. The difference of steps between manual addition of a concept in an ontology and by using OntoFast to populate a new ontology

For example, if a user wants to add a concept with n synonyms then he/she has to repeat the same steps n times. Further, if he/she wants to add references then the same practice has to be done. The same goes with the definition and any other annotation and all this is only for one concept. If you are considering to construct an ontology with many concepts which are having dozens of synonyms (as in biological domain) then it would probably take weeks to months to do the simple task of populating an ontology which is not attractive for domain experts. With the help of OntoFast the same task can be performed within couple of minutes while constructing a new ontology. It works only for new ontology because we assumed that massive population of concepts only needed when an ontology is started to be constructed. The tool's output is an OWL/XML file in which the concepts are stored as Classes.

2   Use

The application provides an easy to use interface where an ontology can be constructed and populate very quickly (see Figure 1). Different options allow users to embed a definition, synonyms and references of the ontology via interface. Here we describe our approach to build an ontology very quickly.

Importing of concepts is very easy, since the list of concepts can be imported by clicking on the load new Txt button (Figure 2). All the concepts of a prospective ontology can be given in a form of list in text file (.txt). Fields in the text file should be separated by carriage return commands. The application reads each new line as a new concept and generates the list of concepts that is visualized in the declarations text box (Figure 2). The associated metadata can be then added by selecting a concept in the list. Selected concepts will be highlighted in purple and yellow. Just after importing the list of declarations, the application asks to choose the output xml file to be then used in Protégé or in any similar application. From this moment the user will not need to take care of manually saving the output xml file, since the application will execute automatically saving every time a different concept is selected, and on exit.

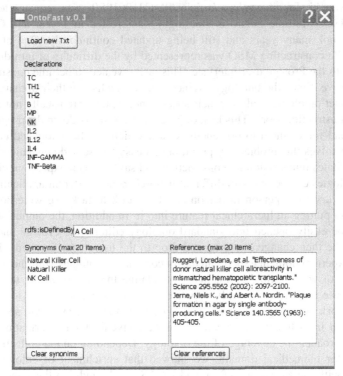

Fig. 2. OntoFast interface. 1: Load button for loading a list of declarations from a txt file. 2: Declarations list which shows concepts loaded by a txt file. A concept can be selected by clicking on it. The selected concept will be highlighted in purple and yellow. 3, 4 and 5: Fields for defining basic properties of the selected declaration. Synonyms and References fields allow to type more than one value.

Metadata can be easily associated with the imported concepts by selecting a concept and providing in the relative fields the associated details. The main attributes required for the ontology were definition, synonyms and references thus there are different text boxes given to incorporate the same. As the goal was to speed up the initial step in the generation of new ontologies, each of the boxes can accommodate copy/paste to quickly populate the ontology. In addition, more than one synonym and reference can be given in different lines. Finally, the hierarchy of the ontology can be arranged later on by user in Protégé, since such an operation can be already carried very quickly in it.

3   Results and Discussion

In this paper we presented an application which allows to construct ontologies quickly in order to speed-up the standard procedure of constructing ontologies and associating metadata. This actually takes time that goes from many months to couple of years and involves many people. For example, PLIO (Protein-Ligand Interaction Ontology) [http://www.ncbi.nlm.nih.gov/pmc/articles/PMC3106195/] was constructed in 18 months, MSO (Multiple Sclerosis Ontology) was created in 1 year and GO (Gene Ontology) took many years and still being updated continuously. One of the main hurdles while constructing MSO was represented by the difficulty of introducing new concepts into the Protégé user interface. This task revealed to be time consuming and labor intensive. Since the ontology engineers are specialists in their domain and they may construct ontologies only for their specific needs, they are usually not experts in ontology construction work. This lack of practice often slows down the progression of the work and forces them to do repetitive task which can be automated easily. Our application solves this problem by providing an easy to use and convenient interface which facilitates quick ontology construction and save domain experts precious time. Since ontologies can be put with different hierarchies and different application scenarios which vary from person to person and from task to task, we were not actually interested in putting an hierarchical feature into it. In addition, the output of our program can be easily opened into standard ontology editors like Protégé and the hierarchy can be then changed by drag and drop to the users specific needs. Hierarchy relies on expert so domain expert can easily construct ontologies with the help of our tool instead of wasting time by manually populating the ontology. Our tool provides an easy to use interface to quickly populate and construct ontology instead of doing repetitive work of adding concepts one by one. More than one synonym and reference can be given in different lines making it more convenient for information retrieval systems to broaden the coverage of the ontology. Depending on the collection of metadata etc for biomedical domain, we showed that enrichment of ontology can be automated with the Knime workflow and UMLS [7]. In addition the same workflow can be used to query any public MySQL database with some minor changes. Ontologies are considered controlled vocabularies for knowledge representation. Our tool is a middle interface between dictionaries and ontologies and provides an easier way to transform one into another.

Acknowledgements. This work has been sponsored by Merck KGaA, a pharmaceutical and chemical company.

References

1. Cimiano, P., Völker, J.: Text2onto - a framework for ontology learning and data-driven change discovery. In: Montoyo, A., Muñoz, R., Métais, E. (eds.) NLDB 2005. LNCS, vol. 3513, pp. 227–238. Springer, Heidelberg (2005)
2. Etzioni, O., Cafarella, M., Downey, D., Kok, S., Popescu, A.-M., Shaked, T., Soderland, S., Weld, D.S., Yates, A.: Web-scale information extraction in knowitall (preliminary results). In: WWW 2004: Proceedings of the 13th International Conference on World Wide Web, pp. 100–110. ACM, New York (2004)
3. Faure, D., Nédellec, C.: Knowledge acquisition of predicate argument structures from technical texts using machine learning: The system ASIUM. In: Fensel, D., Studer, R. (eds.) EKAW 1999. LNCS (LNAI), vol. 1621, pp. 329–334. Springer, Heidelberg (1999)
4. Gruber, T.R.: A translation approach to portable ontology specifications. Knowledge Acquisition 5(2), 199–220 (1993)
5. Hahn, U., Romacker, M., Schulz, S.: medsyndikate—a natural language system for the extraction of medical information from findings reports. International Journal of Medical Informatics 67(1-3), 63–74 (2002)
6. Khondoker, M.R., Mueller, P.: Comparing ontology development tools based on an online survey. In: Proceedings of the World Congress on Engineering (WCE 2010), London, U.K, vol. I (2010)
7. Rajput, A.M., Gurulingappa, H.: Semi-automatic approach for ontology enrichment using umls. Procedia Computer Science 23, 78–83 (2013)
8. Saric, J., Jensen, L.J., Ouzounova, R., Rojas, I., Bork, P.: Extraction of regulatory gene/protein networks from medline. Bioinformatics 22, 645–650 (2006)
9. Velardi, P., Navigli, R., Cucchiarelli, A., Neri, F.: Evaluation of OntoLearn, a methodology for automatic population of domain ontologies. In: Buitelaar, P., Cimiano, P., Magnini, B. (eds.) Ontology Learning from Text: Methods, Applications and Evaluation. IOS Press (2006)
10. Yamaguchi, T.: Acquiring conceptual relationships from domain-specific texts. In: Maedche, A., Staab, S., Nedellec, C., Hovy, E.H. (eds.) Workshop on Ontology Learning. CEUR Workshop Proceedings, vol. 38. CEUR-WS.org (2003)

Mathematical Content Semantic Markup Methods and Open Scientific E-Journals Management Systems

Alexander Elizarov, Evgeny Lipachev, and Denis Zuev

Kazan Federal University, Russia
{amelizarov,elipachev,dzuev11}@gmail.com

Abstract. The paper discusses the approach to automate the processing of electronic mathematical documents and their transformation into semantic documents. Structuring electronic storage of periodical issues in mathematics and multi-volume works conferences was performed.

Keywords: Information and communication technologies, information resources, technologies of the Semantic Web, electronic scientific collections, metadata extraction, mathematical notation, electronic publications, Open Journal System.

1 Introduction

Internet and computer technologies have changed dramatically the ways of exchanging of science knowledge and research results. Mobile devices are used in every part of our life, especially in production activities and evolution of Cloud computing technologies. This discovered a challenging task to create a uniform information space, which could integrate all science resources and keep certain semantic relations between them. The key moment of such integration task is that we must semantically markup this scientific content. A large number of known xml-based markup languages gives us a possibility to use them in order to increase the effect of semantic structuring during automated processing of information. This is the main scope of the Semantic Web as a part of global process of Evolution of the Internet.

Nowadays traditional ways of disseminating research results are replaced by the technologies of the Digital Era. Printed-paper form has been the engine of culture and education during the past 500 years but today it is no longer competitive with the digital technology. Therefore, publishing in general, and scientific, in particular is actively reconstructed. Maintaining the traditions, that are historically in scientific journals (peer review, discussion of the editorial board, etc.) new methods to support publishing are developed. The idea of creating Worldwide Digital Library of Mathematics (WDML) is discussed [1].

Most of modern scientific publications are presented on the Internet; periodicals often have web portals with electronic versions of published materials or summaries of articles. All these portals are supported by a management system

P. Klinov and D. Mouromtsev (Eds.): KESW 2014, CCIS 468, pp. 242–251, 2014.

that provides navigation to the content or they are part of a bigger overarching information system (e.g, the administrative system of the whole organization).

One of the main trends of the information society is creating a new type of information systems known as digital libraries (DL). DL is a distributed information system that enables reliable and effective use of different collections of electronic documents that are available for the end user via the global data network. Components of DL are specialized electronic collections of information resources.

Electronic scientific publications management systems are not limited only by providing remote paper submission services to scientific journals and further processing to final publication. They also may be responsible for discovering and granting access to all existing content and provide advanced search services (by author, article title, keywords, etc.) in the appropriate digital collections, in other words they fully implement the functionality of digital libraries. It means that, electronic scientific journal can be considered as a scientific DL, which operates on journal articles as information objects.

Creation of an information system that must support the processing of mathematical electronic collections has essential differences and is more complicated. This is primarily due to the presence of formulas in the article text, which have many technologies for their typing and displaying. Most of the available electronic sources of scientific mathematical information contain texts, where automatic processing is difficult because of the complexity of data retrieval and lack of the information about structural skeleton of the text.

The paper discusses the approach to automate the processing of scientific electronic documents and converting them to structured e-documents. Emphasis is placed on the key moments of processing of mathematical texts. Using services created by the proposed method, we performed structuring and marking up of a large volume of electronic storage containing the periodical issues in mathematics.

2   Semantic Markup

Correct keyword selection and correct metadata creation that describe properties and content of information object affects dramatically searching results relevancy and even on efficiency of the search process as a whole. It means that methods of extraction and creating metadata from scientific content are crucial for the quality of searching services. Usage of metadata, which are created using both Dublin Core and RDF, can increase the effectiveness of searching services in digital scientific journals.

In journals of mathematics, an important part of searching service is a searching using formula fragments. Search, using fragments of formulas, for example, in digital repository of Lobachevskii Journal of Mathematics[1] was done [2]. The technology of converting mathematical texts and documents into XML format and rewriting formulas from those documents using MathML-notation lies at the

---

[1] http://ljm.ksu.ru/

base of the search algorithm [3]. The Algorithm provides several XML/MathML streams of discovering, converting and preservation. One of those streams is responsible for transformation of documents from original author's TEX format to XML with MathML insertions

Most popular publishers that are working with mathematical texts (e.g. www.ams.org and Russian academic journals) use only TEX-notation. The biggest archive arXiv.org mostly consists of articles, that are TEX-files or of *.pdf and *.ps files, that are in fact also compiled TEX-files.

Nowadays there are many program tools for semantic marking electronic documents and for saving them into XML (e.g. for TEX-MathML conversion) [4], but many of them cannot work properly with real author's documents. This happens because several documents in one collection may have too many different style compositions and do not have any common structural elements. That's why firstly we need to transform electronic documents without any structure to the documents with certain structure, which is suitable for collection. Only after this action, some automated parsing procedures can be applied. The transformation algorithm of mathematical e-documents is based on their syntax analysis [5]. This is the key difference of our algorithm from other ones that are described in Lemon8-XML Public Knowledge Project [6] or TeamBeam Project [7]. As a result we also created a standard style sheet with definition of some common semantic TEX-constructions (e.g. \autor{}, \journal{}, \title{} or \udk{}).

The algorithm can be divided into several steps. On the first step the whole collection of documents is split into several homogeneous clusters based on the used style sheet. Since the collection consists of journal articles and articles from composite books there cannot be many different clusters with their own style sheets. Then we prepare special version of the algorithm for each cluster, considering its style sheet or style sheet of group of similar clusters. All author's syntax structures are replaced by the standard ones. On the next step, the algorithm extracts necessary data for filling semantic TEX-structures. This successful transformation of a collection documents gives us a chance to apply to the documents such structural and semantic mark-up formats as OpenMath, OMDoc and STEX (semantic TEX) [8,9]. Moreover, the transformation is also used for building a mathematical ontology and creation of semantic search service [10,11]. Much of the semantic content in TEX-documents is represented only implicitly, and we must decode it only manually for understanding and further processing. For machine-processing this implicit content must be made explicit, which is a non-trivial task.

Despite TEX-system has wide functions for document-structuring, authors often use only semantically simple tools for creating structure of a document. The Documents in archives, which were written years ago, when electronic form of document was used only for preparation for printing, are the most complicated ones for machine processing. Anyway, we can try to extract structure of such documents automatically by analysing font selection or text unit sequences. Defined structure and metadata extraction of e-document automatically gives us ability to transform it into suitable formats of Semantic Web [3].

Set of requirements for scientific articles, which are defined by journals' style sheets, was used as a base set of attributes for the metadata extraction algorithm. Tags of the documents allow selecting some text units automatically. Using semantic tags such as \author or \title in articles and applying a standard style sheet to the documents of the collection make the machine-processing algorithm of mathematical texts much easier.

The vast amount of scientific literature constitutes a difficulty for authors and researchers in finding and using all relevant information in their work. Partially this problem can be solved by using metadata. In a digital library framework, we can find multiple kinds of metadata, which usually are created during the registration process [12]. Descriptive metadata, a more generic name for the traditional bibliographic metadata, relates to the description and identification of the information objects, such as titles, authors, indexing terms, classification codes, abstracts, etc. References also are an important part of the metadata section [13]. Extraction of the whole bibliography block is a relatively simple task – usually at the beginning of the list, the relevant keyword is located. Separation of each bibliography record and its' internal structural analysis is much more difficult problem.

Automatic extraction process of bibliographic data from articles of an e-mathematical collection consists of finding bibliographic block in the document and then parsing strings into bibliographical components. For example, tag \begin{thebibliography}, which is used in most journal articles in TeX-notation, can uniquely identify bibliographic objects. It should be noted, that usage of structural tools of TeX-system is not common practice. Many electronic documents, in particular, materials of scientific conferences, do not have no any structural markup; moreover, even the bibliography block may be not structurally separated. For those electronic documents, the automatic parsing algorithm uses typography features and order of text units in the document.

The algorithm of bibliography elements extraction can be divided into several steps:

- Extraction of individual bibliographical records from the bibliographical section. For proper separation of records the rules of references accepted in the journal (brackets, numbering) are used;
- Using developed regular expression patterns (e.g. [14]), each bibliographical record is parsed to select list of authors, title of the article, year of issue and other publisher's imprints.

The algorithm is implemented on C# language. We tried to use this algorithm to process the electronic collections of "Proceedings of Lobachevskii Center of Mathematics", and a part of archive of "Uchenye Zapiski Kazanskogo Universiteta". Important to say, that these journals use different systems of rules of references, and we had to construct an individual set of patterns for each of data array. For searching for an \bibitem block in bibliography section we used the pattern:

```
string pattern =
        @"item{.*?}(.*?){.em(.*?)}.*?[--|//](.*?)
                (\d\d\d\d).*?--(.*?)[bib|end".
```

Next pattern used for metadata extraction for two journals – "Russian Mathematics" and "Uchenye Zapiski Kazanskogo Universiteta":

```
string pattern =
        @"item.*?{.[em|it](.*?)}(.*?)[--|//](.*?)
                (\d\d\d\d).*?--(.*?)[bib|end]".
```

Another one used for metadata extraction of "Proceedings of Lobachevskii Center of Mathematics":

```
string pattern =
    @"[0-9](.*?){\\it(.*?)}(.*?)
            (\d{4}).*?([CP].~\d+--\d+|\d+~[cp]).".
```

There are examples of source files of papers for semantic analyzing (See figures 1, 2).

Differences between style sheets of scientific journals increase difficulty of extraction process. We can see this on figures 1 and 2.

Fig. 3 shows a fragment of the resulting xml-file.

The practical application of the described algorithm showed its effectiveness. About 10% of e-documents from collections were processed incorrectly or incompletely. This is due to the fact, that there was not any stylistic validation at the stage of receiving articles and authors' design (including the bibliography) of articles in some cases did not meet the prescribed rules of journals.

3   Scientific E-Journal Management Systems

Since libraries are increasingly involved in journal publishing, a shared preservation quality digital repository is a natural place to archive and provide access to journal literature to ensure its long-term preservation and discoverability [15].

Modern scientific e-publication management systems are not limited by the submission services of articles into a scientific journal and their further processing for final publication, but provide access to the generated content and advanced search (by author, title, keyword, etc.) in corresponding electronic collections, i.e. completely implement functionality of digital libraries. From this point of view, a scientific e-journal can be considered as a scientific DL operating on the articles of the e-journal as with information objects. Analysis of existing scientific e-journal management systems was carried out in [16]. We can use DL technologies to automate editorial processes in scientific journals. This was demonstrated on the example of the introduction of software platform OJS (Open Journal Systems). Public Knowledge Project[2].

---

[2] http://pkp.sfu.ca/ojs/

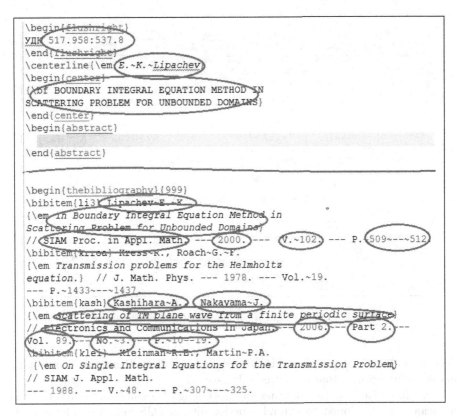

Fig. 1. Paper fragment of Journal 1 and its structure

The functions of modern scientific e-journal management systems contain services, regulating the peer review process and ensuring the collective editing of electronic documents. In addition, these systems should provide such editorial services as classification, annotation, metadata selection, publication, long-term preservation, conversion, distribution, syndication, usage statistics, harvesting, combining into a collection, interaction with institutional repositories, access control, subscription and sending out notices, new arrivals.

Since 2013, a scientific e-journal management system is created in the Republic of Tatarstan with the participation of the authors. In this project, we chose The Open Journal System OJS as a software environment that provides all functions of automation of editorial and publishing processes. Taking into account of the specifics of each particular journal editorial processes is based on the completion of the program code contained in the OJS. The system has a modular architecture that allows you to develop your own classes and modules. It implements the Model-View-Controller (MVC)-structure and, therefore, data storage, user interfaces and control functions are separated to different layers of interaction. The functionality of the system can be extended with the help of

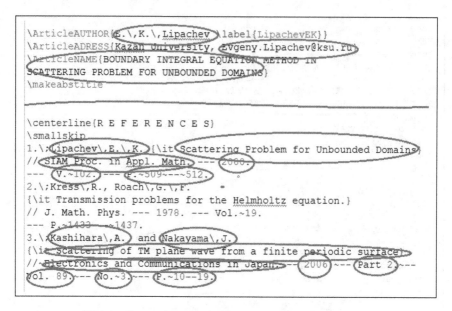

Fig. 2. Paper fragment of Journal 2 and its structure

special modules and plug-ins. The system has a gallery of modules containing many useful features that empower OJS (see [17]).

A module of automation of semantic processing of documents written in TEX-notation was developed to extend functionality of OJS instance. The module solves following main problems:

- downloading of a TEX-document to the OJS journal system;
- checking for compliance of the loaded document with the editorial rules (validation process);
- generation of reports on the results of validation and alert system;
- compilation of the TEX-document by the OJS server and generation of reports;
- extraction of metadata from the TEX-document.

4   Using Services of Semantic Markup in E-Journal Management Systems

Widespread web-based applications developed using the technology of Cloud Computing allow to create a new type of workspace, providing access to corporate resources and services from any device all over the world. A prerequisite for such service is only the access to the Internet. In particular, a new scientific communication system is formed, for example, in mathematics. The development of cloud technologies has also affected the ways the research results are published. At the same time, systematic access to scientific content presented in

```
  - <bibitem>
        <author id="1"> Kress R. </author>
        <author id="2"> Roach G.F. </author>
        <rtitle> Transmission problems for the Helmholtz equation </rtitle>
      - <journal>
            <jtitle> J. Math. Phys. </jtitle>
            <year> 1978 </year>
            <vol> 19 </vol>
            <number> </number>
            <pages> 1433-1437 </pages>
        </journal>
    </bibitem>
```

Fig. 3. Metadata extraction – resulting xml-file fragment

electronic form, is impossible without a special automated system of publication of scientific works. The architecture of this system proposed in [16] and contains three levels – physical level, basic level and the level of services.

The physical layer describes the hardware component of the system, ensuring the functioning of the upper layers, and includes system and application software. All of these components must be provided with technical support including the virtualization and cloud computing technologies, although implementation without the use of virtual machines is also possible.

The basic layer is responsible for providing of main scientific e-journals management services ensuring, in particular, the registration of authors and users, the initial reception and processing of articles, including automatic check of compliance with the editorial rules and the rules of reviewing. There should be also the control of compliance with a deadline for the article consideration, of referee appointment and of distribution of various notifications. There also should be services of remote interaction and interoperation, search in the electronic information resources and automated extraction of metadata and structuring of the input information. User management support, access rights differentiation and a possibility for providing the paid access to the content are also necessary. On the basic layer, it is advisable to use one of the known scientific e-journals management systems. In particular, we propose to use the OJS, with the help of which all the business processes of the electronic publishing as well as the content preservation are implemented.

The layer of the services contains additional add-ons and functions, taking into account the specific of the e-journal topical area. For example, for the mathematical e-journals the services of conversion into specialized formats (TeX, MathML and others) are essential. This is a front-end of the systems where all the interaction with the end user takes place. At this level, all discussed scientific collection integration services and, possibly, some ontology constructing services should be placed. In particular, we install here a service, which extracts metadata from articles in TeX format and uploads them into the storage subsystem. This service allows to markup resources, hosted by the system with use of the described algorithm.

The user interaction with scientific e-journals management system can be arranged either through an own web portal, or through special software adapters from the web portal of the specific journal that stores its content in the repository of the system.

In the case of the first type of the interaction, a registered user gains an access to all e-journals, hosted by the system and the web portal serves as a single entry point. This method is most convenient for new journals that have not had their own web sites.

For the e-journals that already have history and support their own sites the second way of the interaction is more acceptable, in our opinion. In particular, it allows to keep usual web link of the e-journals' site and its "history" in the Internet, although the editorial processes are automated as much as possible.

Acknowledgments. The authors would like to thank Dmitry Akhmetov and Alexey Gerasimov, who have contributed to scientific the e-journal management system (`science.tatarstan.ru`). The authors are also very grateful to the three anonymous reviewers for their valuable suggestions.

The work is supported by the Russian Foundation for Basic Research and the Government of the Republic of Tatarstan (project №12-07-97018) and by the Russian Foundation for Humanities (project №14-03-12004).

References

1. Rocha, E.M., Rodrigues, J.F.: Disseminating and preserving mathematical knowledge. In: Borwein, J.M., Rocha, E.M., Rodrigues, J.F. (eds.) Communicating Mathematics in the Digital Era, pp. 3–21. A K Peters, Ltd. (2008)
2. Malakhaltsev, M.A.: Lobachevskii Journal of Mathematics (1998-2007). Portable electronic collection of mathematical documents. Kazan University, Kazan (2009)
3. Miner, R.: The importance of MathML to mathematics communication. Notices of the AMS 52, 532–538 (2005)
4. Elizarov, A.M., Lipachev, E.K., Malakhaltsev, M.A.: Web-technologies for Mathematician: MathML Bases. Practical Guidance. Fizmatlit, Moscow (2010)
5. Elizarov, A.M., Lipachev, E.K., Hohlov, Y.E.: Semantic methods of structuring mathematical content providing enhanced search functionality. Information Society 1-2, 83–92 (2013)
6. Suhonos, M.J.: Semi-automatic citation correction with Lemon8-XM. Code4Lib Journal, 6 (2009), http://journal.code4lib.org/articles/1011
7. Kern, R., Jack, K., Hristakeva, M., Granitzer, M.: TeamBeam – meta-data extraction from scientific literature. D-Lib Magazine 18(7/8) (2012)
8. Kohlhase, M.: STeX: Semantic markup in TeX/LaTeX. Jacobs University, Bremen (2008), http://kwarc.info/kohlhase
9. Kohlhase, M.: Using LaTeX as a semantic markup format. Math. Comput. Sci. 2, 279–304 (2008)
10. Lange, C.: Ontologies and languages for representing mathematical knowledge on the Semantic Web. Semantic Web 4(2), 119–158 (2013), http://www.semantic-web-journal.net/sites/default/files/swj122_3.pdf

11. Birialtsev, E., Elizarov, A., Zhiltsov, N., Ivanov, V., Nevzorova, O., Solov'yev, V.: Model of semantic search in the collections of mathematical documents based on ontologies. In: 12th All-Russian Scientific Conference "Digital Libraries: Advanced Methods and Technologies, Digital Collections", Kazan, Russia, pp. 296–300 (2010) (in Russian)
12. Borbinha, J.: Digital libraries and the rebirth of printed journals. In: Borwein, J.M., Rocha, E.M., Rodrigues, J.F. (eds.) Communicating Mathematics in the Digital Era, pp. 97–110. A K Peters, Ltd. (2008)
13. Kogalovsky, M.: Metadata, their properties, functions and classifications. In: Proceedings of the 14th All-Russian Scientific Conference "Digital libraries: Advanced Methods and Technologies, Digital Collections", pp. 3–14. Pereslavl-Zalessky, Russia (2012), http://ceur-ws.org/Vol-934/paper3.pdf (in Russian)
14. Friedl, J.: Mastering regular expressions. O'Reilly Media Inc. (2008)
15. Hawkins, K.S.: A model for integrating the publication and preservation of journal articles. In: Selected Papers of the 15th All-Russian Scientific Conference "Digital Libraries: Advanced Methods and Technologies, Digital Collections", Yaroslavl, Russia, pp. 112–116 (2013), http://ceur-ws.org/Vol-1108/paper14.pdf
16. Elizarov, A., Zuev, D., Lipachev, E.: Electronic scientific journal management systems. Scientific and Technical Information Processing 41(1), 66–72 (2014)
17. Elizarov, A., Zuev, D., Lipachev, E.: Open scientific e-journals management systems and digital libraries technology. In: Selected Papers of the 15th All-Russian Scientific Conference "Digital Libraries: Advanced Methods and Technologies, Digital Collections", Yaroslavl, Russia, pp. 102–111 (2013), http://ceur-ws.org/Vol-1108/paper13.pdf (in Russian)

Author Index

Artemova, Galina   1

Blokhin, Yury M.   150
Boyarsky, Kirill   1

Chicaiza, Janneth   15

Dautov, Rustem   29
Dobrenko, Natalia   1
Drobyazko, Grigory   76
Dyachenko, Oleg   219

Elizarov, Alexander   242

Foteyeva, Viktoria   44

Galieva, Alfiya M.   57
Gatiatullin, Ayrat R.   57
Gorshkov, Sergey   67
Gouzévitch, Dmitri   1
Gusarova, Natalia   1

Hladky, Daniel   76

Kanevsky, Eugeny   1
Kirillovich, Alexander   105
Kovalchuk, Sergey V.   175
Kozlov, Fedor   229

Le Grange, Jon Jay   76
Levashova, Tatiana   184
Lipachev, Evgeny   105, 242
Lomov, Pavel   90
Lopez-Vargas, Jorge   15

Maltseva, Svetlana   76
Motta, Santo   237

Nand, Parma   128
Nevzorova, Olga A.   57, 105

Ogorodniychuk, Dmitriy   76

Panteleyev, Michail   44, 208
Pappalardo, Francesco   237
Paraskakis, Iraklis   29
Pennisi, Marzio   237
Perera, Rivindu   128
Petrova, Daria   1
Piedra, Nelson   15

Rajput, Abdul-Mateen   237
Reshmy, Krishnan   120
Roos, Nico   160
Rubtsova, Yuliya   140
Rybina, Galina V.   150

Schadd, Frederik C.   160
Sherimon, P.C.   120
Shilov, Nikolay   184
Shishaev, Maxim   90
Smirnov, Alexander   184
Smirnov, Pavel A.   175
Stannett, Mike   29

Teslya, Nikolay   184
Tovar-Caro, Edmundo   15

Ustalov, Dmitry   196

Vinu, P.V.   120
Voigt, Martin   76

Yelagina, Nataliya   208
Youssef, Takroni   120

Zagorulko, Yury   219
Zhiltsov, Nikita   105
Zuev, Denis   242